BLUE GUIDE   OXFORD AND CAMBRIDGE

BLUE GUIDE

OXFORD AND CAMBRIDGE

Mercia Mason

Maps by John Flower

Plans by Hilary Wright

A & C Black
London

W W Norton
New York

Third edition 1987

Published by A & C Black (Publishers) Limited
35 Bedford Row, London WC1R 4JH

© A & C Black (Publishers) Limited 1987

Published in the United States of America by
W W Norton & Company, Inc.
500 Fifth Avenue, New York, NY 10110

Published simultaneously in Canada by
Penguin Books Canada Limited,
2801 John Street, Markham, Ontario L3R 1B4

British Library Cataloguing in Publication Data

Mason, Mercia
  Oxford and Cambridge.—3rd ed.—(Blue
  guide)
  1. Oxford (Oxfordshire)—Description—
  Guide-books   2. Cambridge (Cambridgeshire)
  —Description—Guide-books
  I. Title   II. Series
  914.25′7404858   DA690.098

  ISBN 0–7136–2840–5
  ISBN 0–393–30363–2   USA

PREFACE

No excuse is needed for bringing Oxford and Cambridge together between the covers of one book. They are the Heavenly Twins of university cities; and their unique status has been emphasised rather than diminished by the great increase since the 1950s in the numbers of other universities. So closely indeed are they identified in the public mind that they are often referred to simply by the composite name of 'Oxbridge'.

Ancient origins, history, organisation, migration of scholars from one to the other throughout the centuries, all these factors do give them a strong family likeness. But the traveller who is fortunate enough to have time to spend in both will before long become aware of almost as many differences as similarities. Some of these, like the 'Backs' of Cambridge, or the gardens of Oxford, are immediately obvious. Others, such as the subtle differences in the styles of the buildings, or the absolute diversity of the two university 'languages', emerge more slowly. To appreciate fully the individuality of each place, an individuality of soul as much as of appearance, needs long familiarity with both, but even on a brief visit it is possible to catch a sense of it, in the studious hush of a secret Oxford quadrangle, or in the fresh astringent airiness of an open Cambridge court.

Not every visitor has the chance to explore both cities. The old editions of Baedeker's famous guide used to say that every tourist to England should visit Oxford 'and, if time allows, Cambridge', and—largely because of Oxford's central position, on the route to other tourist centres—this still tends to remain the pattern. But even for those who can only visit one or the other, it is still interesting to be able to make connections and comparisons, and so, with the visitor to both and the visitor to only one in mind, the introductory articles on history, organisation and architecture all treat of both places together, and in the detailed descriptions that follow frequent cross-references between the two are made.

Unlike many castles, ancient monuments, and 'stately homes', whose principal purpose nowadays is to encourage and provide for the needs of the tourist, and which are therefore organised for the tourist's convenience, the colleges of Oxford and Cambridge are essentially private places, whose raison d'être is to provide for the needs of those engaged in academic study, research, and teaching, and are therefore organised for the scholar's convenience. That visitors are allowed to wander through their quadrangles and courts—usually without even the payment of any fee—is a generous courtesy, not an obligation. It is a courtesy which should never be abused. Since the rise of mass tourism the huge numbers of visitors to both Oxford and Cambridge have caused the colleges severe problems; many have to restrict their opening hours, and the parts that visitors may see; some are finding it necessary to close entirely during the weeks of the summer examinations to ensure peace and quiet for intensive study. Sadly, too, for reasons of security and protection from damage, many halls and even chapels are open only under supervision, some not at all. So visitors may be disappointed, but they should not be surprised or resentful, if they cannot always see what they want.

The essentially private nature of the colleges, their aloofness, even, from the affairs of the citizens and visitors around them, are typified by the fact that they neither declare their identity, nor make it easy to discover their charms and treasures. It is rare to find a college with its name displayed; often the only way to discover where you are is to study the notice-board inside the gatehouse and deduce from its many flapping layers of literature which college you have reached. And once inside do not expect labels on chapel, hall, or other places of special interest. You will seldom find them. However, there are always kindly people about who will direct you, or even take you there, if the directions given in the book fail.

The detailed descriptions of colleges concentrate mainly on what the ordinary unaccompanied visitor can see. Sometimes, however, places not normally open to the public, such as the Bodleian Library Arts End at Oxford, or the Thomas Gray rooms at Pembroke College, Cambridge, are also described, either because they have particular importance, or have a particular relevance to the architectural history or the personalities associated with a college. But in communities as rich in history and personalities as Oxford and Cambridge it is inevitable that almost as much has to be left out as put in. Selection has been one of the author's major problems.

At the end of the entry on each college is a list of famous people connected with it. Very stringent standards have been applied and the result is inevitably somewhat subjective and will probably satisfy no-one. Honorary fellows are not normally included, and reluctantly it has been decided, to avoid any invidious choices or wounding omissions, not to include any living persons (members of the royal family only excepted), although often no doubt their names might be of more immediate interest than those of Elizabethan poets, or Victorian statesmen. The decision also results in women being almost totally excluded, university education for women having such a comparatively short history, and their numbers until recently having been so small. The colleges founded for women have many nationally distinguished daughters, but most of them (happily) are still alive.

Observant readers will notice that sometimes the same name occurs in more than one list. This is because the person concerned has been an undergraduate at one college, and later a fellow of another (or others).

Perhaps no book in the Blue Guide series will be subject to such informed and critical scrutiny as this one, dealing as it does with the very well-springs of scholarship and criticism. Every effort has been made to achieve absolute accuracy, but the author is only too well aware of the gap between intention and achievement. Readers will no doubt discover (perhaps with pleasure?) many mistakes. They are asked to point these out, so that future editions can be corrected. Any suggestions for improvements will be welcomed and acknowledged.

CONTENTS

Maps and Plans

NOTE ON THE THIRD EDITION

In this third edition of *Blue Guide Oxford and Cambridge* the sections on the two cities themselves remain substantially the same as in the second edition, although of course thoroughly revised and updated. The sections on their environs, however, have been greatly expanded, and now provide information on many places of interest and beauty within about a twenty-mile radius of each city, for those who want a change from intensive sightseeing and perhaps a day in the country.

ACKNOWLEDGEMENTS

Any guide book writer leans heavily on the work of others. The books I chiefly consulted while working on this guide are listed in the bibliography. I fully acknowledge my debt of gratitude to their authors. In preparing the new sections on Environs, I have made much use of guides to parish churches and houses open to the public; to their (usually unnamed) writers my thanks are also due. I am indebted to Keith Spence, author of *Blue Guide Cathedrals and Abbeys of England and Wales*, for much of the description of Ely Cathedral.

In preparing this third edition I have once again had the most generous help. College authorities and museum directors have meticulously checked and updated entries, and made many helpful suggestions, all in the most kind and encouraging manner. City authorities, transport managers, and tourist offices have patiently answered my questions. I should like to thank them all individually, but as that would almost require another book, I hope they will accept this acknowledgement as an expression of my gratitude.

Finally, I want to thank my husband, Oliver Mason, who has taken much of the hard work of this revision off my shoulders, while leaving me with all the credit.

MERCIA MASON

PICTURES
Thanks are due to the following for providing illustrations:
City of Cambridge Planning Department: pages 21, 151
Thomas-Photos: pages 64, 74, 91, 106
The National Trust (John Bethell): page 125
John Leigh: pages 161, 200
Donald O.F. Monk: page 187
English Heritage: page 196

THE HISTORY OF THE UNIVERSITIES

The Middle Ages

ORIGINS

Oxford and Cambridge are two of the oldest universities in Europe, although neither is so old as they used to claim in the heady contests to establish seniority which enlivened the Middle Ages. Oxford then traced its origins to a mythical King Memphric, who founded the city in 1000 BC, and to Brutus, an equally mythical grandson of Aeneas, who came to England after the fall of Troy, and founded the university with a group of Greek and Latin scholars who accompanied him. Less ambitiously, Oxford also claimed Alfred the Great as their founder. Cambridge countered with Prince Cantaber of Spain, in the 'year of the world' 4321, and even in the more sober assessments of 1820 a guide book to Cambridge could state that 'Its establishment as a place of instruction for youth, probably soon followed the introduction of Christianity into this island, in the fourth century, during the Saxon heptarchy'.

In fact neither university was 'founded'. Both grew up in the 12C, and began with groups of scholars congregating around famous teachers of the day. In 1167, as the result of a royal quarrel, English students were expelled from Paris, and it is probable that many migrated to Oxford, a conveniently accessible place which already had several monastic schools (St. Frideswide's and Osney Abbey). Certainly by 1200 Oxford was providing a regular course of study, similar to that followed in the University of Paris.

There must also have been famous teachers at Cambridge at this time, perhaps, again, connected with monastic schools (Barnwell Priory and St. Radegund's), because when in 1209 a number of students fled from Oxford after a quarrel (the first of many) with the townspeople, it was chiefly in Cambridge that they settled. Both universities grew rapidly in reputation and numbers, and received the protection and patronage of the King and, as essentially ecclesiastical establishments, of the Pope.

In the early days there were no colleges. Students lived in lodgings, or in Halls or Inns presided over by a Master. The university's affairs were regulated by the Chancellor, who also had wide authority over town matters, assisted by the Proctors, Masters, and Regent Masters (teachers in charge of a 'school'). Lectures were held in hired rooms, while the parish churches were used for ceremonial occasions and meetings. It was not until 1320, when Oxford built the Congregation House, and 1350–1400 when Cambridge built the Old Schools, that either university had any property of its own.

COLLEGES

Meanwhile, however, the first colleges had appeared: at Oxford Merton, University, and Balliol, and at Cambridge Peterhouse, were all founded by 1300; many others followed, mostly owing their establishment to rich benefactors. They provided for the communal accommodation and financial needs of teachers and masters; in effect they were 'graduate' colleges. Such undergraduates as there were continued to live mostly in hostels and Halls until the 16C. The buildings followed the monastic model, and all the members were in religious orders, and of course celibate. The academic gowns of today are the descendants of their clerical robes. Simple and austere in their inception, many of the colleges became eventually both wealthy and powerful. Indeed, their influence, as great landowners and as ecclesiastical patrons, extended far beyond the confines of their respective universities.

LEARNING

Education was directed to the needs of the Church; theological studies, however, embraced logic, philosophy, and mathematics. Students entered at about sixteen for a seven-year course in the Liberal Arts, divided into the Trivium—Grammar, Rhetoric, and Logic—and the Quadrivium—Arithmetic, Geometry, Astronomy, and Music. Their names still appear above doorways of the Old Schools in Oxford. After taking his Bachelor of Arts degree the student had to study and teach for at least a further two years to qualify for his Master's degree. To achieve a doctorate required in all about sixteen years. In days when books and writing materials were scarce and expensive both teaching and examination (of which the 'disputation' was an important part) were oral. Latin was spoken throughout. Although other subjects, notably Law and Medicine, were added to the curriculum as time went on, this pattern continued little altered until the mid 16C.

During the 14C and 15C Oxford became one of the intellectual centres of Europe and took a leading part in the development of scholastic philosophy, the revived study of Aristotle (albeit in Latin translation), and the beginnings of experimental methods of enquiry. With this period are associated the great names of Grosseteste (the first Chancellor), Roger Bacon, Duns Scotus, and William of Ockham.

In the mid 14C the university was torn by the controversies surrounding the teaching of Wyclif and his followers, known as Lollards. Regarded as heretical by conservative church authorities, they came under severe episcopal displeasure, and for a time Oxford was in considerable disfavour, and suffered some decline.

TOWN AND GOWN

The story of the universities throughout the Middle Ages is punctuated with conflicts, often bloody, between town and gown, conflicts aggravated by the growing ostentation of college wealth, and the exemption of members of the university, who came under ecclesiastical law, from lay jurisdiction. Antagonism reached its climax in Oxford in 1355 with the Massacre of St. Scholastica's Day, when townsmen, summoned by the bells of St. Martin's, and students, summoned by the bells of St. Mary's, joined battle till the streets ran with blood. Although triumphant in the field, the townspeople later paid dearly for their victory, in fines and a yearly penance before the Vice Chancellor in St. Mary's church. This ceremony was discontinued only in 1825.

At Cambridge a somewhat similar event took place in 1381 during the feast of Corpus Christi, which was an occasion for the display of much collegiate wealth. Rioters attacked colleges, seized the treasures of Great St. Mary's, raided the university chest, and made a bonfire of documents outside the church. University and college authorities were forced to sign away their rights and privileges. But, as at Oxford, the university soon triumphed. The townsmen were severely punished with loss of rights, while the university's were all restored, and in addition it was given control over the town trade in food and drink, a control exercised until 1886.

The Renaissance and the Reformation

Interest in the New Learning grew throughout the 15C, stimulated by contact with the Italian universities where the Renaissance was already in full flower. At Oxford the movement towards humanistic studies and away from scholasticism was led by John Colet (who strongly influenced Erasmus during his sojourn in Oxford in 1498), by William Lily, Thomas Linacre, and William Grocyn, who first taught Greek publicly in the early 1500s, and one of whose pupils was Sir Thomas More, the 'man for all seasons'. In Cambridge the way was led by John Fisher (Vice Chancellor and later Chancellor of the university, and Bishop of Rochester, martyred in 1535). At his invitation Erasmus came to Cambridge, where he was the first to teach Greek, and in 1511 became Professor of Divinity. His presence much enhanced the university's European standing.

The religious upheavals of the 16C greatly affected Oxford and Cambridge. Many of their monastic students were dispersed and heads of colleges who would not recognise Henry VIII's supremacy (1534) were ejected. Oxford, always more religiously conservative, suffered more severely. Cambridge, under the influence of Thomas Bilney, Hugh Latimer, Nicholas Ridley, and the German protestants Martin Bucer and Paul Fagius, was in the forefront of the Reformation. After the execution of Bishop Fisher, Thomas Cromwell became Chancellor, and royal favour was shown in the establishment of five new professorships and the university's largest college—Trinity.

In 1555–56, when under Mary Tudor attempts were being made to restore the old faith, Oxford was the scene of the trial for heresy, and death at the stake, of the three bishops, Cranmer, Latimer and Ridley (the 'Oxford Martyrs', though all Cambridge men). At Cambridge John Hullier endured the same terrible death on Jesus Green.

After these storms Elizabeth I's reign provided a period of tranquillity. Protestantism gradually became the established religion and from 1581 all members of the universities had to assent to the Thirty-nine Articles; Roman Catholics and Nonconformists were thus excluded for the next 300 years. The Queen took a close interest in both places, visited them several times, and provided them with new statutes, which remained in force until the 19C.

UNDERGRADUATES
During the late 16C and the 17C the number of students increased greatly, and the range of studies widened to prepare young men for the professions and public life as well as the Church. There were considerable social distinctions between the various types of students, who ranked as follows:

Gentlemen or Fellow Commoners, who paid high fees and received many of the privileges of fellows. They wore special gowns and tasselled caps.

Scholars, paid for by the foundation, but not necessarily poor.

Commoners (Oxford) and *Pensioners* (Cambridge), who paid lower fees.

Servitors (Oxford) and *Sizars* (Cambridge), who received free board and lodging and some tuition and in return acted as servants to Fellows and Fellow Commoners.

The Civil War

The Civil War of 1642–46 had disastrous effects. Oxford, always royalist and High-Church, naturally supported the King. Cambridge did likewise, though, owing to its strong Puritan elements, with less enthusiasm. Almost all the colleges surrendered their plate to provide funds for the royalist cause. Both towns became deeply embroiled in the war, Oxford as the King's headquarters, Cambridge as a Parliamentary military stronghold. At Cambridge those Masters who were suspected of High-Church or royalist leanings were expelled, and chapels were stripped of their ornaments by the notorious iconoclast William Dowsing (though some, anticipating this purge, prudently removed or concealed their treasures). During the Commonwealth similar treatment was meted out to Oxford, though it did escape the activities of Dowsing. At the Restoration in 1660 the whole process was, of course, reversed.

From the Restoration to 1800

This was initially a time of great activity, with much building and rebuilding, and some widening of the range of studies, particularly in the sciences (the Royal Society, founded in 1660, consisted largely of Oxford and Cambridge men). But during the 18C both universities sank to a low ebb; there are many contemporary comments on the idleness, heavy drinking and lack of scholarship among Fellows and undergraduates alike. Examinations deteriorated into a farcical repetition of stereotyped questions and answers; any change or reform was obstinately opposed. 'The two universities were, in the opinion of the wit and cleric, Sydney Smith, like "enormous hulks confined within mooring chains, everything flowing and progressing around them" whilst they remained immovable and decaying in mid-stream' (V.H.H. Green, 'A History of Oxford University', p 107). They became more and more the preserve of the wealthy and privileged, as numbers dwindled and expenses increased.

Nineteenth-century Reform

At the beginning of the 19C Oxford and Cambridge were thus virtually still medieval universities. Amazing changes were to take place in the next hundred years, though reform came slowly, and often reluctantly. Some improvements were made in the examination system and some new subjects were introduced in the early 1800s, but progressive ideas were still strongly resisted, and Oxford in the 1830s and 1840s was largely absorbed in the controversies which raged round the *Tractarian* (or *'Oxford'*) *Movement*. This High-Church group, so called from the series of tracts in which its principal adherents propounded their views, was dedicated to a revitalisation of spiritual life and the refutation of the rationalist philosophies of the time. The leader of the movement, which was centred on Oriel College, was John Keble, and among its members were E.B. Pusey, Hurrell Froude, Isaac Williams, and the immensely influential John Newman. To conservative churchmen the Tractarians appeared dangerously Papistic (Newman did in fact join the Church of Rome in 1854, and eventually became a cardinal), and they rallied in opposition. In the words of the great contemporary Oxford scholar Mark Pattison, the struggle between the two factions 'entirely diverted our thoughts from the true business of the place' (Green, op.

cit., p 140).

No such doctrinal battles were fought in Cambridge. There the activities of the so-called *Camden Society* (or '*Ecclesiologists*'), who like the Tractarians drew their inspiration from the pre-Reformation church, were largely confined to matters of church architecture and furnishings, though even these caused fierce controversy on occasions.

In the end reform was forced on the universities through the Parliamentary Commissions of 1850 and 1874. There were widespread changes in the fields of administration, finance, subjects of study, and examination requirements. Religious tests were abolished in 1871, and from 1874 Fellows were allowed to marry. By 1900 Oxford and Cambridge were moving into the modern world.

Women in the Universities

These liberalising measures made possible the emergence on the scene of an entirely new character—the academic woman, although it was to be a long time before her presence made much impact on these strongholds of masculinity. As late as 1938 Sir John Betjeman could write: 'I suppose it is only right to bring in undergraduettes, but in bringing them in, it would be wrong to give the impression that they play a large part in the social life of the university'. And again: 'Whether there should be women dons, or whether women should be allowed a university training at all, is a question ...' ('An Oxford University Chest', pp 39 and 57).

The movement for the education of women had been gathering momentum since the 1840s. In their acceptance at the old universities it was for many years Cambridge which took the lead. Its Local

No Degrees for Women! The Scene outside the Senate House, 1897

Examinations were opened to girls in 1863 and it was a group of forward-looking Cambridge men-that helped and encouraged Emily Davies to open her college for women at Hitchin in 1869. Four years later it moved to Girton, two miles from Cambridge, and its members were able (very much on sufferance and closely chaperoned) to attend university lectures, although any social mixing was strictly taboo. Newnham College (then Hall) opened in 1878, and in 1881 women were allowed to sit the Tripos examination. And there, in Cambridge, the matter rested for over sixty years. Petitions for the admission of women to degrees and university membership were determinedly rebuffed, most violently in 1897 and 1920, when the controversy achieved national notoriety. Although titular degrees were granted in 1923 it was only in 1948 that women were fully admitted and in 1952 that their colleges achieved equal status with men's, and women were able to take their part in university counsels. In 1975 the first woman Vice Chancellor was elected. It seems somewhat ironical that gowns, proud symbol of the so hardly-won status of undergraduate, are now almost never worn by girls.

Oxford, always conservative, made a slower start. There the Association for the Higher Education of Women was not set up until 1878, nine years after the beginnings of Girton; the first women's colleges were established in 1879, and university examinations were not fully open to women until 1894. Thereafter, however, Oxford overtook Cambridge rapidly. Degrees for women were approved in principle in 1909, although not actually granted until 1920, when women became full members of the university. It was, however, 1959 before their colleges achieved equal status with men's. As at Cambridge this opened the doors of university office, and the first

woman Proctor was elected in 1979. This had one unforeseen result. Up to then female academic dress had consisted of the appropriate gown and a soft square black cap. Such headgear cannot be raised in ceremonial greetings, so Oxford's women took to the hard 'squares' long worn by their brothers, though now seldom seen on the heads of either sex.

The women who pioneered these achievements are mentioned in the accounts of the colleges with which they are associated. Among the many men who championed their cause a few must be named: at Cambridge Henry Tompkinson, Professor Fawcett, and pre-eminently Henry Sidgwick; at Oxford Professor T.H. Green, Dr Talbot (of Keble), Dr Mark Pattison, and Professor Arthur Sidgwick (Henry's brother). In the controversies surrounding their campaign the most extraordinary arguments were brought against them, ranging from the theory that the female brain could not survive long periods of study, to objections that female hats obscured the view during scientific demonstrations. Yet within a hundred years nearly all the colleges at both universities were equally open to men and women alike.

Modern Times

Changes as far-reaching as those of the late 19C affected Oxford and Cambridge after the Second World War. State aid for higher education brought a huge increase in the number of undergraduates, and graduates reading for advanced degrees. This, and the new emphasis on scientific studies, necessitated not only much expansion and reorganisation of the university facilities and administration, but vast new building programmes as well. In all these projects the universities have had help from munificent benefactors; colleges, individual buildings, professorships, fellowships, scholarships and research programmes bear witness to their names. At Oxford Lord Nuffield, who made a fortune in motor manufacture, poured the benefits of his wealth on to the university, in spite of his well-known aversion to academics, and his low opinion of the value of academic education. On the other hand a Frenchman who had made a fortune in the Middle East, M. Antonin Besse, had such a high opinion of Oxford graduates that he gave a complete new college (St. Antony's) and handsome endowments to a number of others. Yet another college (Green College) has been largely funded by Dr and Mrs Cecil Green of Dallas, Texas, two of many, many American benefactors, while the Nissan Motor Company of Japan has established and endowed a Centre for Japanese Studies.

Prominent among Cambridge benefactors are Mr David Robinson, a Cambridgeshire businessman, who has given the college of that name, and the Cripps family, donors of new buildings at Queens', St. John's, and Selwyn. Both Oxford and Cambridge have their Wolfson colleges, as well as a number of other buildings bearing this name. Both have also received much help from the Ford Foundation. These are just a few; industry has been generous to both universities, and so now, as in past generations, have countless individuals. The universities, for their part, have responded to the challenge of new needs in exciting and imaginative ways, and to changing attitudes and social 'mores' with—on the whole—sympathy and humour, so that seven hundred years of buildings, traditions, learning, and manners seem able to live together in tolerance—even in friendship.

OXFORD	CAMBRIDGE
The book which is always open at the same page	The book which is never opened

UNIVERSITY ORGANISATION

A distinguishing feature of Oxford and Cambridge is their combination of the communal life of the colleges with the teaching and degree-conferring functions of the university. There is no university building as such, nor anything in the nature of a university campus. Both university and colleges are corporate bodies with their own quite distinct endowments, though the colleges do now contribute to the funds of the university. Each college has its own staff of tutors, enabling pupils to receive individual attention (in *tutorials* at Oxford, *supervisions* at Cambridge), but its members are entitled to attend also all university lectures. The honours lectures of the colleges are open to all members of the university.

The college community. This consists of a Head, Fellows, and Undergraduates. The Head is known as Master (the almost invariable term at Cambridge), Warden, Principal, Provost, Rector, Dean (at Christ Church), or President (at Cambridge this title occasionally denotes the Vice-Master). The Fellows are selected from distinguished graduates, not necessarily of the university or college in which they hold a fellowship. The Fellows and Tutors are popularly known as Dons. Most colleges also have a number of honorary fellows, and graduate students reading for higher degrees.

Most undergraduates live in their college or one of its hostels, and are expected to dine in Hall a specified number of times during the week. The old regulations governing the time by which they had to be in their rooms in the evening, when the gates closed, have now largely vanished into history, and so, in consequence, has the ancient sport of climbing in after hours.

As it is the college rather than the university which is the focal point in Oxford and Cambridge life, it is the *Junior Common Rooms* (Oxford) and *Junior Combination Rooms* (Cambridge) and their committees which largely fulfil the functions performed at other universities by the student unions. In recent years Student Representative Councils have been established, to voice undergraduate opinion on general matters affecting daily life, and most faculties have liaison committees on which senior and junior members can meet to discuss academic affairs.

University authorities. The ultimate governing authority of the universities, consisting of all MAs who have kept their names on the books, is known as *Convocation* at Oxford, the *Senate* at Cambridge. In the past these bodies had wide voting rights, but since 1926 their function has been limited to formal matters, such as the election of the Chancellor. Legislative authority effectively rests with *Congregation* (Oxford) and the *Regent House* (Cambridge), made up of all resident doctors and MAs who hold teaching or administrative posts in the university or colleges. Measures submitted for their approval are called '*statutes*' at Oxford, '*graces*' at Cambridge. Administrative authority is exercised by the smaller elected bodies known as the *Hebdomadal* (weekly) *Council* (Oxford) and the *Council of the Senate* (Cambridge); the relationship is roughly comparable to the Government and the Cabinet.

The *Chancellor of the University*, elected (for life) by Convocation or the Senate as the case may be, is usually an eminent public figure. His rôle nowadays is purely ceremonial. In practice his executive duties are carried out by the *Vice-Chancellor*, normally (though at Oxford not necessarily) the head of one of the Colleges, who is elected by Congregation or the Council of the Senate and holds office for four years at Oxford, two at Cambridge.

University discipline is the particular responsibility of the two *Proctors* (though they have a variety of other duties), who are Fellows of colleges and hold office for a year. At Oxford they are assisted by *Pro-Proctors* and an *Assessor*.

Courses of study, appointments of teachers, and examinations are controlled by *Faculty Boards*. The range of courses open to students is extensive, and always growing; full details of everything to do with admission, courses, first and higher degrees, are given in the university handbooks, calendars and prospectuses.

The **University Year** begins in October and is divided into three terms of about eleven weeks, at Oxford *Michaelmas*, *Hilary*, and *Trinity*, at Cambridge, *Michaelmas*, *Lent*, and *Easter*. 'Full Term', during which undergraduates are required to be in residence, begins about two weeks after 'term', and ends about a week earlier. Undergraduates normally remain at the university for three or four years, depending on their course of study, and read for an honours degree (Bachelor of Arts).

In contrast with the procedure at other universities, entrants to Oxford and Cambridge (who may not apply to both universities in the same year) have to apply not to the university itself, but to the college of their choice. Colleges are mostly arranged in groups for entrance purposes, and candidates may be considered by another college within the same group if not accepted by their first choice. Places are awarded either on the outcome of a special examination and interview or on local examination results and interview. The old examinations of 'Responsions' at Oxford and 'Little Go' at Cambridge, which qualified an applicant for admission to the university, have been superseded by exemptions granted on satisfactory local examination levels. The old system of entrance awards has also (recently) been abolished; in the past new students might be granted scholarships or exhibitions (at Cambridge, scholars were known as 'pensioners'). Now such awards are given on the results of several terms' work (usually after the first year). At neither university is Greek or Latin any longer necessary. Compulsory Greek as an entry requirement was abolished in 1919 at Cambridge and in 1920 at

Oxford; Latin was finally dethroned (not without a struggle) in 1960.

Examinations are held in late May and June; at Oxford Finals or 'Schools' are taken all together, at Cambridge normally in two parts, one at the end of two years, the other at the end of the third (or fourth) year. These parts need not be in the same subject, although they are normally related; together they are known as the 'Tripos' (perhaps from the three-legged stool on which the examiner sat in the days of oral examinations). Results are graded into classes; those passing out in mathematics at Cambridge are classed as *Wranglers* and Senior and Junior *Optimes*, though since the introduction of alphabetically-arranged lists no longer graded as 1st, 2nd, 3rd, etc, within their class.

No further examination is required for a Master of Arts degree (MA) which can be obtained for a modest fee seven years after matriculation (acceptance into the university).

Ceremonies and Dress. Degree-givings take place at intervals throughout the year, at Oxford in the Sheldonian Theatre, at Cambridge in the Senate House. The ceremonies, conducted in Latin, are ancient and impressive, especially when higher or honorary degrees are being conferred and the scene is enriched with the gorgeously-coloured robes and hoods of those holding or receiving doctorates. The highlight of academic ceremonial at Oxford is *Encaenia*, or *Commemoration*, held on the Wednesday following the end of the Trinity term (early July). The name dates from the dedication of the Sheldonian in 1669, and the occasion is the last surviving remnant of the 'Act', the medieval ceremony of confirming degrees granted over the previous year, and of remembering founders and benefactors.

The grand summer degree-givings at Cambridge are known as *General Admissions*, those throughout the year as *Congregations*. The old name of Commencements was abandoned in 1926.

Full **academic dress** consists of the appropriate gown, for graduates a hood (slung round the neck and hanging down the back, not worn on the head) and a square hard black cap. Men wear dark suits, white shirts, white bow ties and at Cambridge 'bands' (short strips of linen at the neck); women wear dark dresses, or dark skirts with white blouses, and dark stockings. This curiously attractive costume is known at Oxford as 'sub fusc'. Academic dress is worn at Oxford for ceremonial occasions: degree-giving, matriculation—when new entrants are formally presented to the Vice-Chancellor—and for examinations. At Cambridge it is worn for degree-giving only. There is no university matriculation ceremony, but some colleges conduct their own. For examinations only a gown is required. Gowns vary according to status. All undergraduate gowns are black (except at the Cambridge colleges of Caius and Trinity, where they are dark blue), and at Oxford little more than loose black cotton waistcoats with long hanging bands in front, although scholars are distinguished by a longer gown. Graduates' gowns are fuller, and those of doctors of different colours, scarlet predominating. In the past undergraduates had to wear gowns for lectures, interviews, tutorials and supervisions, Chapel (surplices on Sundays, at Cambridge for all, at Oxford for Heads, Fellows and scholars), for meals in Hall, and out-of-doors in the evening. These formalities have largely disappeared, though some colleges still require gowns in Hall.

Sport and Leisure. Sport plays a large part in university life, although its position has perhaps declined as the importance of examination results has grown. All games are played, most colleges having their own sports grounds, but the athletic activity most connected in the public mind with Oxford and Cambridge is perhaps rowing. This takes place at Oxford on the Isis (Thames), mostly between Folly Bridge and Iffley, at Cambridge on the Cam between Midsummer Common and Bait's Bite Lock, beyond Fen Ditton. Rowing began in the early 19C, and the first inter-university boat race took place at Henley-on-Thames in 1829. This race (now rowed in London between Putney and Mortlake in late March or early April) gradually became a national sporting event, people who had no connection with either university being passionate supporters of one or the other boat, and flaunting dark blue favours for Oxford, light blue for Cambridge, according to a wholly arbitrary allegiance. History was made in 1981 when the Oxford crew included a woman coxwain. Inter-collegiate races, in which women now have an official part, although they do not compete against the men's crews, take place in February (known as *Torpids* at Oxford, *Lents* at Cambridge), and in early summer during *Eights Week* (Oxford, late May) and *May Week* (Cambridge, mid June). The object, except in the case of the Torpids, is not to overtake but to 'bump' the boat ahead; the college crews race in several divisions on four successive days, and the top boats of the lower divisions ('sandwich boats') row also at the bottom of the divisions immediately above them. The boats start at intervals of 160ft: if a boat succeeds in 'bumping' the one in front of it, it takes that boat's place in the next day's contest. Members of crews which move up four places or end up 'Head of the River' are awarded an oar on which is recorded the event and the names of the oarsmen and coxwain. Those who represent their university in rowing, or any other sport, are awarded a *'blue'*, or for minor sports, a *'half-blue'*.

During Eights Week and May Week the colleges hold sumptuous balls, usually in specially erected marquees within the grounds. Evening dress is de rigueur, and after dancing all night the tradition is to punt up or down the river in the dawn light to a bacon and egg breakfast.

Drama flourishes at both universities. Although the *Oxford University Dramatic Society* (OUDS) has a very high standard, it is Cambridge that seems to produce the actors and the shows (notably the Footlights Revue) which go on to achieve a national reputation. The *Amateur Dramatic Club* (ADC) was founded in 1855 and has its own theatre just off Jesus Lane.

In politics it is Oxford which is pre-eminent, and many famous politicians have served their apprenticeship in the Union, as the university debating societies are called. Distinguished public figures are invited as guest speakers at debates, which are sometimes regarded as being of sufficient moment to be reported in the national press.

For those who aspire to journalism there is a wide variety of publications, notably at Oxford the magazines 'Cherwell' and 'Isis', and at Cambridge 'Stop Press', 'Broadsheet', and the undergraduates' vade mecum 'Varsity Handbook' (all still in publication in 1986).

Indeed, whatever the interest, a club or society seems to exist to cater for it, and the multiplicity of meetings and entertainments offered on college notice boards is bewilderingly various. There are, too, amusements which are not announced: the thrilling hazards of night-climbing, and the associated recreation of undergraduate 'pranks'. It is perhaps less commonplace than it used to be for chamber pots, umbrellas, and gowns to appear on spires and roof-tops, but over the past years Cambridge has excelled itself with a banner slung between the pinnacles of King's College Chapel, and a car slung under St. John's 'Bridge of Sighs', while Oxford successfully entrapped motorists in an inescapable circulation of the one-way road system by the judicious re-arrangement of a few traffic signs.

Among all these activities is one enjoyed and indulged in by every right-minded Oxbridgean—going on the river. Punting on the willow-lined Cherwell or Cam on sunny afternoons, or twilit evenings in early summer, must be one of the most 'unforgettable, unforgotten' memories of undergraduate days. Even here the universities must differ; Oxford punts from the sloping end, Cambridge from the flat.

Oxford punts from the sloping end, Cambridge from the flat.
Above: On the Cherwell. Below: On King's Backs

THE ARCHITECTURE OF OXFORD AND CAMBRIDGE

by *Stephen Games*

Oxford and Cambridge offer an ideal introduction to the history of English architecture. They have both seen an almost continuous growth and development over the last 700 years, and buildings from most periods still remain. Individual buildings are among the finest anywhere in the country; together they add up to a fascinating architectural tapestry.

At heart, both Oxford and Cambridge are medieval townships and although apparently similar they have distinct identities which appeal to different people in different ways. Oxford with its noble colleges along the High Street is the more urbane of the two, Cambridge with its colleges stretching gracefully down to the river Cam the more romantic.

Cambridge lacks Oxford's busy skyline. It is flatter and smaller and has always had fewer colleges, though within each one there may be a wider variety in the size of courts and the styles of building. Only Christ Church, Oxford, comes near to the spaciousness of King's and Trinity, and many of Cambridge's smaller colleges achieve a sense of airiness by opening up their courts on one side to give views of the outside world.

At Oxford, the colleges themselves are smaller and more tightly enclosed. There are high stone walls, including the old city wall which runs down Merton Walk and skirts the grounds of New College, and they fence the colleges off from the town, shutting out prying eyes. By contrast, Cambridge college gardens are famed for their planting and welcome the curious gaze of students and visitors as they punt past on the river or stroll along the Backs.

Oxford colleges are divided into a larger number of smaller quadrangles, making the precincts of the Bodleian Library and Oriel Lane into a dense maze of secret worlds. There is a greater similarity of buildings, partly because until the mid 19C all Oxford colleges were built in the same oolitic limestone, a good quality stone found locally.

Cambridge, whose only local stone was a poor quality clunch rubble, used red, then white, brick, or less often a stone imported from further afield. This gives it a greater variety of buildings and a less uniform, less consistent atmosphere. In this it is perhaps the more truly typical of the picturesque character of English architecture.

The location of Oxford in the area of the Cotswold Hills, and of Cambridge in the flat marshes of East Anglia, has proved a decisive factor influencing the architectural identity of each town. Cambridge colleges were built on reclaimed land outside the existing medieval town and at the convergence of two main roads, the London Road and the Colchester Road. The area between them is triangular, and triangular planning is invariably muddled and complex.

Oxford was built on slightly rising ground, well above flood level and some distance from the river Isis (Thames) and its tributary the Cherwell. In spite of its huddle of narrow streets and alleys, Oxford has a rectilinear street pattern which lends itself easily to simple, urbane planning, with ample opportunities for creating dramatic spaces.

Many Cambridge colleges are built between road and river, which gives them an ambiguity. They have to look in two directions: they have a hard face, with tough brick walls and castellated gatehouses built straight up against the street; and they have a soft face with the lawns and river gardens which give the Backs their wide open quality.

Because of their distance from the river, Oxford colleges are not distracted from their simple relationship with the street. Instead, they have a single entrance which is marked by a square stone gate tower, developed from Saxon towers. Everything else is bounded by a wall. Even at Magdalen, the only college which does front the river, there is a hard edge of buildings against the waterfront.

Oxford also has a hierarchy of streets with broad major roads intersecting at right angles and minor roads behind. The smallest are the lanes—Queen's Lane, Logic Lane, Oriel Lane—little more than alleyways dog-legging between one college and another. The grandest street, the High, is a slowly curving thoroughfare across which college buildings face each other.

Then there is St. Giles, wide enough for a whole fairground in the summer, and the Broad, once the site of the town ditch but later the scene of a noble civic forum dominated by the Bodleian Library, the Sheldonian Theatre and the Old Ashmolean Museum, all university, rather than collegiate, buildings.

Cambridge has nothing like it. The college buildings face not other colleges across the narrow streets, but rambling old town buildings, which used to dominate the town far more than they do today, now that so many have been lost, and which impeded the expansion of the university. There are no major streets. The road along which most of the colleges are threaded, Trinity Street, winds about and changes its name four times within a few hundred yards. The only attempt to create a university forum—rather than the town market-place—is a small lawn in front of the Senate House.

Both universities began the same way, with teaching masters who took paying students who would later provide the trained manpower that ran the Church and the Court. An early example of their buildings can be seen in the remains of Gloucester College, founded in Oxford in 1283 and now incorporated into Worcester College. Built by Benedictines, the undressed limestone walls are typical of ordinary Cotswold housing of the day.

The Church dominated medieval society, and the earliest college buildings took the form of monastic institutions. The two largest buildings were the Hall, where everyone ate, and the Chapel. Then there would be studies and lodgings, a library, a kitchen and a lodge for the master. This order has survived to modern times at both the universities.

The first college to organise itself in this way was Merton in 1264, and Oxford continued to develop along fairly conservative lines. In a period of 200 years, from 1379 to 1566, Oxford built nine new colleges, of which eight were founded by powerful bishops and the ninth, Christ Church, by a cardinal, Thomas Wolsey. Not surprisingly, these church foundations conformed to an architectural orthodoxy, though one which was elaborated in considerable depth.

New College, built between 1379 and 1386 by William of Wykeham (Bishop of Winchester), was the first grand version of this model, with a chapel and raised hall side by side on the north of the quad, and a fortified gatehouse on the west. There are separate rooms for sleep and study, distinguishable by the alternating two- and three-light windows. Although all the rooms were part of the college community, they continued to be grouped around separate staircases each with its own front entrance, as if they were private row houses. Even grander in scale was Magdalen, built by another Bishop of Winchester nearly 100 years later, with a cloister all round the main quadrangle. Many regard it as the finest collegiate building at either university.

The Merton model, which had been so successful at Oxford and which the Bishop of Ely had recommended in the building of Cambridge's first college, Peterhouse, in 1284, had little impact on later buildings at Cambridge. Over the same 200-year period, excepting the foundation of Jesus College by a later Bishop of Ely in 1496, colleges were built by many people apart from the Church—especially clerical academics, the Crown, and women close to the Court. The result was a far greater variety of buildings, but of poorer architectural quality.

Cambridge saw six new colleges founded in the 14C but it was not until well into the 15C that planned courts came to be built—at Magdalene, King's, Christ's and Queens'. Until then, college building was crude—Old Court at Corpus Christi gives some idea still—and disorganised.

When the Crown founded colleges at Cambridge it frequently made use of existing buildings, as at Trinity, or built cheaply. Queens', founded by the Rector of St. Botolph's in 1446 but taken over almost immediately by the queen of Henry VI, then by the queen of Edward IV, is a good example. Built in a reddish brick with two cloistered wings in the second court, it may look quaint to us now but it lacks any of the extravagance of Oxford. It was simply a serviceable building, based on a manor house of the period with a ceremonial gatehouse, rather than a monastery.

Cambridge continued to build sensible, generally modest, buildings on a scale that was domestic rather than grand. Henry VI's Chapel at King's College seems to be an exception—it is not. For all its soaring beauty it is a very simple building, a unique free-standing single-space structure based on a medieval hall and quite unlike the Oxford chapels, with their transepts and choir inspired by the unfinished chapel at Merton.

Other Cambridge buildings continued to break the rules to which Oxford conforms. When Dr Caius refounded Gonville College in 1557 he built the first three-sided court in the style of what were at the time the most modern French country houses. They were open on the fourth side to encourage ventilation and so prevent disease, and this was copied soon after in the new buildings of Emmanuel and Sidney Sussex.

Disease must have been combated at Cambridge fairly successfully, for Third Court at St. John's, 1669, was the first college building to be built two rooms deep, meaning that they could only be ventilated on one side. According to Pevsner, the doubling-up was an afterthought after building work had begun. It is another sign of the makeshift nature of Cambridge buildings—invariably the result of lack of funds, sometimes lack of foresight, and frequently at the expense of urban cohesion.

We therefore have to take Cambridge buildings as we find them—at random: the Fellows' Building at Christ's was the first semi-Classical free-standing residential block in the 17C; Clare College, built by the Grumbold family, was a deliberately played-down reaction against Jacobean excess; Wren's chapels show the restraining influence of the Dutch; Rickman and Hutchinson's Fourth Court and Bridge of Sighs at St. John's, however, show a lavish example of picturesque scene-setting though the rear is plain brick.

Perhaps because a very satisfactory architectural style was established at Oxford from early on, its development was cautious and slow. We see fan-vaulting at King's College Chapel in Cambridge in 1508, designed by John Wastell. It takes 125 years before it appears at Oxford, above the beautiful staircase to the side of Christ Church Cathedral, and it was only adopted, presumably, when it was considered safely archaic. At University College, the 1716 Quad was built as an almost exact copy of Front Quad, designed in 1634 by Richard Maude with a series of little Dutch gables and Perp hood mouldings over each window.

Gothic architecture survived far longer at Oxford than anywhere else in England, let alone Europe. Even Wren, architect of St. Paul's Cathedral in London, and a man with an inquiring mind who felt more at home with Italian Baroque architecture, grudgingly returned to a kind of Gothic when asked to complete Tom Tower at Christ Church, and Hawksmoor followed his example at All Souls thirty-five years later.

Wren's earlier work, the Sheldonian Theatre, can be seen less as a contribution to mainstream Oxford architecture than as an archaeological reconstruction of an ancient Roman theatre built as an academic curiosity, just as the botanist John Tradescant brought exotic plants back from his travels abroad for the purpose of study.

Taking English architecture as a whole, there have been waves of extravagance followed by waves of simplicity. Almost without exception, Oxford benefited by the former, Cambridge by the latter. The pattern of Oxford's building activity peaked during the Middle and Late Gothic, then the Jacobean, Palladian, Baroque, and High Victorian periods, all periods of exceptional grandeur and force. The phases of Cambridge's building activity are, by contrast, Tudor, Dutch Classical, Georgian, Picturesque, and Arts and Crafts.

This does not mean, however, that there was not a certain amount of overlap and by the time we get to the 19C the divisions become less precise, especially with the Neo-Classicism of the 1820s and the Neo-Traditionalism that began in the 1890s and carried right through to as late as the 1950s.

Of those periods, the one in which Oxford is utterly unmatched is that of Jacobean Baroque in the early 17C, an architectural style which combines the heraldic devices and intricate strapwork and panelling of the Elizabethans with the Classical architecture of the Italian Renaissance. There are many small examples but the two masterpieces are Wadham College (1610–13) and the Bodleian Library (1613). The feature they share is the monumental gateway, a vast elaboration of the medieval gate towers typical of Oxford but dressed up to look Roman.

The frontispiece of the Bodleian is the grander. It is five-tiered to show each of the Classical orders (Tuscan, Doric, Ionic, Corinthian and Composite) used by the Romans. Each tier is increasingly elaborately carved, rising past a panel showing James I being attended by Fame and the University, and topped by two unequal crocketed pinnacles with a pierced strapwork crest between them.

Compare what Cambridge was doing in the same period.

Cambridge had actually made its excursion into Renaissance architecture as early as 1567 with Caius's Gate of Virtue, but had no idea how to develop the idea. The Gate of Honour, 1575, is an ingenuous muddle of wrong proportions and confused motifs. And even fifty years later, in 1628, Peterhouse Chapel is still an unholy mixture of eccentric elements and fancy curves, not helped by alterations in 1709. And yet by 1631, Canterbury Quad at St. John's Oxford showed a far more accurate attempt at Classical architecture, while the next year Nicholas Stone's gateway to the Botanic Garden had finally got it right.

A similar episode took place in the 18C. The growing antiquarian interest among university dons turned its attention to Andrea Palladio, the 16C Italian architect. Dean Aldrich of Christ Church and Dr Clarke of All Souls turned amateur architects and, with William Townesend, a builder, and others, provided Oxford with a wealth of Palladian buildings from 1705 until about 1770. Their purity was only matched at Cambridge with the Fellows' Building at Peterhouse, 1738.

By this time, Oxford was already creating one of the best pieces of Baroque townscaping ever seen in England, with the building by Gibbs of the Radcliffe Camera. This magnificent circular domed building sits between the semi-Gothic buildings of All Souls by Hawksmoor, for whom Gibbs had worked and who had planned a Camera of his own, and the medieval Brasenose College, now rebuilt. Though it was completely different from anything seen in Oxford before, with curved buttresses around the dome taken from Longhena's Santa Maria della Salute in Venice, it was completely at home.

It was around this time that Cambridge began to look over its shoulder at Oxford and realise that architecturally it was failing to compete. Various architects were aware of the problem and came forward with schemes of their own to transform the university. Hawksmoor, again, suggested turning Cambridge into an Italian Baroque city with monumental vistas linked by the existing church spires. It came to nothing. Nor did a project by Capability Brown, the landscape designer, to turn all the little college gardens on the Backs into one big parkland. As with Henry VI's plans for King's College in the 16C, Cambridge's architectural history was proving to be more important for what was not built than for what was.

Another scheme which failed to materialise was Gibbs' plan for a university centre, also designed to unify the town. One part of it however was built, the Senate House 1722–30, though it looked so out of place that in 1754 the Master of Caius College next door built a pretty Palladian facade for the medieval Old Schools building by its side in an attempt to bring some Classical order to the scene.

If these ambitious schemes got nowhere, it was because Cambridge was nowhere near as rich as Oxford, where large endowments enabled college Fellows to indulge themselves in good food, good wine, good hunting and good architecture, untroubled by trifling academic concerns. The reduction in student numbers was hitting both universities severely throughout the 18C, but whereas Oxford spent its way out of the recession, Cambridge went into decline.

Some colleges at Cambridge, however, were shamed into improving the appearance of their decaying medieval buildings, and there was a strong reaction against Cambridge's traditional building material, brick, now thought second-rate. In the absence of any need for new buildings, Peterhouse refaced its old buildings in stone in 1754, followed by Christ's in 1758, Emmanuel in 1764 and several other colleges. The result was invariably an unsatisfactory combination of medieval buildings with Georgian sash windows but lacking the simple proportions which even the humblest Georgian building can boast. It was a typical case of Cambridge's make-do-and-mend attitude to building.

Colleges that did not have enough money to afford stone facings covered their brickwork or clunch in Roman cement (stucco) instead. This is what happened at Sidney Sussex College, where in the 1820s Wyatville hid the existing Elizabethan buildings behind a fake skin of gables and battlements. Had the colleges been wealthier and had to serve a larger student population, all these buildings would have been demolished and replaced.

The only way for Cambridge to stop worrying about what its existing buildings looked like was for it to turn its attention to new buildings instead. This had to wait for the climb in student numbers that affected both universities in the 19C and which in turn gave rise to calls for educational reform and a new approach to university-based, rather than collegiate, teaching.

Reform was in fact imposed on Oxford and Cambridge by Act of Parliament and it is at this point, with the universities bowing to national pressures, that their separate identities begin to blur. Yet Cambridge continued to leave its best ideas unfulfilled, especially in the neo-Greek buildings of Cockerell, Burton, and Rickman and Hutchinson, for which it was argued that Greek architecture best represented the new ideals of freedom and enlightenment being discussed in education. William Wilkins, a don at Caius, did manage to build the new college of Downing as a series of Grecian pavilions linked around three sides of a wide campus. Although it became the standard plan for American colleges, it was ignored by the rest of Cambridge.

Reform had an architectural impact in several directions: the new emphasis on science teaching at Cambridge resulted in the university laboratories on the Pembroke and Downing sites; the lifting of the restriction on marriage for dons saw the creation of a whole suburb of large brick villas in north Oxford in the 1870s and a smaller suburb of more individual houses in west Cambridge around the turn of the century; finally there was the establishment of the women's colleges.

Oxford's strong conservative church links responded to threats of progress with an overwhelming call to revive the ecclesiastical architecture of the 14C, a movement which it pursued with its invariable vigour, insensitively destroying or improving buildings not considered sufficiently Gothic but also putting up a fantastic variety of very stylised new buildings.

For many architects working at Oxford, the Gothic revival meant the opportunity to be inventive, without the restrictions of proportions and symmetry which Classical architecture imposed on them. Among the most imaginative work was that of Butterfield, who at the new Keble College created huge expanses of flat wall in polychromatic brickwork.

Butterfield's use of brick, a material foreign to Oxford, was just one symptom of the enormous shake-up which architecture suffered under the Victorians. Even John Ruskin, the Oxford social reformer who preached about ornament, colour and texture in architecture and who commended the Gothic of Venetian palazzi and French cathedrals, found himself approving the cast-iron frame and glass roof of Woodward's University Museum.

Salvin, Waterhouse, and later Champneys and Caröe, created equally strident buildings which were frequently damaging to the character of both universities. Particularly badly hit were Balliol at Oxford, which was almost entirely rebuilt, and Caius and Pembroke at Cambridge; Waterhouse had a hand in all of them. Cambridge also had its traditions turned upside down when in 1863 Scott built a copy of Merton Chapel at St. John's, Cambridge's first transeptual chapel, and one of a number of Victorian stone churches—lovely in the Midlands, wrong for East Anglia.

Victorian Gothic, however, was less well represented, and appeared later, at Cambridge although the medieval revival of the 1820s pre-dated the Oxford Tractarians. Butterfield, Burges and Street —powerful architects at Oxford—had no luck at Cambridge. Instead, Cambridge waited to develop its more domestic Arts and Crafts work, with Morris creating sumptuous medieval interiors at Jesus, Queens', Peterhouse and All Saints Church, while Blomfield's new Selwyn College was a typically sensible, modest, contrast to Keble.

There is an argument that with the abandonment of celibacy for masters of colleges in the reign of Elizabeth I, Cambridge acquired a variety of charming Master's Lodges and that the presence of women close to the university influenced its architectural decisions. True or not, it was the building of women's colleges in the 1870s and 1880s with their softer, less aggressive, designs—medieval almshouses at Girton, Queen Anne at Newnham—which contributed again to Cambridge's romantic rural atmosphere.

In the 18C and early 19C, and after the First World War, most colleges locked up their rooms and bolted the shutters for lack of students. But in the 1930s a massive expansion in student numbers began, leading to huge pressure on space. Both universities responded with a major programme, after the war, of new colleges and faculty buildings, mainly outside the historic centres, and by the conversion and enlargement of old town buildings which were adopted for modern college use.

In many cases, new buildings have proved more important in the repertoire of the architects who built them than for any contribution they might have made to the universities, though more recent buildings have captured some feeling for tradition and continuity. In general, in spite of an initial insensitivity and destructiveness in their handling of new architectural techniques, architects have quickly learnt how to slip new buildings on to difficult sites with great ingenuity, adding depth to the historic fabric of the towns.

	OXFORD	**CAMBRIDGE**

SAXON

England's earliest surviving, most basic architecture. Square towers, crude stone. Openings few and small. Plan small, square.

St Michael's Church, Cornmarket

St Bene't's, Trumpington St. Shows vestiges of Roman-style architecture, with round-headed doorway and square capitals.

Top tier of St Bene't's Church tower, Cambridge

NORMAN

Brought to England from France in 1066. Seen at best in churches and castles. Massive walls, large heavy roofs. Dressed stone provided flat surfaces for wall painting, now rare. Carved decoration, based on painting, seen in zig-zag mouldings round tops of columns, doorways, arches. All openings round-headed.

St Fridewide's Priory, now part of Christ Church Cathedral. **St Peter-in-the-East,** Queen's Lane, fantastic birds' head mouldings on south doorway. **Iffley Church,** zig-zag mouldings. **St George's Tower,** part of Oxford Castle, 1071.

Church of the Holy Sepulchre, Cambridge

Round Church (Holy Sepulchre), Bridge St. Early 12C. Rare. Only four other round churches of period in the country. Drastic re-building in 19C when conical roof added.

DOMESTIC NORMAN

Houses consisted of single room, or hall, often at first floor level, for all living, sleeping, eating. Stores in undercroft. Became major feature of all college buildings.

School of Pythagoras, St John's, Cambridge

School of Pythagoras, grounds of St John's College, c·1200. May have been home of a teacher, or master, with paying resident students.

GOTHIC

Pointed arch and spire. Main structure in buttresses. Walls thinner with larger windows than before. First windows were narrow lancets, but from early 14C lancets combined and stone shafts between them thinner, ending in elaborate tracery in window heads. Planned layout of buildings. Monastic communities in first colleges, with buildings arranged round court (Cambridge) or quadrangle (Oxford).

Merton College, 1308-78. First college to lay down quadrangle plan. **Chapel,** 1290, without nave, became Oxford model. [Exeter: Chapel, 1854-60, brilliant copy of this period by Scott. Large rose windows, steep pitched roof, statues on buttresses, decorated trefoil parapet.]

Exeter College Chapel, Oxford

[**St John's: Chapel,** copy of Oxford Gothic chapel by Scott, 1863-69.]

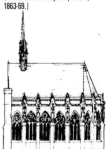

EARLY PERPENDICULAR

Emerging preference for straight lines, verticality and distorted forms. Arches flatter, quatrefoils stretched, windows larger.

New College, 1379-86. Classic example of planned quadrangle. Also **Funerary Cloister,** 1400. **All Souls: Chapel,** hammerbeam roof, 1442. **Merton College,** square stone tower, 1448, developed from Saxon towers. See also numerous square gate towers at other colleges.

Merton College Chapel, Oxford

PERPENDICULAR

Peculiarly English development of Gothic. Avoids curves. Emphasis on height. Complex intersecting patterns. Flat walls divided up by ribs and string courses as if windows. Intricate vaulted ceilings became fan vaults. Intricate hollow parapets. Huge glass windows, often coloured, with numerous thin shafts supported by horizontal bars. Pinnacles, square-plan spirelets, crockets.

Divinity School: lierne vault by master-mason William Orchard, c 1483, with complicated rib and pendent bosses.

King's College: Chapel, begun 1446 by Reginald Ely. Completed 1515. Unique as free-standing building. Superb fan-vaulting. Early 16C. by John Wastell.

Divinity School, Oxford

King's College Chapel, Cambridge

DOMESTIC PERPENDICULAR

St John's College, Cambridge

Magdalen, 1474-1510, perfect example of cloistered quad, with gargoyle string course round parapet hiding gutter. Statuary and bestiary on buttresses as alternatives to spirelets. Upper storey later than lower.

Queens' College, 1448, by Reginald Ely, builder of King's Chapel. Scale smaller than anything at Oxford. Cambridge's first planned college, based on manor house rather than monastery as at Oxford. Same red brick as Magdalene, and Trinity Hall. Huge turreted gatehouses —Cambridge feature. See also **St John's** (two), **Trinity** (two plus chapel), **Old Schools, Christ's** (now stone-faced), and **Jesus** (square with stepped corners).

Magdalen Cloister, Oxford

TUDOR

After Reformation, style dictated by landed families instead of the Church. Unfortified manor houses, with castellations and other vestiges of castles used as decoration. Windows grouped into several lights. Perp. heads, but set in rectangular frame. Square hood mouldings over windows. Ornamental lanterns instead of spires.

Queens' College: President's Gallery, c 1540. Half-timbered in original yellow and brown, not false white and black. Squarish flat-capped appearance. Tall vertical timbers, few diagonals. Leaded glass, bay windows.

President's Gallery, Queens' College, Cambridge

ELIZABETHAN

Mania for intricate flat decoration. Copious examples at both universities, mostly interiors and so difficult to find. Heraldic devices, strapwork, linen-fold, lozenges, and motifs clumsily copied from Italian Renaissance.

Main gate, Christ's College, Cambridge

Jesus: First Quad, 1571, with symmetrical windows and mullions.

Gonville and Caius, 1565-67. **Second court** (Caius), open on one side and screened by wall. Shows influence of French country houses. Became popular in later Cambridge buildings. See also **Emmanuel, Sidney Sussex, Caius: Gate of Virtue** and **Gate of Honour. Trinity Hall,** mid 16C, shows Dutch influence in stepped gable.

| | **OXFORD** | **CAMBRIDGE** |

JACOBEAN

Elements of Roman architecture employed as motifs on medieval buildings, but still essentially as decoration; columns, pediments, porticos used more sculpturally, less flat, than before. Excessively lavish at Oxford, displaying Royalist sympathies. Architectural tableaux centred round openings—fireplaces, gateways, and flat-fronted Oxford gate towers. Cambridge more eccentric, less exotic.

Wadham, 1610, grand four-storey frontispiece with paired columns, triumphal arch, heraldic shield. **Bodleian Library,** 1613-24, five-storey frontispiece with Tuscan, Doric, Ionic, Corinthian and Composite columns and strapwork pediment on buildings still boxy-Tudor. **St John's: Canterbury Quad,** 1631-36, shows Tudor castellated parapet and persists with hood mouldings incorporated into string course. Also elegant Renaissance cloister. **University College,** 1634-77, and **Oriel College,** 1620-42 **Front Quads** show Jacobean gables.

Peterhouse: Chapel, 1628-32, Gothic and Renaissance motifs eccentrically combined. Ogee Perp. niches, crocketed, Corinthian pilasters, rusticated facade. **Magdalene: Pepys Library,** date unknown, mock projecting gable fronts, round-arched cloister.

Detail of Bodleian Library, Oxford

EARLY RENAISSANCE

Reaction against excess, seen only at Cambridge. New mood of simple Classicism in which forms previously used with abandon now brought under control.

Fellows' Building, Christ's College, Cambridge

Trinity: Nevile's Court, 1612. Early attempt at Classical restraint. Windows regular in bays. Elegant cloister. Uninterrupted balustrade. Little decoration. **Clare College,** 1638-1700s by John Westley and the Grumbold family. Order, rhythmical facade. Tall, narrow, square bays. Regular dormer windows with hipped roofs, or pedimented gables. **Christ's: Fellows' Building,** 1640-43.

WREN

First English architect with academic knowledge of Italian Renaissance who built widely. Also influenced by Dutch, especially, and by French sources to adapt Italian and Roman models for English needs. College chapels are simple boxes, main facade on short side. Pilasters, niches, garlands, pediments, parapet urns, and lanterns used with restraint. Little other decoration.

Sheldonian Theatre, 1663-69. Faithful reconstruction of ancient Theatre of Marcellus in Rome. Ceiling painted as sky and interior meant to resemble canvas structure. **Trinity College: Chapel,** 1691-94.

Pembroke College: Chapel, 1665, Wren's first Cambridge building. **Emmanual College: Chapel,** 1666-77. **Trinity College: Library,** 1676-90, retains the cloisters and style of Nevile's Court. Excellent carving inside by Grinling Gibbons. Also fine plasterwork.

Sheldonian Theatre, Oxford

PALLADIAN

Academic interest in architecture of Andrea Palladio, 16C Italian, first published in English editions around early 18C. Palladio's country villas were rectangular boxes with main facade on long side. Proportional, symmetrical facade with central feature—portico, pediment, flight of stairs, etc. Town palazzi heavier, without central feature. Length, proportions unimportant. Windows round-headed or keystoned, large, regular, shorter at each storey.

Three amateurs led Oxford Palladianism earlier than rest of country: Dean Aldrich of Christ Church, Dr Clarke of All Souls, Wm Townesend, experienced builder. **Christ Church: Peckwater Quad,** N., E. and W. sides, 1705-14, by Aldrich. Probably also his **All Saints Church,** 1706, and (with Townesend) **Corpus Christie: Fellows' Building,** 1706. **Christ Church: Peckwater Quad** S. side (library), 1717-21, by Clarke. **Magdalen: New Building,** 1731, probably by Townesend.

East Range, Worcester College, Oxford

Senate House, 1722-30, and **King's College: Fellows' Building,** 1724, both by Gibbs. **Peterhouse: Burrough's Building,** 1738-42. **Old Schools** (E. side), 1754-58, by James Burrough, Master of Caius, and Wright. Palladian screen to mask old building and match Senate House.

OXFORD

CAMBRIDGE

GEORGIAN

Simple Palladian. Terraced housing with plain rectangular fronts. Sash windows. Successful throughout Britain.

First Court and Master's Lodge, Christ's College, Cambridge

Trinity Hall, Peterhouse, Emmanuel College and others refaced their decaying medieval brick and clunch stone buildings behind new Georgian facades around 1740s.

BAROQUE

Extravagant, dramatic use of Classical elements. Expensive, and seen only at Oxford.

The Queen's College: Front Quad, mostly 1730s, three-sided quad fronting the street. Possibly by Hawksmoor. Cupolas; rusticated and banded vermiculated columns on gatehouse. **Radcliffe Camera**, 1737-49, by Gibbs. Venetian in character. Curving buttresses round dome recall Longhena's church in Venice.

Radcliffe Camera, Oxford

PICTURESQUE

Growing interest in archaeology led to 200-year revival of old styles, especially Gothic. At first, used superficially as surface decoration on buildings really Georgian underneath. Created romantic settings to evoke the past.

Fourth Court, St John's College, Cambridge

All Souls: North Quad, 1715-40, by Hawksmoor in pseudo-Gothic inspired by Wren's Tom Tower at Christ Church. Also **Library**, with classical interior.

Sidney Sussex College: 16C buildings gothicised by Wyatville with stepped castellations, and stucco with raked joints to imitate stonework. **King's College: screen and hall** in flamboyant Perp. style, 1824-28, and **New Court**, 1823-27, in domestic Perp., both by Wilkins.

St John's: Bridge of Sighs and **'Wedding Cake' Cloister Court**, 1825-31, by Rickman and Hutchinson. St John's first college to require a fourth court and, for lack of space, to cross the river.

Radcliffe Observatory, Green College, Oxford

NEO-CLASSICISM

Styles from ancient Greece and Rome used by reformers to express new spirit of enlightenment in buildings that served whole university, not just colleges.

St Paul's Church, 1836, in Ionic style. Now converted to Arts Centre. **Ashmolean Museum**, 1841-45, by Cockerell. Imaginative handling of Greek elements.

Downing College, planned 1784, built 1800s and on, by Wilkins. Linked Grecian villas round three sides of campus. **Squire Law Library**, 1831-42, by Cockerell. **Fitzwilliam Museum**, 1837, by Basavi. Elongated portico.

Fitzwilliam Museum, Cambridge

GOTHIC RESTORATION

Religious movement, at first led by Cambridge Ecclesiologists, then Oxford Tractarians, aimed at rekindling medieval Christian society by recreating 14C architecture. Many buildings cruelly restored, or demolished, in misguided attempt to improve them.

Many colleges rebuilt facades, 100 years after Cambridge, in Gothic style, not Georgian. **Lincoln**, 1824, **Pembroke**, 1829-30, **All Souls**, 1826. **Balliol** almost entirely rebuilt from 1850s by Salvin, Butterfield and Waterhouse. Not a success.

Balliol College, Oxford

Round Church disfigured by Salvin.

| | **OXFORD** | **CAMBRIDGE** |

HIGH VICTORIAN

Imaginative experimental use of Gothic in new configurations, shapes and colours. Made external appearance and planning of rooms much easier because of new freedom. Essential when designing for new needs, especially science laboratories.

University Museum, 1855, by Woodward. Influence of Ruskin in Venetian Gothic brickwork. Interior has early cast-iron Gothic nave, with glass roof. **Keble College,** 1868-82, by Butterfield. Open quads, flat expanses of polychrome brickwork. First college with corridor access. **Worcester College: Chapel and Hall,** lavish Gothic decoration by Burges, and by Kempe at **Pembroke.** North Oxford, large villas for dons, now allowed to marry and live out of college. Large estates built all at once.

Jesus: Chapel; Queen's: Hall; and **Peterhouse: Hall,** redecorated by William Morris 1864-75. **Pembroke: South Range,** 1871 and **Union Society,** 1866, all by Waterhouse.

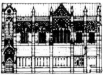

Keble College, Oxford

North Oxford villa

ARTS AND CRAFTS

Medieval revival, but more domestic flavour. Special appeal at Cambridge, where women's colleges first built.

Girton College, Cambridge

Girton College, 1873, by Waterhouse and others. Half-timbered gables, plain brickwork. More like cottage almshouses. Expansion of Cambridge later than at Oxford, dons moving west across Backs into cottagey suburb. Individual houses by Bailey Scott and others, 1900s.

JACOBEAN REVIVAL

Eclectic style, able to absorb the best features of Gothic and Classical architecture. Can be grand or domestic in flavour, highly decorative.

Town Hall, 1890s, by H. T. Hare. **Oriel,** 1908-11, by Basil Champneys.

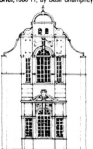

Newnham College, Cambridge

Newnham College, 1875-1910, by Basil Champneys in mix of Jacobean and Queen Anne styles with large chimneys, dormers, small-paned windows. **Pembroke: New Building,** 1878, by G. G. Scott, and 1907 extension by Caröe with balustrading and ornamental gables. **Sidney Sussex: Garden Range,** 1891, by J. L. Pearson.

NEO-TRADITIONAL

After final Jacobean fling and shock of Great War, interwar buildings settled down to be reassuring, familiar, simple.

Campion Hall, by Lutyens, 1936. **New Bodleian Library,** 1937-40, by Scott, in square undressed limestone blocks. **Nuffield College,** designed 1939, by Harrison in Cotswolds style.

Nuffield College, Oxford

Clare: Memorial Court, 1923-24, by Scott, neo-Georgian. **Magdalene: Benson Court,** Lutyens Building, by Lutyens, 1930, in a mixture of Tudor and Jacobean styles. **Queens': Erasmus Building,** 1959, by Sir Basil Spence. Unpopular.

OXFORD

CAMBRIDGE

MODERN
Vast increase in student numbers plus international trends in architecture turned Oxford and Cambridge into testing grounds for new ideas on building, planning. Late 1950s and 60s, monumental scale with new colleges and faculty buildings. Emphasis on planning. As demands met, goals grew smaller, looking at new forms of layout, organisation, then new techniques, and finally fitting in with surroundings.

St Catherine's College, 1960, by Danish architect Arne Jacobsen. Designs included furniture and cutlery.

Arts Site, 1950s, by Casson and Conder. Based on new-town shopping precincts, raised off ground on piers. **St John's: Cripps Building**, by Powell and Moya, 1963-67, superb example of same idea but more romantic. **New Hall**, founded 1954 for women, built 1962-66 by Chamberlin, Powell and Bon.

New Hall, Cambridge

ORGANISATION

English Faculty Library and Law Library, 1964, and **Zoology Laboratory**, 1970, both by Sir Leslie Martin.

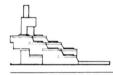

Peterhouse: William Stone Building, by Sir Leslie Martin, 1963; Cambridge's only high-rise residential block. **Gonville and Caius: Harvey Court**, by Martin and St John Wilson, 1960, three-dimensional puzzle. **Christ's College: New Building**, by Denys Lasdun, 1970; multi-layered, facing one way.

New Building, Christ's College, Cambridge

MATERIALS

Thomas White Building, St John's College, Oxford

The Queen's College, Florey Building, by James Stirling, 1968-70. Red tiles, five-sided glass wall on concrete A frame. **Keble College**, 1970, and **Catholic Chaplaincy**, 1970, by Ahrends, Burton & Koralek. Curving brick. **St John's**, Arup Associates, 1974, concrete units.

History Faculty Library, Cambridge

Leckhampton, 1964, by Arup Associates. Use of prefabricated concrete. **History Faculty Library**, 1964-67, by Stirling. Red tiles, and glass.

FITTING IN

Christ Church Picture Gallery, 1964-67, by Powell & Moya. **Wadham College**, 1972, by Gillespie Kidd & Coia.

Robinson College, 1980, Gillespie Kidd and Coia. Reworking of red brick Cambridge themes. **Trinity Hall**: new building 1976, and **Darwin College** extensions 1980, both by Roberts.

New Building, Lady Margaret Hall, Oxford

CONVERSIONS
Growing congestion led to conversion of old buildings, cottages, etc. for undergraduate accommodation, creating new trend.

Trinity College, 1967, Civic Trust Award for cottage conversions. . **Blackwell's Music Shop** and **Wadham College scheme**, 1971-72, by Gillespie Kidd & Coia.

Magdalene: Mallory and Benson Courts, where Redfern, then David Roberts, architecture don of college, converted old tanneries and shop backs into undergraduate village. 1930s, then 50s. **Kettle's Yard**, art gallery and house, by Sir Leslie Martin. Darwin College, by Howell, Killick, Partridge and Amis. 1966.

Kettle's Yard, Cambridge

SOVEREIGNS OF ENGLAND

Anglo-Saxons
827–836   EGBERT
837–858   ETHELWULF
866–871   ETHELRED I
871–899   ALFRED THE
             GREAT
899–925   EDWARD THE
             ELDER
925–940   ATHELSTAN
959–975   EDGAR
978–1016   ETHELRED II (THE
             UNREADY)
1016   EDMUND
             IRONSIDE
[1016–1035   CANUTE THE
             DANE
1035–1040   HAROLD I
1041–1042   HARDICANUTE]
1042–1066   EDWARD THE
             CONFESSOR
1066   HAROLD II

Normans
1066–1087   WILLIAM I (THE
             CONQUEROR)
1087–1100   WILLIAM II
             (RUFUS)
1100–1135   HENRY I
1135–1154   STEPHEN

Plantagenets
1154–1189   HENRY II
1189–1199   RICHARD I
1199–1216   JOHN
1216–1272   HENRY III
1272–1307   EDWARD I
1307–1327   EDWARD II
1327–1377   EDWARD III
1377–1399   RICHARD II

Lancastrians
1399–1413   HENRY IV
1413–1422   HENRY V
1422–1461   HENRY VI

Yorkists
1461–1483   EDWARD IV
1483   EDWARD V
1483–1485   RICHARD III

Tudors
1485–1509   HENRY VII
1509–1547   HENRY VIII
1547–1553   EDWARD VI

1553–1558   MARY I
1558–1603   ELIZABETH I

Stuarts
1603–1625   JAMES I
1625–1649   CHARLES I
[1649–1660   COMMON-
             WEALTH]
1660–1685   CHARLES II
1685–1688   JAMES II
1688–1694   WILLIAM III AND
             MARY II
1694–1702   WILLIAM III
1702–1714   ANNE

Hanoverians
1714–1727   GEORGE I
1727–1760   GEORGE II
1760–1820   GEORGE III
[1810–1820   REGENCY]
1820–1830   GEORGE IV
1830–1837   WILLIAM IV
1837–1901   VICTORIA

House of Saxe-Coburg
1901–1910   EDWARD VII

House of Windsor
1910–1936   GEORGE V
1936   EDWARD VIII
1936–1952   GEORGE VI
1952–   ELIZABETH II

BIBLIOGRAPHY

The literature on Oxford and Cambridge is enormous. This bibliography touches only the fringe, and represents the books most often (though by no means exclusively) consulted during the writing of this guide. They are for the most part fairly easily available, and will probably provide for the needs of the general reader wanting further background information, or anecdotal entertainment.

Oxford

Oxfordshire	Nikolaus Pevsner and Jennifer Sherwood. Penguin Books, Buildings of England Series 1974.
New British Architecture	Robert Maxwell. Thames and Hudson 1972
Clarendon Guide to Oxford	A.R. Woolley. Oxford University Press 1979
A History of Oxford University	V.H.H. Green. Batsford 1974
Oxford	Jan Morris. Faber and Faber 1965 OUP Paperback 1978
The Oxford Book of Oxford (Anthology of comments on Oxford)	Jan Morris. Oxford University Press 1978
Portrait of Oxford	Hal Cheetham. Robert Hale 1971
An Oxford University Chest (A lighthearted and idiosyncratic personal view)	John Betjeman. Reprinted by Oxford University Press 1979
The Woman at Oxford	Vera Brittain. Harrap 1960
Oxford and its Colleges	J.W. Wells. Methuen, Little Guide Series, 1897 (long out of print)

Cambridge

Cambridgeshire (2nd edn)	Nikolaus Pevsner. Penguin Books. Buildings of England Series 1970
Cambridge New Architecture / A Guide to Cambridge New Architecture	N. Taylor and P. Booth. Leonard Hill Books 1970 and 1972 (out of print)
Cambridge	F.A. Reeve. Batsford 1976
Portrait of Cambridge	C.R. Benstead. Robert Hale 1968
The Colleges of Cambridge	Bryan Little. Adams and Dart 1973
Cambridge and its Colleges	Edmund Vale. Methuen, Little Guide Series 1959 (out of print)
Period Piece (Reminiscences of Cambridge and the Darwin family at the turn of the century)	Gwen Raverat. Faber and Faber 1952
That Infidel Place (History of Girton)	M.C. Bradbrooke. Chatto & Windus 1969
Women at Cambridge	Rita McWilliams Tullberg. Gollancz 1975

Much use has also been made of the University Handbooks published by OUP and CUP and the many excellent Visitors' Guides (usually anonymous) to the individual colleges and churches. These are more frequently to be found at Cambridge than at Oxford. 'Blue Guide England' by Stuart Rossiter (Ernest Benn 1980) has also been a mine of information. Two delightful books unlikely to be found, but which have given the author much pleasure, are: 'A Pictorial and Historical Gossiping Guide to Oxford' by Jas. Moore, undated but probably about 1897, and 'A Guide through the University of Cambridge', anonymous, 1820.

Nearly all the houses and churches described in the Environs sections have their own guide-books or leaflets (also usually anonymous), which have been very useful, and which provide much fuller information than it has been possible to give in this Blue Guide.

EXPLANATIONS

TYPE. Large type is used in describing the main outline and principal points on each route; it is also used for the introductory comments on and history of each building. Smaller type is used for diversions from the main route, places of lesser importance, and in describing architectural details where these are dealt with at length.

ASTERISKS indicate points of special interest. They are used sparingly; lack of an asterisk does not imply lack of interest or beauty. Their distribution is necessarily somewhat subjective.

PLANS (Pl.A1) after the name of a place or building refers to the grid-plan on the appropriate map. Plans of buildings, where given, are self-explanatory.

ABBREVIATIONS. In addition to those generally accepted the following also occur:

General

Abp	Archbishop
adm	admission
Bp	Bishop
c	circa (about)
C	century
exc	except
Pl.	plan
pron	pronounced

Architectural

EE	Early English
Dec	Decorated
Perp	Perpendicular
Vict	Victorian

The term Gothic is applied both to medieval styles (EE, Dec, and Perp) and also to the later reproductions of the style (eg Vict Gothic). Gothick indicates the romantic fantasy medievalism fashionable in the late 18C–early 19C.

OXFORD

The City of Oxford

Oxford University

Practical Information

Transport

BY CAR, from London: A40/M40; about 1¼ hours, longer at busy times.

BRITISH RAIL: Railway Station, Park End St (8–10 minute walk from Carfax, or 3 minutes by bus). Good service to most major centres; to and from London (Paddington) about every hour during the day (approximate time 50 minutes–1 hour). Tel 722333; Oxford–London talking timetable tel. 249055.

BUS AND COACH SERVICES: Bus and coach station *Gloucester Green*. A comprehensive network of frequent local buses is operated by Oxford and South Midland bus companies, serving the city and the surrounding area. There is also a network of longer-distance coach services (CityLink) linking Oxford with London, Heathrow, Gatwick and Stratford-upon-Avon. Between London (Victoria Coach Station) and Oxford the 190 Motorway express coach service operates every half-hour during the day with a journey time of 100 minutes. There is also a frequent Motorway express service (X70) linking Oxford with Heathrow and Gatwick.

   Full details available from Oxford Motor Services Ltd, 395 Cowley Road, Oxford OX4 2DJ. Bus and coach enquiries tel 711312.

   National Travel World, 138 High St, provides information on trains and buses to personal callers.

   A Park and Ride service from the outskirts to the city centre operates Monday to Saturday as follows:

   North Side: Pear Tree, Woodstock Road
   West Side: Seacourt, Botley Road
   South Side: Redbridge, Abingdon Road
   East Side: Thornhill, London Road

Parking. Car parks are shown on the map. The more central ones are apt to be full after about 9.30 am. There is a limited amount of street parking in the centre (meters; maximum stay 2 hours) and further out free (maximum stay as indicated).

Main Post Office: St. Aldate's, tel 812581.

Information Office: St. Aldate's, Oxford OX1 1DY, tel 726871. Open all the year Mon–Sat 9–5.30 (Tues 9.30–5.30), Sun and BH 10.30–1, and 1.30–4 June, July, August. Tickets for local coach tours and theatres, concerts, etc, both in Oxford and elsewhere may be booked.

Accommodation, of which there is a great variety from large hotels to bed and breakfast, may be difficult to find in the height of the season and particularly during Eights Week (late May) and Commemoration (late June/early July). Whenever possible bookings should be made well in advance. The Information Office will help.

Theatres: Apollo Theatre, George St, tel 244544; Playhouse, Beaumont St, tel 247133.

Cinemas: ABC 1, 2, and 3, George St, tel 244607; ABC Magdalen St, tel 243067; Penultimate Picture Palace, Jeune St, tel 723837; Phoenix 1 and 2, Walton St, tel 54909; Not the Moulin Rouge, New High St, Headington, tel 63666.

Boating is a very popular summer pastime on both rivers, and so much part of the Oxford experience that all visitors should try to fit a punt or canoe trip into their schedule. Boats may be hired on the THAMES at Folly Bridge, Combe Road Wharf, Medley Boat Station (Port Meadow), and Cardigan St. On the CHERWELL, punts and canoes are available at Magdalen Bridge and Bardwell Rd. Punting is not as difficult as it looks. The first principle is to keep the pole as close as possible to the side of the boat; let it go if you are in danger of falling overboard, there is usually someone about who will retrieve it for you. A wise precaution is always to have a paddle as well. At Oxford you stand in the sloping end of the boat to punt.

Salter's run regular motor cruiser passenger services and excursions from Folly Bridge (tel 243421).

Bathing: in the THAMES at Long Bridges, reached by towpath from Folly Bridge; Tumbling Bay, reached by towpath from Botley Rd, and at Wolvercote, Port Meadow. In the CHERWELL at Parson's Pleasure, reached from South Parks Rd (men only; fee). There are *swimming pools* at Hinksey Pool, off Abingdon Rd (open air; fee); Ferry Pool, Marston Ferry Rd and Temple Cowley Pool, Cowley (heated, indoor; fee).

Skating: Ice rink, Oxpens Rd.

Sightseeing

General Advice. All the colleges display notices at their gates giving the opening times currently valid. They also indicate where the visitor may go. These directions should be strictly respected. Staircases and working libraries are **never** accessible to sightseers unless special arrangements for a particular purpose have been made in advance in writing. Visitors are particularly asked to be quiet.

Opening times. Where these are more or less permanently fixed, as with museums, galleries, old libraries round which visitors are conducted, etc, details are given in the appropriate place. The colleges themselves pose more of a problem, their opening times being liable to vary from year to year. As a rough guide, many are closed in the mornings, most are open for a few hours in the afternoon. To help in planning a tour a list (1986) is given below, but there is no guarantee that it will remain correct. The times apply only to college quadrangles and grounds; chapels, halls and other points of interest may or may not be open; where they are regularly open at fixed times this is noted in the appropriate place.

fixed times this is noted in the appropriate place.

All Souls	2–5
Balliol	variable; parties over 8 by appt only
Brasenose	10–dusk
Christ Church	9.30–6; fee
Corpus Christi	term 1.30–4.30; vacation 10–6
Exeter	9–dusk
Green	all day, but access to Radcliffe Observatory restricted
Hertford	9.30–dusk
Jesus	2–4.30
Keble	summer 10–7, winter 10–sunset
Lady Margaret Hall	all day; closed Aug, Christmas, and Easter
Lincoln	2–6
Magdalen	2–6.15; fee
Manchester	term 9–5, vacation 9–1
Mansfield	9–dusk
Merton	Mon–Fri 2–5, Sat and Sun 10–5; closes one hour earlier Nov–Feb
New College	term 2–5, vacation 11–6
Nuffield	7.30–dusk (Sun 10–dusk) quadrangles only
Oriel	2–5
Pembroke	2–6
Queen's	term 2–6, vacation 9–5
St. Anne's	all day, grounds only
St. Antony's	Mon–Sat 2–5
St. Catherine's	9–dusk
St. Edmund Hall	9–dusk
St. Hilda's	2–5
St. Hugh's	all day; closed mid Aug–mid Sept
St. John's	Mon–Fri 2–5, Sat and Sun 10–1
St. Peter's	chapel in term 10–6
Somerville	grounds 2–5.30, hall and chapel by arrangement
Trinity	2–5.30 or dusk if earlier
University	10–6
Wadham	1.30–4.30
Wolfson	all day, grounds only, not quadrangles
Worcester	term 2–dusk; vacation Mon–Sat 9–12 and 2–dusk, Sun 2–dusk

Colleges may be closed during the summer examination period (mid May–late June); many are also closed at times in vacations when in use for conferences and in August, at Christmas and Easter for holidays.

For visitors with very limited time there are guided walking tours, in groups of not more than 25, lasting about 2 hours, organised by the Information Centre: morning and afternoon daily except in winter when they take place on Saturdays only.

History

Oxford is the meeting place of two rivers. Flowing from the north-west is the Upper Thames, or Isis, and from the north the Cherwell ('Char'). Their waters join to the south of the old city centre, and together flow on south-east towards London as the Thames. These rivers still play an important part in Oxford's leisure life; in the past they were the city's raison d'être. The first settlement probably grew up at the river-crossing ('the ford for oxen') and must have been important as a meeting place of both roads and waterways, and as a defensive strongpoint in times of trouble, commanding as it did these means of communication. Even today Oxford is in some sense the crossroads of England.

Its name first appears in the Anglo-Saxon Chronicle in the year 912, when Edward the Elder 'held Lundenbyrg and Oxnaford and all the lands pertaining thereto'. By then it was one of the principal towns in the country, a busy trading centre and frequently the place where kings and their councils of state foregathered. Religious orders too had establishments here; according to legend St. Frideswide had founded her priory at Oxford some time in the 8C, because it was there that a well-aimed thunderbolt rescued her from the undesired attentions of King Algar. Nothing remains of her church or convent buildings, which were burnt down by the Danes very early in the 11C.

When William of Normandy arrived in 1066 Oxford was handed over to Robert d'Oilly. He built the castle (see p 85 for details) and began work on the massive walls which by the 13C enclosed the city. Churches were built, and monastic houses proliferated. St. Frideswide's Priory was refounded in 1122; Osney, Godstow and Rewley abbeys followed. Various orders of friars established themselves in the area just south of the town which is now a wilderness of ring roads and car parks. Trade flourished and Oxford prospered.

But there was a cuckoo in the nest—the infant university, which soon began to dominate its adopted home. From the mid 13C the town declined as the university increased, and the history of Oxford becomes to all intents and purposes the history of Oxford University.

Town and gown were at loggerheads almost from the beginning. All through the Middle Ages the townspeople complained of the students' riotous behaviour, the university complained of the townsmen's grasping dishonesty, and the ill-feeling erupted into frequent battles. On practically every issue they supported different sides; in the Civil War the town was for Parliament, the university for the King; in the 19C the town wanted the railway, the university opposed it, and frustrated too the proposed siting of the chief GWR works near the town, which greatly needed some such source of employment. The university had a stranglehold on development and change.

Now the tables are turned, and in the 20C Oxford has become a large industrial, commercial and residential centre, where the ancient university probably impinges very little on the lives of most of its citizens apart, perhaps, from the number of visitors it attracts. This tremendous change was largely brought about in the first place by one man—William Morris (later Lord Nuffield), designer and man-ufacturer of the Morris car. He began, shortly before the First World

War, with a small bicycle and then motor bicycle business in Longwall Street. This led in the 1920s to motor car production, first on the outskirts of Oxford itself, later in the (then) village of Cowley. Morris Motors (now part of BL) took over Oxford in the 20C as it had been taken over in the 12C by students. Indeed the old city is sometimes referred to as 'The Latin Quarter of Cowley'.

Low-lying and damp, Oxford is supposed to be an enervating place. This is not the impression it gives as traffic roars unceasingly along the streets, shopping crowds hurry along the pavements, cyclists weave their way through the narrow lanes, and tour guides whisk their charges at breathtaking speed from college to college.

OXFORD UNIVERSITY has 35 colleges, of which seven are for graduates only: All Souls, Green, Linacre, Nuffield, St. Antony's, St. Cross, and Wolfson. Five were founded for women: Lady Margaret Hall, St. Anne's, St. Hilda's, St. Hugh's, and Somerville. All colleges are now mixed except St. Hilda's and Somerville. St. Hugh's accepts only women as junior members, but senior members may be women or men. There are five Permanent Private Halls: Campion Hall, for Jesuit students, Greyfriars and St. Benet's, for Franciscan and Benedictine students respectively (though both accept a few lay students also), Mansfield College, founded for Congregationalist (United Reformed Church) students, but now offering a wide variety of courses, and Regent's Park College, principally for Baptist students, but with a small number of places for non-theological studies. The various other theological colleges and 'houses' are not part of the university.

There are about 9400 undergraduate students (1985/6).

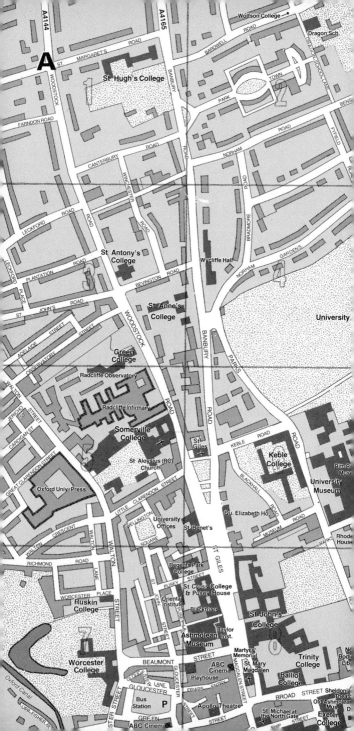

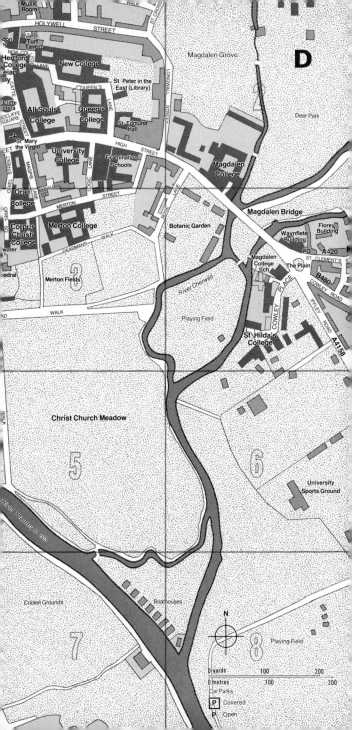

D

Magdalen Grove

Deer Park

Music
Room

HOLYWELL STREET

ST CROSS

Turf
Tavern

NEW COLLEGE LANE

Hertford
College
eian
ry

New College

St Peter in the
East (Library)

QUEEN'S

LONGWALL STREET

All Souls
College

Queen's
College

St Edmund
Hall

Magdalen
College

St Mary
the Virgin

University
College

Examination
Schools

HIGH STREET

Oriel
College

MERTON STREET

Magdalen Bridge

ROSE LANE

Florey
Building

Corpus
Christi
College

Merton College

Botanic Garden

Waynflete
Building

A420

ST CLEMENT'S

edral

DEADMANS WALK

Merton Fields

Magdalen
College
Sch

The Plain

COWLEY PLACE

B480

COWLEY ROAD

River Cherwell

WALK

Playing Field

St Hilda's
College

IFFLEY ROAD

A4158

Christ Church Meadow

River Thames or Isis

University
Sports Ground

WALK

Cricket Grounds

Boathouses

N

Playing Field

0 yards 100 200

0 metres 100 200

Car Parks

P Covered

P Open

1   Carfax, and South and South-East of Carfax

The centre of Oxford is CARFAX (Pl.C2; the name possibly derives from the Latin 'quadrifurcus', four forks, or the French 'quatre voies', four ways). The roads that cross here are: (N) *Cornmarket* (buses and taxis only), which beyond Broad St becomes Magdalen St and then widens out into St. Giles; (S) *St. Aldate's*, leading to Folly Bridge (over the Thames); (E) *High St* ('the High') leading to Magdalen Bridge (over the Cherwell, pron Charwell and usually referred to as 'the Cher'); (W) *Queen St* (pedestrians only) leading towards the modern Westgate Shopping Centre and the railway station.

It is helpful in finding the way about, and round buildings, to have this pattern and the points of the compass firmly in mind.

The majority of Oxford's most beautiful and interesting buildings, both ancient and modern, are within a half-mile radius of this crossroads, and of these the greater number are concentrated in the quarter-mile square immediately E of Carfax, on each side of the High. Explorations can conveniently be divided into four groups, taking as a starting-point Carfax itself.

The 14C tower (open late March–end October, weekdays 10–6, Sun 2–6), on which is a clock with striking quarter-jacks, is all that remains of *St. Martin's Church*, demolished 1896. In this church Orlando Gibbons the composer (1583–1625) was baptised, and Shakespeare is supposed to have stood sponsor to the infant William Davenant (playwright, 1606–68) whose father was landlord of the Crown Tavern opposite (now No. 3 Cornmarket), where Shakespeare almost certainly used to stay on journeys between London and Stratford. John Aubrey, the historian, records that Shakespeare 'was wont to go into Warwickshire once a yeare, and did in his journeye lye at this house in Oxon where he was exceedingly respected'.

The former inn guest room on the second floor is now known as *The Painted Room* (used by a tutorial establishment, but open Mon–Fri 9–1, 2.30–5, subject to availability; donation appreciated). In the course of alterations in 1927, when the premises were occupied by a firm of tailors, early 17C oak panelling was discovered under the layers of wallpaper and canvas. Beneath this panelling were well-preserved wall-paintings dating from about 1550, an elegant design of trellis-work enclosing bunches of fruit and flowers. Similar paintings dating from the 1550s and 1560s were found in 1948 in several rooms of the *Golden Cross* next door (seen on application to the Manager's office).

The Golden Cross has been an inn since the 13C, and still retains its old enclosed yard; the buildings date mostly from the 15C and 17C.

As one goes S down ST. ALDATE'S (Pl.C4) the *Information Office* is on the right with the main Post Office and a row of telephone booths just beyond. Opposite is the Town Hall, which houses the *Museum of Oxford* (open Tues–Sat 10–5). This tells the history of Oxford in a series of pictures, models, old maps, prints etc, excellently explained in English, French, German, Spanish, Japanese and Arabic. The displays are complemented by a series of furnished period rooms, including an Elizabethan inn parlour and an 18C student's study.

On the corner of Pembroke St (right) is St. Aldate's Bookshop, and just beyond it, *St. Aldate's Church*, largely rebuilt in the mid 19C, vigorously evangelical in its worship. On the right at the other end of Pembroke St is the small *Museum of Modern Art* (open Tues–Sat

10–5, Sun 2–5). Across the road in St. Ebbe's St is *St. Ebbe's Church*, also largely rebuilt in the mid 19C, but with a massively carved Norman W door. Beyond is the huge Westgate shopping precinct (Pl.C3/4). For more on this part of Oxford see p 86.

Behind St. Aldate's Church is the entrance to **Pembroke College** (Pl.C4), founded in 1624, and named after the Earl of Pembroke, Chancellor of the University at the time; it replaced a number of medieval halls, chief of which was Broadgates Hall, whose refectory is now the Senior Common Room. Old Quad is mostly 17C but much altered about 1830, and to the W (right) is Chapel Quad, spacious early Vict; both are colourful with flowers. At the far end, approached up a flight of steps, is the very handsome *Hall*, with hammerbeam roof and tall Perp windows. On the left of the quad is the *Chapel*, a simple early 18C building elaborately decorated in 1884 by C.E. Kempe, who also designed the windows. It was colourfully restored in 1972. The altarpiece is a copy by Cranke of Rubens' 'Risen Christ'.

To the right is the North Quad (1962); it consists of the Besse Building (named after Oxford's French benefactor M. Besse, see also pp 16, 90), a row of old houses originally facing Pembroke Street but now turned back to front, and a new building (1976) named after the Rt Hon. Harold Macmillan, Chancellor of the University since 1960. The former Beef Lane is now within this quad. On the S side are three striking bronze statues, 'Mourning Women' by J.W. Harvey (1946), a memorial to members of Pembroke's JCR who died in the Second World War.

Back in Old Quad a passage to the left of the entrance leads to the Master's Lodgings, originally almshouses built by Wolsey, and to the new *Library* (1974–75) given by the McGowin family of Alabama (no adm except as stated below).

Pembroke's most famous son was Dr Johnson, who studied here for four terms in 1728–29 till poverty forced him to leave. He occupied the second-floor rooms over the gateway. Johnson retained a great affection for Oxford in spite of his brief and not always happy sojourn. His portrait by Reynolds hangs in the Senior Common Room; his teapot, cider mug, one of his 'themes' (essays), and some books are displayed in the library, and the college possesses various other Johnson memorabilia. They can only be seen however by special permission on written application.

FAMOUS MEMBERS. Broadgates Hall: Francis Beaumont, playwright, 1584–1616; John Pym, parliamentarian, 1584–1643; Sir Thomas Browne, author of 'Religio Medici', 1605–82.

Pembroke: Samuel Johnson (see above), 1709–84; William Shenstone, poet, 1714–63; George Whitefield, leading Methodist, 1714–70; Sir William Blackstone, author of 'Commentaries on the Laws of England', 1723–80; John Lemprière, author of 'Bibliotheca Classica', 1765–1824; James Smithson, founder of the Smithsonian Institution in Washington, 1765–1829.

To the S of Pembroke, in Brewer St, are the *Cathedral Choir School* and *Campion Hall*, a centre for Jesuit students, designed by Sir Edwin Lutyens in the early 1930s, and named after Edmund Campion, the Roman Catholic martyr (1581). In Rose Place is the *Old Palace* built in 16C for Robert King, last abbot of Osney and first Bishop of Oxford. With striking modern additions (1970–71, by Ahrends, Burton and Koralek), it now houses the Roman Catholic Chaplaincy to the University, and a bookshop.

No. 83 St. Aldate's is supposed to be the shop in Lewis Carroll's 'Through the Looking Glass'; its charming sign commemorates the connection. A quarter of a mile beyond is Folly Bridge (formerly

Grand Pont, rebuilt 1825–27 by Ebenezer Perry; Pl.C6). Until the late 18C a tower and gatehouse stood on the bridge, where traditionally Roger Bacon (early scientist and astronomer, c 1214–94) had his study (see also p 86).

Almost opposite Pembroke is the entrance to *Christ Church Meadow* (Pl.D5). Broad Walk, formerly lined by elms, runs E to the Cherwell. A path running N between Corpus Christi (left) and Merton (right) across Merton Field, where parts of the old city wall can be seen, links it with Merton St. New Walk runs to the Isis and the college boat houses (which replace the erstwhile and more picturesque college barges), where there is a pleasant riverside walk shaded with lime trees; in summer the air is heavy with their scent.

Between New Walk and St. Aldate's is the *Music Faculty* building, originally St. Catherine's Society and subsequently Linacre College (see p 96).

*Christ Church (Pl.C4; entry through Meadow Gate— fee—exc Sun, when the main gate should be used), known familiarly as 'the House', from its Latin Name 'Aedes Christi', is the largest college in Oxford and has many points of comparison with Trinity College, Cambridge (see p 140). It was founded by Wolsey as Cardinal College in 1525, on the site of St. Frideswide's Priory, most of which he demolished. Of the vastly ambitious buildings he planned, few were completed when he fell from favour in 1529. Henry VIII refounded it as Henry VIII College (an ecclesiastical establishment only) in 1532; this in turn was suppressed, to be refounded yet again, in 1545, as Christ Church. What Wolsey had left of the old priory church became Oxford Cathedral as well as the college chapel (a unique situation), and the Dean head of both the cathedral chapter and the college. The Dean is appointed (for life) by the Crown; the reigning sovereign is also the college Visitor. The royal connection was strengthened during the Civil War, when Charles I made the deanery his residence. Fellows of Christ Church are known, confusingly, as 'students'. The college has a long line of most distinguished members, including thirteen prime ministers, and formerly had strong traditional links with Eton and the English aristocracy.

From St. Aldate's a wide pathway leads through the beautiful War Memorial Gardens (1926; wrought-iron gates by R.M.Y. Gleadowe) to *Meadow Buildings*, built in 1863 in Vict/Venetian Gothic style, and to the visitors' entrance. The buildings ahead (right) are what remains of St. Frideswide's Priory; the original 'frater' (later the Old Library, now undergraduate rooms), the cloister and the cathedral.

The small *Cloister*, whose W side was pulled down in 1525, is in the Perp style (1499). It was here that Cranmer was formally 'degraded' in 1556, being publicly insulted, stripped of his vestments, and having his hair shorn. A Norman doorway leads into the EE *Chapter House*, where there is an exhibition of old plate, and a small bookstall and shop.

The ***Cathedral** (open 9.30–4.30), the smallest in England, is predominantly late Norman in appearance (rebuilt 1141–80), although many additions and alterations have been made at various times, notably the 13C spire, one of the earliest in England (hence perhaps its rather squat appearance), and the 19C W front and E end by Sir George Gilbert Scott (1870). The visitors' doorway leads into the S AISLE, the E end of which is the *Lucy Chapel*. The *E window (c 1330) shows, in the upper lights, the arms of England and France still separate, and in the central light the martyrdom of Becket, his head replaced, presumably in deference to Henry VIII's dislike of

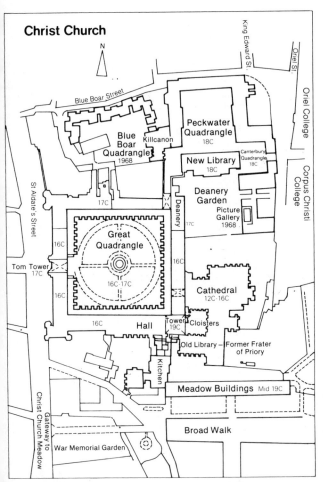

Christy Church

N

Blue Boar Street

King Edward St.

Oriel Street

Oriel College

Corpus Christi College

Blue Boar Quadrangle 1968

Killcanon

Peckwater Quadrangle 18C

New Library 18C

Canterbury Quadrangle 18C

Deanery Garden

Picture Gallery 1968

Deanery

St Aldate's Street

17C

17C

16C

Great Quadrangle

16C-17C

16C

Tom Tower 17C

16C

16C

Cathedral 12C-16C

Hall

Tower 19C

Cloisters

Old Library — Former Frater of Priory

Kitchen

Meadow Buildings Mid 19C

Gateway to Christ Church Meadow

Broad Walk

War Memorial Garden

the saint, by a piece of plain glass. Other interesting windows are a memorial to Bp King (see Old Palace, p 49), and one by Burne-Jones portraying Faith, Hope and Charity. In this aisle are many monuments, to cavaliers killed in the Civil War and to cathedral dignitaries, and the regimental chapel of the Oxfordshire and Buckinghamshire Light Infantry.

In the NAVE the massive piers of the arcades are alternately round and octagonal, and an illusion of height is given by the unusual placing of the triforium inside the main arches, with a secondary arch below (as at Romsey Abbey and Jedburgh). The roof is 16C timber-work, the pulpit and organ screen 17C, the stalls 19C. There are monuments to Bp Berkeley (the philosopher, 1685–1753) and Dr Pusey (high-Anglican reformer, 1800–82).

Oxford Cathedral: the nave arcade. From an early nineteenth century print

The CHOIR has a gloriously vaulted late 15C *roof (similar to the Divinity School, p 73). The E end, by Scott, is in Norman style.

On the N side (left) are three parallel aisles: the North Choir aisle, the Lady Chapel, and the Latin Chapel. Between the first two are the remains of St. Frideswide's shrine, and between the Lady Chapel and Latin Chapel the finely carved oak watching-chamber (15C) from which guard was kept on the treasures of the shrine. The putative saint is commemorated every 19 October in a special service attended by dignitaries of the cathedral, university and city, in fully-robed splendour. The Latin Chapel is so called because the daily service was said here in Latin until 1861 (except for a break during the Commonwealth); it was also used for Divinity lectures till the late 19C. It has massive oak stalls, some probably 14C, others 16C, interesting monuments including a bust of Robert Burton (author of 'The Anatomy of Melancholy', 1577–1640), and in the N windows some 14C stained glass. All three N aisles have E windows by William Morris and Burne-Jones. At the W end of the N aisle is a spectacular window by Abraham van Linge (c 1630) depicting Jonah and Nineveh.

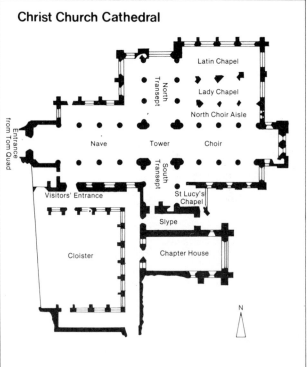

Christ Church Cathedral

Latin Chapel

North Transept

Lady Chapel

North Choir Aisle

Entrance from Tom Quad

Nave   Tower   Choir

South Transept

Visitors' Entrance

St Lucy's Chapel

Slype

Cloister

Chapter House

N

The entrance to the *Hall* is in the SE corner of the Bell Tower (Bodley, 1879), up a stairway, built by Wyatt in 1805, beneath a beautiful fan-vaulted *roof (1640, a very late example of the style). The Hall, the largest in Oxford (115ft by 40ft), which was completed in Wolsey's time, has a sumptuously carved and gilded hammerbeam roof, whose central bosses bear the arms of the see of Winchester, of which, inter alia, Wolsey was bishop, encircled by the Garter. The arms of five more of Wolsey's sees, Lincoln, Bath and Wells, Durham, York, and St. Alban's, and his cardinal's hat, appear in the heraldic glass (partly original) of the W window. An impressive array of portraits includes work by Lely, Kneller, Reynolds, Gainsborough, Romney, Lawrence, Millais, Watts, Herkomer, and Graham Sutherland. Henry VIII dominates the scene, flanked by Elizabeth I and Wolsey. A bust of the reigning sovereign (college Visitor) is traditionally placed immediately below him.

Wolsey's vast kitchen, below, has been modernised and is still in use (no adm). An election slogan of 1829 reading 'No Peel' is burned into a doorway at the stair foot.

Wolsey also built the S and two-thirds of the E and W sides of the GREAT QUADRANGLE (Tom Quad), including the massive gateway in whose vaulted roof are forty-eight coats of arms. The statue of Wolsey was not put up until 1791. The famous cupola-topped *Tom Tower*, designed by Wren in 1681, carries a huge bell (Great Tom, 6¼ tons, last recast 1680) taken from Osney Abbey. It rings 101 times every evening at 9.05 (9 pm by the Oxford meridian), once for each member of the original foundation, and was formerly the signal that all undergraduates should be within their colleges and the gates closed. 'It need hardly be said that the signal is not obeyed', says a guide book of 1897. The great pool, originally the college reservoir, is known as 'Mercury' from its central statue, a 1928 replacement of the 17C one by Giovanni da Bologna, toppled from its plinth by Lord Derby in 1817.

In the NE corner of Tom Quad is Fell's Tower (statues of John Fell, Dean 1660–86, and H.G. Liddell, Dean 1855–91). It was Dean Fell who completed the building and lay-out of Tom Quad in the late 17C. He was an energetic educational reformer and disciplinarian, hence perhaps the well-known verse beginning 'I do not like thee, Dr Fell'. Beneath it Kill Canon Passage (so called for its draughty cold) leads into PECKWATER QUAD, built on the site of Peckwater Inn, 1705–13. Here (S side) is the *Library* (open only by special arrangement), built 1717–72 to be 'the finest library that belongs to any Society in Europe'. It has beautiful plasterwork ceilings, 18C woodwork and furnishings (including 24 stools by Chippendale) and some of the earliest wall bookcases to be built. It houses a priceless collection of books and MSS, and such interesting relics as Wolsey's cardinal's hat (acquired from Horace Walpole) and chair, John Evelyn's diary, Gibbon's miniature travelling library, Lewis Carroll memorabilia, and two copper braziers for charcoal. In the vestibule are busts of past royal Visitors and distinguished members of the college (one of J.L. Lowe, Dean 1939–59, by Epstein).

On the W side is the entrance to the modern BLUE BOAR QUAD (by Powell and Moya, 1968), on the E is CANTERBURY QUAD, built 1773–83 on the site of the old Canterbury College.

The *Picture Gallery* (open Mon–Sat 10.30–1, 2–4.30, Sun 2–4.30; entry can be made direct through Canterbury gate) contains the finest college collection in Oxford of paintings and drawings, mostly 14C–17C Italian.

FAMOUS MEMBERS are so numerous it is impossible to mention more than a random sample. Royalties: Edward VII; politicians (some Prime Ministers): Canning, Peel, Gladstone, Lord Salisbury, Lord Halifax, Lord Avon. Other notabilities: Sir Philip Sidney, poet and soldier, 1554–86; Robert Burton, writer, 1557–1640; William Penn, Quaker, founder of Pennsylvania, 'sent down' for nonconformity, 1644–1718; John Locke, philosopher, 1632–1704; John Wesley, founder of Methodism, 1703–91, and his brother Charles; John Ruskin, art pundit and social philosopher, 1819–1900; C.L. Dodgson ('Lewis Carroll'), 1832–98; W.H. Auden, poet, 1907–73.

The gate of Canterbury Quad leads out into Oriel Sq. Immediately opposite is **Oriel College** (Pl.D1) founded as 'St. Mary's College' in 1324 by Adam de Brome, almoner to Edward II, and rector of St. Mary the Virgin church, which was used in the Middle Ages as the college chapel, and of whose living the college is patron; de Brome is commemorated in one of its chapels. In 1326 the college was refounded by Edward II, who gave it the Hospital of St. Bartholomew in Cowley as a source of income. Thereafter it was known as 'The King's College'. The name Oriel derives from a building on the site named 'La Oriole' acquired in 1329. In the 19C it was the centre of the Tractarian Movement (see History, p 13, and Famous Members, below).

The front quadrangle, built 1620–42, is in the 17C Gothic style pioneered by Merton and Wadham, with pretty Jacobean shaped gables above the windows on both outer and inner sides. A flight of steps leads up to the *Hall* (usually locked), which has a handsome hammerbeam roof. Over the hall porch are statues of Edward II and James I or Charles I, surmounted by one of the Virgin and Child, all canopied.

The *Chapel* (right; visits by appointment) has its original 17C furnishings, with richly carved communion rails and a recently restored bronze lectern. All the glass, except in the ante-chapel, is late 19C.

Oxford Jacobean Gothic: Oriel College, Front Quadrangle. From an early nineteenth century drawing by J.M.W. Turner

The N side of Back Quad (left) is formed by the Library, a Palladian building by Wyatt (1788). Beyond is *St. Mary's Quad*, formerly St. Mary's Hall ('Skimmery'), absorbed into the college only in 1902. Its attractive little hall and chapel (c 1640) are now respectively the Junior Common Room and Junior Library. Opposite is the *Rhodes building* (1901–11), which faces out on to the High. Rhodes was already diamond mining when he came up to Oriel, and owing to frequent absences in Southern Africa took eight years to get his degree. He left the college £100,000 and his statue adorns the High St front, gazing down benevolently from a lofty height on to those of Edward VII and George V.

FAMOUS MEMBERS: the great leaders of the 19C Tractarian Movement were Fellows: John Keble, Richard Whateley, Thomas Arnold (headmaster of Rugby), John Newman (afterwards cardinal), E.B. Pusey, R.H. Froude, R.W. Church. Others include: Sir Walter Raleigh, courtier, explorer, poet, 1552?–1618; Gilbert White, naturalist, and vicar of Selborne, 1720–93; Samuel Wilberforce ('Soapy Sam'), Bp of Oxford, who opposed Darwin's theories, 1805–73; Thomas Hughes, author of 'Tom Brown's Schooldays', 1822–96; Matthew Arnold, poet, 1822–88; J.A. Froude, historian, 1818–94; Cecil Rhodes, 1853–1902.

Corpus Christi College (Pl.D3) was founded in 1517 by Richard Foxe, bishop in turn of Exeter, Bath and Wells, Durham, and Winchester, Lord Privy Seal to Henry VII and Henry VIII, and a great benefactor not only of Oxford but also Cambridge (where he was Chancellor, and Master of Pembroke College). Corpus is a small, intimate college with a strong tradition of learning established by its founder, who wished it to be 'as a hive', that 'the scholars night and day may make wax and sweet honey to the honour of God, and the advantage of themselves and all Christian men'. Provision was made for lectures in Greek, Latin, and Hebrew, whence Erasmus (a friend of Foxe) named it 'bibliotheca trilinguis'.

The gateway roof has beautiful vaulting of 1517. Above in the tower are the original rooms of the President, one with Tudor panelling and plasterwork, and an oriel window (no adm). The *FRONT QUAD is paved; in the centre is a tall sundial (1581) topped by the college emblem, a pelican (a modern replacement). The perpetual calendar round the plinth dates from 1606. On the E side (left) is the small *Hall* with its original hammerbeam roof, and beyond it a passage leads to the *Chapel*. Its particular features are the handsome late 17C stalls and baroque screen, the altarpiece 'after' Rubens, a striking E window of St. Christopher (1931) and a brass eagle lectern (pre-Reformation and the earliest in Oxford). The *Library*, opposite the entrance (no adm), has rich early 17C plasterwork and furnishings; the bookcases still have the rods to which books were formerly chained. Beyond, to the SE (left), are a narrow quad cloistered on one side, the Fellows' or Turner buildings of 1706, and lovely gardens. Further buildings have been added at intervals, including some across Merton St in Magpie Lane.

Unlike the other Oxford colleges Corpus did not surrender its plate to Charles I in 1642, and therefore has many priceless early pieces, including Bp Foxe's gilt and enamelled pastoral staff.

FAMOUS MEMBERS: Nicholas Udall, scholar, teacher, dramatist, 1505–56; Richard Hooker, theologian, author of 'Laws of Ecclesiastical Polity', 1554?–1600; General Oglethorpe, founder of Georgia, 1696–1785; John Keble and Thomas Arnold as undergraduates (see Oriel); Sir Henry Newbolt, poet, 1862–1938; Robert Bridges, poet, 1844–1930.

Immediately next door is *Merton College** (Pl.D3), in all essentials the oldest in Oxford, although both University and Balliol were endowed a few years earlier. Merton was founded in 1264 by Walter de Merton, principally for the study of theology. The original deed, complete with seals, is in the college archives. The enlarged statutes of 1274, and the whole organisation, served as a model for subsequent colleges at both Oxford and Cambridge. In 1380 a former fellow, John Wyliott, provided scholarships whose recipients were known as 'portionistae', hence their designation as 'postmasters', still used. Across the street is a house called 'Postmaster's Hall'.

The buildings are among the oldest and most interesting in Oxford, although many drastic alterations and additions were made in the 19C. The gatehouse, with carvings depicting St. John the Baptist, dates from 1418. Its statues of Walter de Merton and Henry III are reproductions.

On the S side of FRONT QUAD (opposite the gate) is the *Hall*, originally 13C but virtually rebuilt by Wyatt in 1794 and again by Scott in 1874. The door, with elaborate ironwork, is 13C. On the W side (right) past the ancient Treasury or Muniment Room (1288) with high-pitched stone roof, is the entrance to the picturesque *MOB QUAD (c 1308). On its N side is the *Chapel, the oldest in Oxford, impressively lofty and large. The choir was built in 1294; the exquisite tracery of its E window contains 13–14C glass, and the glass in the side windows is contemporary. The beautiful lectern is of spun brass of c 1500; in the floor are memorial brasses to various Wardens, made c 1400 and 1471. The altarpiece, a Crucifixion, is of the school of Tintoretto. Between choir and ante-chapel is a handsome Baroque screen, part of one designed by Wren, removed in the 19C and restored in 1960. The ante-chapel is formed by the transepts (14C Perp); the intended nave, whose arch is the W window, was never built. This window contains 15C glass, but is partly hidden by the organ.

In the S transept (right) is a 14C piscina, curiously set high on the wall, and in the N transept (left) a monument to Sir Thomas Bodley (d 1613), founder of the Bodleian Library, and Anthony à Wood (d 1695), historian of Oxford and chronicler of his times.

In the SE corner of Mob Quad, opposite the chapel, is the *Library (guided visits lasting ½ hr, 2–4 on weekdays; apply to the Verger, in passage between Front and Mob Quads. Closed for six weeks at Christmas and New Year), perhaps the most interesting medieval library in England. Built 1371–78, it was the first to house the books upright in shelves, instead of lying flat in chests (one of which can

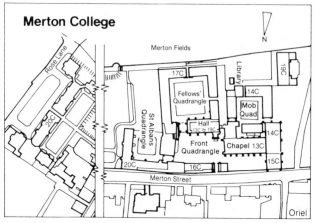

Merton College

be seen near the stairway). One volume is still chained to the shelves, which are fitted with reading boards. The furnishings, panelling, plasterwork and dormer windows are late 16C–early 17C. In some of the small side windows are fragments of 15C stained glass originally in the chapel. In addition to MSS, the library's historic treasures include two 14C astrolabes, an early Welsh Bible, and a massive chest with a complicated threefold locking mechanism in the lid. The original floor level was lower than the present one, so the traditional ghost can be seen only from his knees up.

Leading off the library are two rooms devoted to *Max Beerbohm* memorabilia.
  To the W (right) of Mob Quad in a small garden are Grove Buildings (1864 by Butterfield, much modified in 1930). E (left) is FELLOWS' or GREAT QUAD, built in 1610, in the elegant late Gothic style shortly copied at Oriel, Wadham,

Life at Oxford in the eighteenth century. From a Rowlandson cartoon

and University Colleges, and adorned with an attractive sundial in 1974. Above Fitzjames Gateway (1497) on its NE side were the original Warden's lodgings, now known as the Queen's Rooms, from their occupation by Queen Henrietta Maria during the Civil War. Merton traditionally provided lodgings for royal ladies visiting Oxford. St. Alban's Quad (rebuilt 1904) on the site of St. Alban's Hall, incorporated into the college in 1881, gives access to the beautiful garden (adm only by special permission in writing) which has a terrace walk overlooking Merton fields and Christ Church Meadow, and a pretty early 18C stone summerhouse. Further buildings, and adaptations of old buildings, towards Rose Lane provide additional accommodation and a new Warden's Lodgings (1966).

FAMOUS MEMBERS: Thomas Bradwardine and other notable 14C philosophers and mathematicians; John Wyclif, Bible translator and religious reformer, 1329(?)–84; Sir Thomas Bodley, 1545–1613; Lord Halsbury, Lord Chancellor, author of 'The Laws of England', 1823–1921; Max Beerbohm, writer, caricaturist, wit, 1872–1956; T.S. Eliot, poet, 1888–1965; F. Soddy, scientist, Nobel prizewinner, 1877–1956. Andrew Irvine (1902–1924) was still an undergraduate when he died climbing Mount Everest with Mallory; his last diary is in the college library.

In *Kybald St*, a cul-de-sac off Magpie Lane (linking Merton St with the High) are the charming old John Parsons Almshouses (1814), now part of University College. New almshouses were built in St. Clement's by Helen and Frank Altschul of New York in 1959. The N end of Merton St emerges into the High; it is worth pausing here to look up and down this beautiful and world-famous street. To the right past Rose Lane, which leads to Merton Field and Christ Church Meadow, is the **Botanic Garden** (Pl.D4, adm free; April–September; weekdays 8.30–5, Sun 10–12 and 2–6; October–March; weekdays 9–4.30, Sun 2–4.30; plant houses 2–4 daily). Originally the Physick Garden, linked with the Faculty of Medicine, it was founded in 1621 by Lord Danby, whose bust is over the impressive portal (by Nicholas Stone, 1630), flanked by statues of Charles I and Charles II. The common wasteland weed Oxford Ragwort was first grown here from seed brought from Mount Etna.

Across the street is ***Magdalen College** (pron 'Maudlin', Pl.D2), one of the most splendid in Oxford, founded in 1458 by William Waynflete, in turn headmaster of Winchester, Provost of Eton, Bp of Winchester, and Lord Chancellor, on the site of the former Hospital of St. John. The scholars are known as 'demies' (because they receive only half the allowances of a Fellow); Magdalen led the way in providing places for fee-paying students. Always of aristocractic birth, they were known as 'noblemen' or 'gentlemen commoners' as appropriate, and wore special silk-braided gowns. The college has always had strong links with royalty, the founder's schools, and the aristocracy. The choir school was part of the original foundation, and the chapel services are famous for their music.

Magdalen was in the forefront of the Revival of Learning and the Reformation, and strongly Puritan in the 17C. Nevertheless, it loyally supported Charles I in the Civil War, giving him nearly all its silver. James II rewarded this sacrifice by forcing upon the Fellows a president unacceptable in morals, qualifications, and churchmanship. Their determined resistance led to their expulsion. Eventually, however, the King had to bow to public opinion and reinstate them. Restoration Day, 5 October 1688, has been celebrated ever since. In the 18C the college had a reputation for sloth and self-indulgence, for which it was severely castigated by the youthful Edward Gibbon (see below).

Being outside the city walls, Magdalen had plenty of room to expand, and both quadrangles and grounds are exceptionally spacious. James I called it 'the most absolute building in Oxford'. The chief feature of the High St front is the graceful Perp ***TOWER**, built in 1492–1505 (traditionally by Wolsey, who was then bursar), as the chapel bell tower. A hymn is sung from the top of the tower at 6 am on May morning; since the late 18C this has been the college grace, though the tradition of the singing long pre-dates this.

The ornate gateway (1885) leads into ST. JOHN'S QUAD; on the W side (left) are the Vict Gothic St. Swithun's Buildings, and beyond them Longwall Quad (Giles Gilbert Scott, 1932), and the New Library built in 1851 as a hall for Magdalen College School. Immediately opposite the gateway are the President's Lodging (also Vict) and (left) Grammar Hall, a 1614 addition to the now-vanished medieval Magdalen Hall. In the S corner (right) is the *outdoor pulpit*, from which a university sermon was preached on St. John the Baptist's Day (24 June; now on the nearest Sunday). Originally the quadrangle was strewn with rushes (to represent the wilderness) for the occasion. Beside the pulpit is a passage to *Chaplain's Quad*, with remains of St. John's Hospital and the blocked-up Pilgrim's Gate into the High.

The buildings on the E side (right) of St. John's Quad are those planned and largely completed by Waynflete: the Chapel (entered under the Muniment Tower), and Founder's Tower, leading to the Cloisters and Hall. The Perp *Chapel* (1480) has suffered numerous destructions and restorations, and is now virtually 19C inside. Some of the old stalls, with carved misericords, survive in the ante-chapel together with other relics, including a 15C cope; also a bronze sculpture of Christ and St. Mary Magdalene by David Wynne (1964). Visitors are welcome to choral services (evensong Sat and Sun 5.15, weekdays exc Tues 6; suspended in Long Vacation). The Founder's Tower (no adm) contains state apartments, and still forms part of the President's Lodgings. A tapestry here depicts the marriage of Henry VIII's elder brother Arthur to Catherine of Aragon. CLOISTER QUAD (1490) was largely rebuilt in the 1820s; on the buttresses are grotesque figures called 'hieroglyphs'. Their symbolic significance, if any, is obscure. They were painted (officially) to honour James I's visit. Up a flight of stairs in the SE corner (right) is the *Hall* (1474, much altered in 1902), which happily retains its linenfold panelling and a set of ornate early Renaissance carvings, five depicting the life of St. Mary Magdalene.

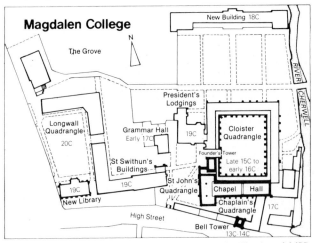

The *Old Library* (no adm), on the W side (left) contains illuminated MSS, Wolsey's copy of the Gospels, and Waynflete's stockings, buskins, and cope. A narrow passage on the N side leads across a wide lawn to the elegant New Building (1733); on the left is Magdalen Grove (not open) where deer have grazed since 1700; on the right a bridge leads to the Paddock, famous for the fritillaries which bloom there in spring, and to the *Water Walks, one of which (N) is named after Addison, the early 18C essayist and poet.

  FAMOUS MEMBERS. Richard Foxe (see Corpus Christi); John Colet, leading light in Revival of Learning, founder of St. Paul's School, 1467–1519; Cardinal Wolsey 1475–1530; Cardinal Pole, controversial Abp of Canterbury, 1500–58; John Foxe (see Brasenose); Sir Thomas Bodley, founder of the Bodleian Library,

1545–1613; John Mason, a founder of New Hampshire, 1596–1635; John Hampden, parliamentarian, 1599–1643; *Joseph Addison,* essayist and poet, 1672–1719; William Collins, poet, 1721–59; Oscar Wilde, dramatist, 1854–1900; Compton Mackenzie, novelist, 1883–1972; C.S. Lewis (see University College); Lord Florey, scientist, Nobel prizewinner, 1898–1968 (also Lincoln and Queen's); Sir John Betjeman, poet, 1906–84. Edward Gibbon, 1737–94, author of 'Decline and Fall of the Roman Empire', left after only fourteen months (1752–53), 'the most idle and unprofitable of my whole career'.

Member of the Royal Family: H.R.H. The Duke of Windsor (Edward VIII), 1894–1972.

Across Magdalen Bridge is a traffic nexus known as *The Plain* (Pl.D4). Immediately on the left is Magdalen's Waynflete Building (1961) and Queen's Florey Building (1970), an astonishing irregular polygon of red tiles and glass on concrete stilts designed by James Stirling (cf History Faculty Building in Cambridge). Beyond, in St. Clement's, is Stone's Hospital, a late 17C almshouse. On the right are Magdalen College School and, along Iffley Road beyond the University Sports Ground, *Greyfriars,* a private Hall for Franciscan students.

In Cowley Place, on a pleasant riverside site, is **St. Hilda's College** (Pl.D4), founded for women in 1893 by Miss Dorothea Beale, one of the great pioneers of women's education. She was an early student at Queen's College, London (see F.D. Maurice, p 134) and afterwards the famous and formidable principal of Cheltenham Ladies' College:

> Miss Buss and Miss Beale
> Cupid's darts do not feel.
> How different from us,
> Miss Beale and Miss Buss.

Named after St. Hilda, the 7C Abbess of Whitby who was one of England's first women scholars, it was recognised as a Hall in 1896, and became a college in 1926. Its first home was an elegant Georgian mansion built for Dr Sibthorpe, then Professor of Botany, about 1780. Additions were made as numbers grew, in the 1880s and 1890s in Gothic style, in 1934 and after the Second World War mostly in neo-Georgian. In complete contrast is *Garden Building* (1968–70 by Alison and Peter Smithson) in markedly modern idiom.

Back across Magdalen Bridge and up the left-hand side of the High, the Vict-Gothic building on the corner of Merton St is *The Examination Schools* (Pl.D1; no adm), extensively used for lectures as well as examinations.

A little further on is **University College** ('Univ.', Pl.D1). It was endowed by William of Durham in 1249 and was at first administered by the University (hence its name). It received its first statutes as an independent foundation in 1280. However, it long held primacy among Oxford colleges on the grounds of a (purely fictitious) claim to have been founded by Alfred the Great. This claim, invented to support a lawsuit in 1381, was upheld as late as 1727, and the college celebrated its millenary in 1882. A bust of King Alfred is still to be seen in the lobby of the Library.

Nothing remains of the medieval buildings. The long curved front of the college, with its two tower gateways, is a good example of Oxford 17C Gothic. The upper (W) gateway carries outside a statue of Queen Anne (a generous benefactor), replacing one of King Alfred, and inside a statue of James II in a Roman toga. This is a reminder of the late 17C Master, Obadiah Walker, who became a Roman Catholic, but managed to retain his post through a dispensation granted by King James. The lower gateway carries outside a statue of Queen Mary, and inside one of Dr Radcliffe, whose generous bequest financed the building in 1719 of the smaller quadrangle, named after him.

FRONT QUAD, built slowly between 1634 and 1677, is little altered, but the *Hall* was extensively remodelled inside in 1802 and enlarged in 1904. It contains some interesting modern portraits. The *Chapel* is also heavily refurbished (by Scott, 1862). The screen, stalls and reredos are late 17C, and there are dramatic windows by Abraham van Linge, 1641. In one is Jonah's ship, loyally flying the college flag. In the NW (right) corner of the quadrangle a passage (doorway 3) leads to the *Shelley Memorial* (1893) where in a gloomy domed chamber a marble statue of the drowned poet rests coldly behind a grille. Shelley was 'sent down' in 1811 for producing, with his friend Hogg, a pamphlet on 'The Necessity of Atheism'.

Beyond Front Quad is a variety of further buildings: New Building, 1842, by Sir Charles Barry (architect of the Houses of Parliament), the Library, 1861, by Scott, and several modern additions tucked into any available spaces. RADCLIFFE QUAD (1716) is reached by a passage E (left), doorway 7, and beyond are more 19C and 20C additions, incorporating the N end of Logic Lane.

FAMOUS MEMBERS: Lord Herbert of Cherbury, statesman and philosopher, 1583–1648; Dr John Radcliffe, popular physician and munificent benefactor of Oxford, 1650–1714; Roger Newdigate, antiquary, founder of the Newdigate Poetry Prize, 1719–1806; Shelley, Romantic poet, 1792–1822; Lord Cecil of Chelwood, international statesman, Nobel prizewinner 1864–1958; Clement Attlee, parliamentarian and Prime Minister, 1883–1967; William Beveridge, Master (see Balliol), 1879–1963; C.S. Lewis, literary critic and Christian writer, 1898–1963 (also Fellow of Magdalen).

Further up the High towards Carfax, just beyond University College, a plaque on the wall marks the site of the house where the scientist Robert Boyle (1627–91) and his assistant Robert Hook worked while in Oxford.

2   North-East of Carfax

Going E down the left side of •THE HIGH, the first point of interest is the Covered Market, lively, colourful, odoriferous and noisy, where anything can be bought from fresh fish to old gramaphone records. Beyond it on the upper corner of Turl St ('the Turl'), is the erstwhile Mitre Hotel, a renowned coaching inn of the 17C and 18C; it is now a restaurant, with undergraduate rooms above. Opposite is *All Saints Church* (Pl.C2) with a spire by Hawksmoor which makes a significant contribution to the Oxford skyline. After the demolition of St. Martin's in 1896 (see p48) All Saints served for a time as the City Church. In the 1970s, no longer needed as a church, it was converted into the library of **Lincoln College**, whose entrance is a short distance down the Turl. Founded in 1427 by Robert Fleming, Bp of Lincoln, as a counterblast to the Wycliffite Movement, its theologians were 'to defend the mysteries of the sacred page against these ignorant laics, who profaned with swinish snouts its most holy pearls'. The religious conservatism of its foundation persisted, and during the Reformation three successive Rectors and many Fellows were expelled. Somewhat ironically Lincoln's most famous member is John Wesley, the founder of Methodism, elected to a fellowship in 1726.

The FRONT QUAD is one of the few in Oxford to retain its 15C appearance; the outer facade has battlements added in 1824, but those added inside in 1852 have happily been removed. *The Hall* (opposite the gateway) dates from 1436; in its ancient beamed roof is the original louvre through which smoke escaped. A fireplace was installed in the late 17C, but the present ornate structure is Victorian (1891). On the right is a passage over which are Wesley's rooms, restored in 1928 with gifts from the American Methodist Church, (adm on application to the Porter's Lodge).

Beyond is CHAPEL QUAD, built in 1608–31. The *Chapel* is unusually light and bright, the panelled roof decorated with shields, swags and crowns, (restored 1958), and the large windows brilliant with glass by Bernard van Linge, c 1630. The beautifully carved woodwork is 17C, including the pulpit from which Wesley preached. In the quadrangle is an attractive modern sundial (War Memorial). The Vict-Gothic Grove Building was added, E of the Front Quad, in 1880, and more buildings between Chapel Quad and All Saints in 1906. Finally need for additional accommodation has made the college spill over the Turl into Lincoln House (1939), and across the High into Bear Lane (1977) while All Saints Church itself (see also above) became the college *Library (open Tues and Thur 2.30–4.30, exc when the college is closed), not inappropriately, since from its foundation Lincoln had a close connection with All Saints, whose living was in the college gift. The interior, on two levels, is remarkably beautiful, light and lofty, the ceiling decorated with elaborate plasterwork, and the giant pilasters picked out in gold. Reminders of its ecclesiastical past are the funeral hatchments, memorial tablets, and tomb of William Levinz, alderman, who died in 1616 aged 100.

  FAMOUS MEMBERS: William Davenant, poet and playwright, Shakespeare's godson (see p 48), 1606–68; John Wesley, founder of Methodism (see above), 1703–91; Dr John Radcliffe, (see University College); Lord Morley, writer and statesman, 1838–1923; Lord Florey, scientist, Nobel prizewinner, 1898–1968 (see also Magdalen and Queen's).

Oxford skyline: the famous 'dreaming spires'

A short way down the High from Turl St, past buildings belonging to Brasenose College (see p 75), is the church of **St. Mary the Virgin** (Pl.D1), whose Dec *tower and spire (188ft high), one of the most splendid in England, is a conspicuous Oxford landmark. Although the parish church of Oxford, it has from earliest times been closely linked to the University. Its chapels were assigned to the different faculties for lectures, and until the 17C meetings of Congregation, examinations, learned disputations, and degree givings all took place here. Its bells summoned scholars not only to study but to battle with the townspeople (see History, p 11); they still mark such University events as the installations of the Vice-Chancellor and the Proctors (who have their own special stalls in the church), Encaenia, and meetings of Congregation and Convocation. A University sermon is delivered by a 'select preacher' on Sunday mornings in term in the presence of the Vice-Chancellor, as are the famous Bampton lectures, endowed by Dr John Bampton (died 1751). In 1555 St Mary's witnessed the trial of the Oxford Martyrs (see History, p 12), and the following year Cranmer's repudiation of his recantation. One of the grooves cut to support the platform on which he stood can be seen on a pillar to the left of the Vice-Chancellor's throne, and damage to the poppyhead pew-ends may also date from this. Wesley worshipped and preached here (the last time in 1744), as in the 19C did the leaders of the controversial Oxford Movement, Keble, Pusey, and Newman, who was vicar in 1828–43 (shortly before he joined the Church of Rome).

Facing the High is the magnificent Italianate Baroque S porch (1637) designed by Nicholas Stone and given by Dr Morgan Owen, Bp of Llandaff and chaplain to Abp Laud. That it carries a statue of the Virgin and Child formed one of the charges against Laud at his trial in 1644. The main entrance is on the N side (in Radcliffe Sq) under the tower (which can be climbed, open all the year 10–5, in summer 10–c 7; fee). The tower and spire, Brome chapel and Congregation House, all on the N side, date from the early 14C. (The statues on the tower replace originals now kept in the Congregation House and the cloisters of New College.) Otherwise the church was largely rebuilt in the Perp style, at the University's expense, in the late 15C. Part of the reredos and stalls are of this date; the rest of the woodwork is mostly 17C. The many monuments include: a slab in the floor of the choir commemorating Amy Robsart (d 1560), neglected wife of Queen Elizabeth's favourite, Leicester; tablets to Dr John Radcliffe (see University College) and the historian John Aubrey (1626–97), and the tomb of Adam de Brome (1328), vicar of the church and founder of Oriel College.

Until the building of Duke Humphrey's Library (see the Bodleian, p 72) in 1488 the upper floor of the Congregation House (NE side of church) was the University's only library. The room was then refurbished and used for Congregation meetings until 1637.

On the corner of Catte St and the High is **All Souls College** (Pl.D1) founded in 1438 by Henry Chichele, Abp of Canterbury, with Henry VI as co-founder. It commemorated the fallen of the Hundred Years' War, and was both a chantry for their souls (its full title is 'The College of All Souls of the Faithful Departed, of Oxford') and an institution for the advanced study of theology and law. It has a Warden and Fellows only and remains unique among Oxford colleges in this respect. Until the reforms of the 1850s its Fellows were reputed to be 'well-born, well-bred' and only 'moderately learned'; nowadays, however, its reputation for scholarship and distinction is high; and to be elected a Fellow is a singular honour. Among its more than sixty Fellows are scholars of international renown in many fields, especially in history and law.

The entrance gateway is in the High; this and Front Quad are largely unaltered 15C work, though the statues of the founders and relief of the Resurrection on the gateway are modern replacements (1940). The Chapel, opposite the gateway, is reached through a beautifully fan-vaulted passage (left). Built in the Perp style (1442) and much restored by Scott in 1872–76, it retains its 15C hammerbeam angel roof, stalls with misericords, and the framework of a magnificent carved stone reredos. The figures in the niches are Vict, some of them being modelled on contemporary members of the college; the originals were destroyed during the Reformation. In 1664 the ruined reredos was decorated with a fresco of the Last Judgement by Isaac Fuller, with accompanying painted ceiling panels above (some of these now hang in the ante-chapel). This fresco was itself replaced in 1715 with one by Sir James Thornhill, who also remodelled the impressive black and gold Baroque screen. The ante-chapel is also 15C. Great (or North) Quad, reached through a passage in the NE (right) corner of Front Quad, is a complete contrast, Baroque Gothic (with Baroque interiors) of 1716–34 by Hawksmoor. The telescope-like towers on the E side and the ogee-capped gatehouse on the W are unique and eye-catching. Between is a lawn of velvet perfection, originally laid down in 1765. The N side is formed by the Codrington Library (no adm), donated together with his great collection of books by Christopher Codrington (d 1710), Governor of the Leeward Islands and once a Fellow of the College. It contains some 120,000 volumes, several hundred MSS and incunabula, and a large number of drawings from the office of Sir Christopher Wren.

Wren designed the beautiful sundial on the library S front (previously on the chapel); its notable accuracy is a reminder that at the time (1659) Wren was already Gresham Professor of Astronomy (he became Savilian Professor at Oxford two years later).

FAMOUS MEMBERS: Thomas Linacre, founder of the Royal College of Physicians, c 1460–1524; Jeremy Taylor, Anglican divine, 1613–67; Thomas Sydenham, pioneer physician, 1624–89; Christopher Wren, architect and astronomer, 1632–1723; Sir William Blackstone, author of 'Commentaries on the Laws of England', 1723–80; T.E. Lawrence, leader of the Arab revolt against the Turks in the First World War, 1888–1935; and a host of other distinguished scholars and statesmen, too numerous to detail.

A short way down the High is the graceful classical facade of ***The Queen's College** (Pl.D1), perhaps the greatest beauty of this beautiful street. It was founded in 1340 by Robert de Eglesfield of Cumberland, chaplain to Queen Philippa, wife of Edward III, under the patronage of his royal mistress; she was the first of a long line of Queens consort to take an interest in the college. His detailed provisions for its constitution were strongly religious: its theology course was to last eighteen years, its Provost and twelve Fellows were to be in Orders. Their numbers represented Our Lord and the apostles,' their scarlet gowns His blood. Seventy 'poor boys' were to represent the disciples sent out to preach (Luke 10). These were the first undergraduates specifically provided for by an Oxford college. Strict rules of discipline were laid down: no bows and arrows, no dogs, no musical instruments except on special occasions, no playing of marbles on the steps. Although most of the founder's arrangements have long been abandoned, several old customs remain: the college is summoned to dinner by the sound of the trumpet; on feast days the founder's drinking horn—an auroch's horn mounted on eagle's feet and banded with silver gilt—is used as a loving-cup; at Christmas a 'boar's head dinner' is celebrated (many of the original scholars were northcountrymen who could not get home for Christmas): at New Year the bursar presents to each guest at the 'Gaudy' a needle and thread ('aiguille' and 'fil', a pun on Eglesfield's name), with the words 'Take this and be thrifty'. Certain senior scholars are called 'Taberdars'.

The college was entirely rebuilt between 1671 and 1765 and is the only one in Oxford of which none of the original buildings survive. *FRONT QUAD (1710–34), 'the grandest piece of classical architecture in Oxford', is partly based on designs by Hawksmoor. Under the entrance cupola is a statue of Queen Caroline, who contributed £1000 towards the completion of the quadrangle. Opposite the entrance (N) the passage leading into Back Quad has on its left the *Hall*, which contains a portrait of Addison by Kneller, and one of Jeremy Bentham, one of the College's most famous members. On the right is the *Chapel*, light and spacious with a highly decorated ceiling (in the apse a painting of the Ascension by Sir James Thornhill), and magnificent Baroque screen. The side windows at the E end are by Abraham van Linge (1635), which together with those at the W end come from the previous chapel (1518).

BACK QUAD was actually built first (1671–1714), the mason-architect being John Townesend, of Oxford. The E range conceals, behind a curtain wall, the Williamson Building of 1671, designed by Wren and paid for by Sir Joseph Williamson, Secretary of State to Charles II, a former Fellow of the college. On the left (W) is the *Library* (no adm), a grand classical building carrying outside an array of statues and inside rich in rococo plasterwork and carved bookcases. From its S end a narrow high-walled passage (cul-de-sac) leads past the old brewhouse into a tiny formal garden opening out on to a lawn, enclosed by cosy-looking house-backs, just behind Drawda Hall and the noisy High. All is peace, flowers, and pigeons. A typical Oxford anomaly, not to be missed.

  Queen's Lane Quad (1967–69, designed by Marshall Sisson) across Queen's Lane, incorporates the facades of houses and shops already on the site. The Florey Building, for postgraduates, is described on p 62.

  FAMOUS MEMBERS: Thomas Middleton, playwright, 1570–1627; William Wycherley, playwright, 1640–1716; Edmund Halley, astonomer, 1656–1742; Joseph Addison and William Collins, who both migrated to Magdalen; Jeremy Bentham, legal and social philosopher, 1748–1823; Walter Pater, critic and essayist, 1839–94 (see also Brasenose); Lord Florey (Provost), see Magdalen. John Wyclif (see also Merton and Balliol) lived in the college as a lodger from 1363 to 1381.

Queen's Lane (middle section closed to traffic) wanders westward into Catte St, becoming New College Lane at its W end. On the right is **St. Edmund Hall** (Pl.D1), familiarly known as 'Teddy Hall', with a history going back, perhaps, to c 1220, and the last survivor of the medieval halls. It is dedicated to St. Edmund of Abingdon, Abp of Canterbury, who taught at Oxford c 1195–1200; the site of the front quadrangle was owned by Osney Abbey until the Dissolution in 1539. It was controlled by Queen's College from 1557 to 1937, and acquired full collegiate status twenty years later. In student numbers it is now among the largest colleges.

  Only a fireplace in the Middle Common Room remains of the medieval buildings; of the charming Front Quad three sides were built in the 16C–18C, and the remaining S side (right of the entrance) in 1927–34. In the centre is the old well (the well head is modern), and on the N (left) side a painted sundial. Opposite the entrance is the tiny panelled *Chapel*; it has 17C stalls and screen (oak on the W side, cedar on the E), glass by Burne-Jones, Morris, and Webb, and a striking altarpiece, 'The Supper at Emmaus', by Ceri Richards (1958). Over the ante-chapel is the Old Library (17C, extended 1931). E of the chapel, ingeniously squeezed into a constricted site between the High and New College gardens, is a new quadrangle (1968–70), providing common rooms, *Hall*, and sets of rooms. Its bold modern buildings (designed by Gilbert Howes) somehow harmonise well with their ancient neighbours. The church of St. Peter in the East, one of the oldest in Oxford, a little further up Queen's Lane and approached through St. Edmund Hall, is now the college *Library*; the crypt can be visited (apply at the Porter's Lodge).

  The unobtrusive entrance to ***New College** (Pl.D1; turn right after

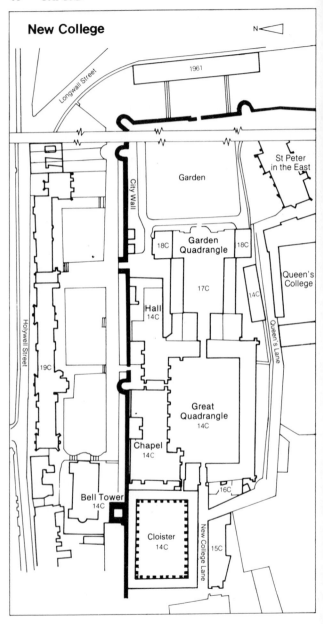

New College

N

1961

Longwall Street

City Wall

Garden

St Peter
in the East

18C   Garden
Quadrangle   18C

17C

Queen's
College

14C

Hall
14C

Holywell Street

19C

Great
Quadrangle
14C

Queen's Lane

Chapel
14C

16C

Bell Tower
14C

Cloister
14C

New College Lane

15C

passing through the archway in New College Lane) belies the splendours within. This is in fact one of the grandest and most prestigious of Oxford's colleges. It was founded in 1379 by William of Wykeham, Bp of Winchester, to provide for the advanced studies of boys educated at his other great foundation, Winchester College (its original name being the St. Mary College of Winchester in Oxford). His object was to repair the ravages among the ranks of the clergy of the Hundred Years' War and the Black Death (c 1345), and produce a supply of 'men of learning, fruitful to the Church ... the King, and the Realm'. Entry was restricted to Wykehamists until the 19C; until 1834 its members were exempt from taking University examinations, and received degrees on the Warden's word alone (a system clearly open to abuse). Although New College played a prominent part in the 16C Revival of Learning, its wealth and privilege afterwards led to a period of decline until with the University reforms of the 19C it gradually regained its pre-eminent position.

William of Wykeham laid down strict rules for its government, and his statutes set two Oxford precedents: compulsory attendance at chapel, and the college tutorial system. In the 20C it set a precedent by being the first of the men's colleges to decide to admit women (1964) although for various reasons this did not happen for another fifteen years.

New College is one of the few colleges where the wealth and prestige of the founder enabled his designs to be carried out in full; the principal buildings, completed about 1386, remain as a superb example of English Perp architecture, and strikingly similar to the sister foundation. It lies just within the old city walls, which are in places incorporated into it. The turreted gate-tower carries statues of the Virgin, the angel Gabriel, and William of Wykeham; the massive oak doors are original. GREAT, or FRONT, QUAD, the first complete quadrangle in Oxford, is impressively large; unfortunately a third storey and battlements, then sash windows, were imposed on the 14C buildings in 1674 and 1711 respectively. On the N (left) is the handsome *Chapel*; although the structure is of the founder's time, the interior (including the raised roof) is almost entirely Vict (by Scott, 1879). The stalls, however, retain their original arm-rests and misericords; both are richly and entertainingly carved. On the N (left) side of the altar are a painting of St. James by El Greco, and the founder's •crozier of silver-gilt set with jewels and enamelwork. In the ante-chapel the stained glass is 14C, with the exception of the great W window, depicting the Nativity and the Seven Virtues, which was painted by Thomas Jarvis to designs by Sir Joshua Reynolds (1777). It is disappointingly brown and wishy-washy. The glass it displaced is in York Minster. In the floor are twenty-three 15C and 16C brasses, and high up on the S wall two 'squints', from which the Warden could observe services and disputations (cf Christ's College, Cambridge). Below are memorials, by Eric Gill, to members of the college, both English and German, killed in the First World War. The whole is dominated by Epstein's compelling •statue of *Lazarus*. The choral services are superb (Sun 6 pm, weekdays exc Wed 6.15; suspended in the Long Vacation).

W (left) of the chapel is the detached Bell Tower and the spacious Cloister, whose building necessitated the right-angled kink in New College Lane. It houses some of the statues from the tower of St. Mary the Virgin church (see p 65).

The *Hall* (usually closed) adjoins the chapel. It is one of the oldest and finest in Oxford, with 16C linenfold panelling, Vict stained glass, and roof by Scott (1877). Above is the Muniment Tower (no adm) which contains the college's title deeds, admission registers, and other ancient records. The remaining 14C building is the Long Room, E of Great Quad and backing on to Queen's Lane. Originally the latrines and cesspool, its upper floor is now a beautiful gallery and reception room.

Opposite Great Quad gateway (E) is GARDEN QUAD, added between 1683 and 1711, and enclosed on its E side by an elegant wrought-iron screen. The chief features of the pleasant *garden* beyond are a well-preserved remnant of the old City Wall and a large artificial mound (1549), perhaps an example of the 'mounts' popular in Tudor gardens. Along the N side of the college, facing Holywell St, are 19C additions, by Scott and Champneys, and on the E side abutting on to Longwall St, the modern Sacher Building (by David Roberts, 1961; cf St. Hugh's). The sculpture on the lawn is by Barbara Hepworth (1964).

FAMOUS MEMBERS: William Grocyn, scholar and humanist, 1446–1519; William Waynflete, founder of Magdalen College (qv), 1395–1486; Thomas Ken, one of the Seven Bishops (1688), hymn writer, 1637–1711; Sydney Smith, journalist, theologian, moral philosopher, 1771–1845; John Galsworthy, novelist and playwright, 1867–1933; A.P. Herbert, writer and politician, 1890–1971; H.A.L. Fisher, historian, 1865–1940; Maurice Bowra, classicist, Professor of Poetry, 1898–1971; numerous archbishops and bishops.

Hertford College (pron 'Harf'd', Pl.D1) lies on each side of New College Lane at its junction with Catte St, the two parts linked by the picturesque 'Bridge of Sighs' (1913). Its present foundation, made possible through the benefaction of the banker T.C. Baring, dates from 1874, and its buildings are almost entirely late Vict, in a variety of styles (by Sir T.G. Jackson). But its history goes back to 1284, when it began life as Hart Hall. It was granted collegiate status in 1740, but subsequently declined, and in 1818 was amalgamated with Magdalen Hall (see p 60), which brought to it useful endowments and distinguished scholarship.

FAMOUS MEMBERS: Of Hart Hall, John Donne, poet and divine, 1572–1631; of Hertford College first foundation, Charles James Fox, liberal statesman, 1749–1806; of Magdalen Hall, William Tyndale, translator of the Bible, pioneer of the Reformation, died at the stake in 1536, and Thomas Hobbes, philosopher, 1588–1679; of Hertford College second foundation, Evelyn Waugh, novelist, 1903–66.

Between Hertford College and Holywell St (N) is the somewhat aggressive Vict-Gothic Indian Institute (Champneys 1896) now the History Faculty Library. HOLYWELL itself has a number of attractive 17C and 18C houses. On the left is the *Old Music Room* (1748), the first room in England to be built solely for musical use. Its beautiful chandeliers were given by George IV, and previously hung in Westminster Hall. The Faculty of Music, formerly housed alongside, is now in St. Aldate's (see p 50). In marked contrast is the modern Blackwell's Music Shop, dramatically lit inside by an inverted cylinder of glass.

Almost opposite is BATH PLACE, with particularly charming little houses, from which a very narrow passage threads its way past the Turf Tavern and, becoming St. Helen's Passage, emerges into New College Lane near the house (No. 7) of Edmund Halley, astronomer and Savilian Professor of Geometry in 1703–42 (see also Queen's College).

On the N side of Holywell is **Wadham College** (Pl.B7) which has its entrance in Parks Rd opposite the spacious garden of Trinity College, of which there is a good view through the 18C iron railings. Wadham, founded in 1610 by wealthy Somerset landowners Nicholas and Dorothy Wadham, is the latest of the old foundations. Its main buildings, almost exactly as they were when completed in 1613, are the supreme example of the Jacobean-Gothic style, with classical touches, so popular in Oxford; their studied symmetry is particularly noticeable.

Wadham's most illustrious phase was during the Commonwealth, when many founder members of the future Royal Society, including Wren and Thomas Sydenham ('the English Hippocrates') gathered round the scientifically-minded Warden John Wilkins, Cromwell's brother-in-law (see also Trinity College, Cambridge).

The gateway to Front Quad is fan-vaulted; immediately opposite is the entrance to the chapel and the hall, a handsome portal with classical columns (cf the contemporary Bodleian Tower of the Five Orders in Schools Quadrangle), and carrying statues of the founders on each side, and James I above. The *Chapel*, actually entered from a passage in the NE corner (left) is of grand and elegant proportions. The east end was considerably altered in 1832, when the reredos, stone panelling, and stalls were put in; the stucco ceiling also dates from then, replacing one of decorated wooden panels. The E window is by Bernard van Linge (1622); the screen, pulpit, communion rail and table are all 17C, the last presented to the college in 1889 by the parish of Ilminster in Somerset, where the founders are buried. The large *Hall* has its original hammerbeam roof and louvre; the heraldic glass in the S window commemorates benefactors of the college, that in the great bay some of its famous members.

A pleasant new copper-roofed block was added on the SE side (right) in the early 1950s, and in 1971–72 old houses in Holywell were adapted and linked to new buildings to complete another quadrangle. The architects, Gillespie, Kidd and Coia, are also responsible for the development behind the old building, in glass and concrete with massive lead-clad roof. The *gardens, with sweeping lawns, stately copper beech and cedar trees, and glorious herbaceous border, are among the loveliest in Oxford. The statue of Sir Maurice Bowra (Warden, 1938–70) is by John Doubleday.

FAMOUS MEMBERS: Robert Blake, admiral, 1599–1657; Thomas Sydenham, pioneer physician, 1624–89 and Christopher Wren, architect and astronomer, 1632–1723 (both afterwards Fellows of All Souls); Arthur Onslow, Speaker of the House of Commons for 35 years, 1691–1768; Richard Bethell (Lord Westbury), 1800–73, Lord Chancellor; T.G. Jackson, architect, 1835–1924; Francis Kilvert, diarist, 1841–79; F.E. Smith (Lord Birkenhead), statesman, 1872–1930; C.B. Fry, sportsman and journalist, 1872–1956; J.A. Simon (Lord Simon), statesman, 1873–1954; Thomas Beecham, conductor, 1879–1961; C. Day Lewis, poet, 1904–72.

Returning from Wadham to the Broad, you see the *New Bodleian Library* (no adm) on the right, a stolid 1930s block in Bladon stone designed by Sir Giles Gilbert Scott, and partly paid for by the Rockefeller Foundation. Of its eleven bookstacks, providing storage for some five million volumes, three are underground, and connected with the old library across the road by a passage and conveyor-belt. A penthouse was added in the 1960s to house the library of the Indian Institute (see above). Across the Broad (S) is the beautiful and impressive group of University buildings which are the very heart of Oxford.

The *Sheldonian Theatre (Pl.C2; open 10–12.45 and 2–4.45; 3.45 in winter) was built 1663–69, at the expense of Gilbert Sheldon, Warden of All Souls and afterwards Abp of Canterbury, to provide a venue for University occasions such as disputations and degree givings, up to that time held in St. Mary's Church (see p 65). It was the first building designed by Sir Christopher Wren, then Savilian

Professor of Astronomy. The annual conferment of degrees and *Commemoration* or *Encaenia* are held here at the end of the summer term (late June), the stately and complicated ceremonies made richly colourful by the full academic dress of the participants, and conducted in Latin (though nowadays translations are provided). The Theatre is also used for large public lectures, meetings and concerts.

The plan of the building, semi-circular in front, rectangular behind, was inspired by pictures of the open-air Theatre of Marcellus in Rome. It is approached up shallow steps, and partly surrounded by railings on whose stone plinths are venerable but unidentified busts, renewed in 1868 and again in 1972. Much of the outside of the Theatre is also modern restoration, the soft stone of the original having succumbed to the ravages of time and weather. The octagonal cupola replaced Wren's smaller one in 1832; it provides an excellent viewpoint (last adm 15 minutes before the Theatre closes). Inside the hall is tiered seating and a gallery supported on wooden pillars painted to simulate marble. The roof is decorated with a large allegorical painting of the Triumph of Religion and Learning over Envy, Hatred and Malice (by Robert Streeter, 1669).

The Theatre housed the University Press until it was moved in 1713 to the *Clarendon Building* (Pl.D1) alongside (left). This was designed by Hawksmoor in the classical style, and largely paid for out of the profits from Lord Clarendon's 'History of the Great Rebellion' published in 1702–04. The statues on the balustrade, by Sir James Thornhill, represent the Nine Muses. Two are modern fibre-glass replacements of the original lead ones. The Press moved to Walton St in 1830, and after many years of use as University offices, the building is now part of the ever-expanding Bodleian Library (see below).

On the right of the Sheldonian is the lovely *Old Ashmolean Museum* (Pl.C2; open Mon–Sat 10.30–1 and 2.30–4) built 1678–83 to house Elias Ashmole's collection of Natural Curiosities (moved to the Ashmolean Museum in Beaumont St in 1840; see p 80 for details) as well as the School of Natural History and a chemical laboratory. It was the first public museum in England. Since 1937 it has been the MUSEUM OF THE HISTORY OF SCIENCE.

The nucleus of the present museum is the Lewis Evans Collection of scientific instruments (given 1925), ranging from astrolabes to photographic equipment, to which was added the Billmeir Collection in 1957. Also shown are items relating to the history of pharmacy and medicine, among them the development of penicillin.

Behind the Sheldonian lies the *Old Schools Quadrangle*, built 1613–19 in familiar Oxford Jacobean-Gothic style. Over the doorways are the names of the disciplines formerly studied here and on the E side is the handsome gate-tower known as THE TOWER OF THE FIVE ORDERS; it is ornamented with columns of the five orders of classical architecture (Doric, Tuscan, Ionic, Corinthian, and Composite) topped by a statue of James I and above him in the parapet the Royal Stuart Arms. All the buildings are now part of the **Bodleian Library** ('Bodley'; Pl.D1). The library, one of the oldest and most important in the world, received its first collection of books and endowments from Duke Humphrey of Gloucester (1391–1447) and was housed above the Divinity School (see below), but these were dispersed during the Reformation excesses of Edward VI's reign, and in 1602 the library was refounded by, and named after, Sir Thomas

Bodley, fellow of Merton College and Ambassador to the Netherlands. Beginning with 2000 books, the Bodleian now contains some $4\frac{1}{2}$ million, as well as over 50,000 MSS. It is one of the six libraries which receive a copy of every book published in the UK, a right negotiated with the Stationers' Company by Sir Thomas Bodley himself. No book may be taken out, no matter how exalted the status of the would-be borrower (Charles I was refused, likewise Cromwell). Readers are admitted by ticket and must be members of the University or suitably sponsored.

The entrance is behind a bronze statue by Le Sueur of the Earl of Pembroke (one time Chancellor of the University), brought here from Wilton in 1722, and leads into the vestibule or *Proscholium* (used as a pig market under Edward VI), now the readers' and visitors' admission-hall and shop (open Mon–Fri 9–5, Sat 9–12.30). Opposite the doorway is the *Divinity School, built mid 15C, whose exquisitely vaulted *roof, enriched with carved coats of arms, figures and natural objects, is one of Oxford's greatest glories. It was the scene in 1555 of the examination of Cranmer, Latimer, and Ridley, the 'Oxford Martyrs' (see History, p 12); later it was used as a corn-store, but was renovated by Wren, who inserted the doorway on the N side and reinforced the walls to support the growing weight of books above. It is now used to display some of the treasures of the Bodleian.

Among important books and manuscripts belonging to the library which are sometimes on display are: the Chanson de Roland; one of the original copies of the revised reissue of Magna Carta, 1217; the manuscripts of T.E. Lawrence's 'Seven Pillars of Wisdom' and Kenneth Grahame's 'Wind in the Willows'; important poetic MSS of Thomas Traherne ('Centuries of Meditations'), John Donne (his only known verse autograph), Shelley (with memorabilia) and Gerard Manley Hopkins (MS B); the only known copies of the first work of Shakespeare's to be printed ('Venus and Adonis', 1593) and of the first edition of 'Tottel's Miscellany', 1557; and the only copy outside North America of the 'Bay Psalm Book', 1640.

Also on view is Sir Thomas Bodley's chest, with its elaborate threefold lock mechanism (cf Merton College Old Library and St John's College Library). There are temporary exhibitions both here and in the old School of Natural Philosophy, on the S side of Old Schools Quadrangle.

At the far end of the room a door leads into the *Convocation House* and *Apodyterium* or Vice-Chancellor's Robing Room (no adm to either); built in the mid 17C, both have fan-vaulted roofs actually inserted much later (1759). They are used for meetings of Convocation and Congregation (see University Organisation, p 18).

In 1681 Charles II summoned his third, and last, Parliament to meet him in Oxford. The Commons sat here in the Convocation House, the Lords in a room across the quadrangle approached up the stairway inscribed 'Schola Geometriae' (now the Classics Reading Room). On the King's arrival Parliament, to its intense dismay, was instantly dissolved.

The oldest part of the Bodleian library is above, in the H formed by the rooms just described, and reached up an insignificant stairway in the corner of the vestibule: 'Duke Humfrey' in the middle, over the Divinity School, the 'Arts End', added by Bodley, over the Proscholium, and the 'Selden End' added mid 17C to house books bequeathed by John Selden (d 1654). Facing the bookshelves of the *Arts End, loaded with venerable and immensely weighty volumes, are high wooden benches and sloping reading desks calculated to keep the sleepiest student awake. The beautiful panelled ceiling is profusely decorated with the arms of the University and of Sir Thomas Bodley. Over all hangs the thrilling hush of centuries of scholarship.

Unfortunately, these riches can only be seen by visitors if accompanied by a senior member of the University who has arranged the visit in advance in writing.

'The thrilling hush of centuries of scholarship', Bodleian Library, Arts End

This group of University buildings is completed by the ***Radcliffe Camera** (Pl.D1; no adm), a handsome classical rotunda rising majestically from the centre of the grass and paved square between the Old Schools and St. Mary's Church, with which older neighbours it is in perfect visual harmony. It was founded as a separate library by Dr Radcliffe (see also University College) whose statue by Rysbrack stands in a niche above the entrance (inside), and was designed by James Gibbs (who also designed, inter alia, the church of St. Martin-in-the-Fields in Trafalgar Sq, London, and the Senate House in Cambridge). Completed in 1749, it was originally a science library, but has long been part of the Bodleian.

On the W side (right, facing St. Mary's) of Radcliffe Sq is **Brasenose College** ('BNC'; Pl.D1) founded in 1504 by William Smythe, Bp of Lincoln, and Sir Richard Sutton (both of Lancashire). It was the direct successor to a Hall of the same name on the site, whose last Principal became the first Principal of the new college. The name probably derives from the 12C or 13C brazen knocker (possibly handle or sanctuary ring, with a lion-like mask) of the original Hall. This was carried off to Stamford in the migration of Oxford students in 1333, and only recovered in 1890. It now hangs above the high table in the Hall, and there is another small one above the main doors. The college has traditionally a great reputation for sporting prowess.

A handsome gate-tower leads into OLD QUAD. This was begun in 1509; a third storey and battlements were added 100 years later. On the N wall (right) is an attractive sundial (1719); instructions on how to read it correctly appear on a new aluminium panel at the entrance to the *Hall* opposite. This room was largely remodelled inside in the 18C, and has a quiet elegance. The *Chapel*, built in 1656 in an interesting mixture of Gothic and Classical styles (the only one dating from the Commonwealth years), is reached through a passage in the SE corner (right) leading into small CHAPEL QUAD. It replaced the earlier chapel alongside the Hall, which then became the Senior Common Room. Its roof is spectacular: colourfully painted and apparently fan-vaulted with elaborate pendants; it is in fact plasterwork of the mid 1660s. Underneath is a 15C hammerbeam roof brought here from the old Augustinian College of St. Mary in New Inn Hall St. In the ante-chapel is a memorial to Walter Pater (Fellow, 1864–94), impressively flanked by Leonardo da Vinci, Michelangelo, Plato and Dante. Beyond Chapel Quad is the Victorian NEW QUAD (Sir T.G. Jackson, 1886–1909), and the striking modern rooms skilfully inserted into the very limited space available by Powell and Moya in 1959–61, the first of their many buildings at both Oxford and Cambridge.

FAMOUS MEMBERS: John Foxe, martyrologist, 1516–87 (see also Magdalen); Robert Burton, author of 'The Anatomy of Melancholy', 1577–1640; Elias Ashmole, antiquary and founder of the Ashmolean Museum, 1617–92; William Petty, political economist, inventor and scientist, 1623–87; Thomas Traherne, mystic and poet, 1636–74; Bp Heber, hymnologist, 1783–1826; Arthur Evans, archaeologist, 1851–1941; Walter Pater, see above and Queen's College; Field-Marshal Earl Haig, (1861–1928), C-in-C of the British Expeditionary Force in the First World War; John Buchan (Lord Tweedsmuir), statesman and novelist, 1875–1940.

John Middleton, a Lancashire giant known as 'The Childe of Hale' visited the college, then full of Lancashire students, c 1613. A life-sized portrait of him was painted, and his huge hand carved on a stone (which Pepys paid two shillings to see on his visit in 1668). The college boat is always named 'Childe of Hale' after him.

Brasenose Lane, which still has its medieval open drain (not of course in use), links Radcliffe Sq with the Turl. On the right is **Exeter College** (Pl.C2), from whose garden a huge horse-chestnut tree leans across the lane towards Brasenose. If the branches touch, it used to be said, Exeter defeats BNC on the river. Exeter was founded in 1314 as Stapeldon Hall by Walter de Stapeldon, Bp of Exeter. From 1405 it was known as Exeter College, and in 1566 it was handsomely re-endowed by a former member, Sir William Petre, whose portrait hangs in the Hall. Like the founder, Bishop Stapeldon, Petre came from rural Devonshire and made his fortune through service to the Crown. The strong West Country link established by Stapeldon continues in the Stapeldon scholarships, only open to West Country candidates.

The college has been much rebuilt and altered at various periods, and is now largely Vict in appearance. On the S side (right) of the quadrangle is the *Hall* (built in 1618, restored in 1818), with large, light, Perp-style windows, fine collarbeam roof, and Jacobean screen. Opposite is the *Chapel*, built in 1856–59 by Sir George Gilbert Scott, and replacing a beautiful 17C predecessor. Scott's design was inspired by the Sainte Chapelle in Paris; its great height overwhelms the rest of the quadrangle, but the lofty multi-arched interior is undoubtedly impressive. It is richly decorated with carvings, mosaics, and a tapestry of 'The Adoration of the Magi' by Burne-Jones and William Morris, who while under-graduates here formed a life-long friendship.

Beyond the E end of the chapel is *Palmer's Tower*, the original gatehouse of 1432, and the only medieval building to survive. From here, passages lead to the right into a 17C–18C quadrangle and the pleasant garden; from the garden there is a good view of the Bodleian and the Divinity School, and to the left into the somewhat cramped and gloomy Margary Quad, bounded on its W side by the modern Thomas Wood building (1964). A gateway leads out into the Broad.

FAMOUS MEMBERS: Anthony Ashley-Cooper, 1st Lord Shaftesbury, politician, associated with the foundation of 'party' government and with the Habeas Corpus Act, 1621–83; Charles Lyell, geologist, 1797–1875; J.A. Froude, see Oriel; Edward Burne-Jones, Pre-Raphaelite artist, 1833–98; William Morris, artist, poet, social philosopher, 1834–96; Ray Lankester, zoologist, 1847–1929; C.H. Parry, composer, 1848–1918; J.R.R. Tolkien, philologist, author, 1892–1973.

Immediately across the Turl is **Jesus College** (Pl.C2), the first post-Reformation college in Oxford, founded in 1571, nominally by Elizabeth I, in reality by Hugh Price, treasurer of St. David's, who persuaded the Queen to lend it her prestige. The college has always had a very close connection with Wales, which even as late as the early 1900s still supplied over half its members.

The Turl St front of the college dates from the founder's time, but was refaced in the Perp style in the 1850s; at this time there was also considerable restoration and alteration of the chapel and of the S side (left), which had been built early in the 17C by Sir Eubule Thelwall (Principal 1621–30) in Jacobean-Gothic. The *Chapel*, on the N (right) side of First Quad, was extended eastwards in 1636; it has a barrel-vaulted roof, late 17C screen, and early 17C pulpit, but is otherwise heavily Vict. On St. David's Day the service is conducted in Welsh. In the ante-chapel is a bust of T.E. Lawrence (a replica of one in St. Paul's Cathedral) who was an exhibitioner of the college in 1907–10. In the *Hall* (opposite the main entrance) the royal founder takes pride of place, with a carved wooden bust over the fireplace, and a portrait over the high table. (She also appears in the Senior Common Room, in a painting by Zucchero.) Other good portraits include Charles I (school of Van Dyck), Charles II (attributed to Lely), John Nash, the architect (by Lawrence), and T.E. Lawrence 'of Arabia' again. The heavily carved screen is decorated with dragons, perhaps a reminder of Welsh loyalties.

The charming INNER QUAD, built between 1646 and 1713, again in Jacobean-Gothic style, remains largely unchanged. It was mainly the work of Sir Leoline Jenkins, (Principal 1661–73), whose munificent benefactions to the college earned him the status of 'second founder'. Through a passage on its N side (right) are further buildings of 1905 and (unmistakably) 1971. The latter was, appropriately, opened by the Prince of Wales.

FAMOUS MEMBERS: Henry Vaughan, mystic poet, 1622–95; Richard ('Beau') Nash, social mentor of 18C Bath, 1674–1762; J.R. Green, historian, 1837–83; T.E. Lawrence, 1888–1925 (see above, also All Souls), and many Welsh prelates and statesmen.

The N end of Turl St (left out of Jesus College) joins Broad St opposite Trinity College. •THE BROAD, as its name implies, is a wide street, gracious, treed, and unhurried. Its few shops are mostly devoted to

University needs—books and academic dress. A cross in the roadway opposite Balliol marks the place where Cranmer, Latimer and Ridley were burnt at the stake in 1555–56.

Trinity College (Pl.A8), with its spacious grounds and varied yet happily harmonising buildings, is particularly attractive. It was founded in 1555 by Sir Thomas Pope, a wealthy civil servant under the regime of Mary Tudor, and was at first strongly Roman Catholic in character. But its history really begins in the late 13C, when Durham College was established to provide for students from the Benedictine priory at Durham. Parts of this first college survive in Durham Quad, which lies, unusually, some distance back from the street, and was originally approached along a narrow high-walled lane (cf Jesus College, Cambridge). Trinity traditionally drew its members from the landed gentry, and has a long list of distinguished sons. It also, in the 17C, had two remarkable and eccentric Presidents, Ralph Kettell, and Ralph Bathurst. Kettell had a particular dislike of long hair; John Aubrey (see 'Famous Members' below) records that he would come into the hall with 'a pair of scissors in his muffe, and woe to them that sate on the outside of the table'.

The beautiful iron entrance gate is a 1737 copy of the one facing on to Parks Rd (see p 70). To the right, beyond some cottages taken over for college rooms in the 19C, and largely rebuilt c 1970, stands *Kettell Hall*, built for himself by the President in 1618–20. It now has the 1920s War Memorial Library (neo-classical) and modern (1964–68) buildings of CUMBERBATCH QUAD on two sides, but seems quite at ease with its 20C neighbours. The quadrangle adjoins Blackwell's bookshop, whose large underground showrooms also extend beneath it. The building along the E side (right) of FRONT QUAD is 19C by Sir T.G. Jackson, as is the President's Lodging just to its left. Next to this (left) is DURHAM QUAD, the oldest part of which is the outer side of the E range (right). Here is the *Old Library* (no adm), whose windows contain some 15C glass. The rest is 17C and 18C. The gate-tower, with its statues of Geometry, Astronomy, Theology, and Medicine, was built by President Bathurst in the 1690s, as was the *Chapel* (right). This has a perfect late 17C Baroque interior, almost untouched except for the insertion of Vict stained glass, and is one of the few college chapels which is 'all of a piece'. The gorgeous plasterwork ceiling has a centrepiece of the 'Ascension' by Pierre Berchet; the richly carved reredos is in the style of Grinling Gibbons, and may even be his work. It is well matched by the beautiful panelling, stalls, and screen. On the N side (left) of the altar is the tomb of the founder and his third wife (1567) transferred from the old chapel of 1406. The *Hall* (left), though built in 1620, has a largely 18C interior, light, lofty, and delicately coloured (extensively restored c 1960). Its chief interest lies in the splendid collection of portraits, which includes a modern group representing 'Arts and Sciences at Trinity 1977'.

A passage at the NW corner (top left) of the quadrangle leads into GARDEN QUAD. On the left, all among flowers, is a bust of Cardinal Newman. The buildings opposite, originally a single isolated block, are by Wren (1688) but much altered since. Open on the E side, this quadrangle and its garden seem particularly gracious and tranquil. A gateway (Dolphin Gate, 1947) leads out into St. Giles through an alleyway between the backs of Balliol and St. John's (not open to visitors).

FAMOUS MEMBERS: Lord Baltimore, one of the founders of Maryland, 1580–1632; Abp Sheldon, Warden of All Souls and builder of the Sheldonian Theatre, 1598–1677; Henry Ireton, Parliamentary leader, Cromwell's son-in-law,

1611–51; John Aubrey, antiquary and biographer, 1626–97; William Pitt, Lord Chatham, statesman, 1708–78; W.S. Landor, writer, 'sent down' for firing at the rooms of the man opposite, 1775–1864; John Newman, theologian and cardinal, 1801–90 (see also Oriel); Richard Burton, explorer, 'sent down' for trying to fight a duel, 1826–90; A. Quiller-Couch, author and critic, 1863–1944 (see also Jesus College, Cambridge); J. Elroy Flecker, poet, 1884–1915; Ronald A. Knox, Fellow (see Balliol); Terence Rattigan, playwright, 1911–79.

Immediately next door (left) is **Balliol College** (Pl.A8). It was endowed c 1260 by John de Balliol, a powerful northern nobleman and father of the Scottish King (1292–96), as a penance imposed by the Bp of Durham for his frequent disputes with the Church. The foundation was actually established by his widow Devorguilla, at first merely as a hostel. The first statutes date from 1282. The college played an important part in the spread of the New Learning in the 15C, when a number of leading Greek scholars were among its members, notably William Gray, afterwards Bp of Ely, who bequeathed to it his superb collection of books, most of which the college still possesses. However, its position of supreme academic pre-eminence, still maintained, dates from the 19C, when it was blessed with a series of outstanding Masters, the best-known of whom was Benjamin Jowett (1870–93). Through his teaching and his brilliant pupils he had a far-reaching influence on Victorian thought. His name is commemorated in Jowett Walk, between Mansfield Rd and St. Cross Rd, and in the contemporary rhyme:

> Here come I, my name is Jowett;
> There's no knowledge but I know it.
> I am the Master of this college;
> What I know not isn't knowledge.

The college was almost entirely rebuilt in the 19C, the architects chiefly involved being Waterhouse (part of the front quadrangle and Hall in Garden Quad), Butterfield (chapel), Salvin and Basevi (part of the W side (left) of Garden Quad). The *Library* and reading-room, originally the Hall, opposite the entrance and left in Front Quad, do in fact date from the 15C but were altered out of recognition by Wyatt in the 1790s. In Butterfield's pink and white striped *Chapel* (to the right of the Library) some Anglo-Flemish glass of 1528 from the ancient chapel was installed in 1912, and other windows are by Abraham van Linge (1637). Its interior is now far less colourful than Butterfield's original, much of his polychromatic alabaster-work having been plastered over, and his Gothic furnishings replaced by modern ones (1937). The spectacular silver-gilt repoussé-work *altar front is a First World War memorial. A passage in the NW corner (left) leads to Garden Quad, whose ancient wooden gates, originally at the Broad St entrance, are now hung on the passage wall. They were to be sold for firewood in the 1860s rebuilding, but were rescued by the Revd T. Harling Newman, who 'deemed it a pity that gates which had witnessed so many deaths by burning should themselves end in flames.' Exiled for some years to Essex, the gates were returned to the college in 1926.

Garden Quad presents a rather random appearance, and the Vict *Hall* looks distinctly uncomfortable, wedged between its 1960s neighbours (by Oxford Architects Partnership). It is approached by a long steep flight of steps; the organ within was given by Jowett, by whom the tradition of regular concerts here was established. The college has additional buildings in Manor Rd (see p 96).

FAMOUS MEMBERS: John Wyclif, Master in 1360, religious reformer and Bible translator, 1329(?)–84; John Evelyn, diarist, 1620–1706; Adam Smith, economist and political philosopher, 1723–90; Robert Southey, poet, 1774–1843; H.E. Manning, theologian and cardinal, 1808–92; both Abps Temple, father 1821–1902, son 1881–1944 (also Fellow of Queen's); Matthew Arnold, poet and critic, 1822–88 (also Fellow of Oriel); Algernon Swinburne, poet, 1837–1909; Arnold Toynbee, historian and expert in international affairs, 1889–1975 (also a Fellow); Lord Curzon, statesman and Viceroy of India, 1859–1925 (also Fellow of All Souls); Hilaire Belloc, writer, 1870–1953; William Beveridge, economist, creator of the Beveridge Report, 1879–1963 (also Master of University College); Julian Huxley, biologist, 1887–1975; his brother Aldous Huxley, novelist ('Brave New World'), 1894–1963; Ronald A. Knox, writer, translator of the Bible, 1888–1957; Sir Seretse Khama of Botswana, 1921–80.

The top of Broad St just beyond Balliol joins Cornmarket St; Carfax is to the left.

3   North and North-West of Carfax

CORNMARKET STREET, running northward from Carfax, consists largely of modern shops. The old Crown Tavern and Golden Cross Inn are described on p 48. In St. Michael's St (left) is the main entrance to the *Oxford Union Society* (Pl.C2), founded as a social and debating club in 1823, a time of increasing political and social awareness and new thinking. It has long been renowned for the quality of its debates and as a training ground for future politicians; numerous distinguished MPs, ministers, and prime ministers first tried their oratorical powers in its hall. A determinedly masculine stronghold, its doors were closed to women as members until 1963. The buildings date mostly from the 1850s and 1860s; the walls and roof of the old library are decorated with scenes from the Morte d'Arthur painted by various Pre-Raphaelite artists; unfortunately owing to inadequate preparation of the plaster they have greatly deteriorated.

Debates are held on Thursday or Friday evenings. Visitors are admitted to the gallery as spectators; application must be made to the General Office at least two days in advance.

Opposite St. Michael's St is the church of *St. Michael at the North Gate* (Pl.C2), whose Saxon tower (pre-1050) once formed part of the city defences. It adjoined the Bocardo (prison), where Latimer and Ridley were held before their deaths at the stake in 1555, and Cranmer in 1556 (see History, p 12). Its oaken door, bearing a brass inscription, is kept in the church. The church itself, though mostly built in the 13C, has been extensively restored since a severe fire in 1953. Some of the glass is 13C, and includes (in the N aisle) a rare lily Crucifixion. St. Michael's is now the city church, and contains the city font (originally in St. Martin's, then in All Saints, see p 63) which must be the one in which Shakespeare's godson was baptised.

Immediately beyond, across Broad St, in Magdalen St, is the church of *St. Mary Magdalen* (Pl.A8), largely rebuilt by Scott, who added the Martyrs' aisle (N) in 1842, when he was building the Martyrs' Memorial. In the S chapel is a memorial to John Aubrey (d 1697) the biographer and antiquarian (see Trinity College).

The *Martyrs' Memorial*, just outside the church at the S end of St. Giles, was designed by Scott in 1841, in the style of the Waltham Eleanor Cross. It commemorates Cranmer, Latimer, and Ridley, whose statues (by H. Weeks) contemplate the swirling traffic at their feet.

On the corner of St Giles and Beaumont St (right) are the imposing neo-classical buildings (Pl.A8) of the *Taylor Institution* (the 'Taylorian', facing St. Giles) and the **Ashmolean Museum** (facing Beaumont St; open Tue–Sat 10–4, Sun 2–4) designed in 1841–45 by C.R. Cockerell, who a few years earlier had worked on the Fitzwilliam

Museum at Cambridge. The Taylorian, whose facade carries statues symbolising the Romance languages of France, Italy, Germany and Spain, was founded for the study of modern languages with a bequest from Sir Robert Taylor, an architect (died 1788). Extensions were added on the N side in the 1930s. The Ashmolean, one of the finest museums in England outside London, houses the University's magnificent archaeological and art collections.

The history of the University museums begins in 1602, with the provision of a gallery for ancient objects within the newly built Bodleian Library. Then, in 1675, Elias Ashmole 'virtuoso and curioso', antiquarian, scientist, expert in heraldry, offered his old University the extraordinary and diverse 'closet of rarities' known as Tradescant's 'Ark', which had been given to him by John Tradescant the Younger (d 1662). These natural and historical curiosities had been collected largely by his father, John Tradescant the Elder (died 1638), naturalist, and gardener to Charles I, during his plant-hunting and other travels; the work was carried on by the son. To house the 'Ark' a new museum was built near the Bodleian and named the Ashmolean after its benefactor. It was the first public museum in Britain, and with its laboratories and library remained the centre of scientific studies in Oxford till the mid 19C. Large bequests in the 18C and 19C led to the building of the present museum in Beaumont St, to which the name 'Ashmolean' was transferred in 1899. The Old Ashmolean (see p 72) is now the Museum of the History of Science. Various extensions have been added to the Ashmolean, and the natural history and ethnographical exhibits transferred to the Science and Pitt-Rivers Museums respectively (see p 94). Reference to the floor plans will show visitors where to find the displays which particularly interest them. While it is impossible here to detail all the more important exhibits, it may be helpful, at any rate to the non-specialist visitor, to mention a few of the highlights.

Ground Floor. To the left of the entrance is the RANDOLPH GALLERY, containing classical sculptures, Greek, Hellenistic, and Roman originals, and Roman copies, mainly from the *Arundel* or *Pomfret Marbles*, including a torso of c 480 BC, a pedimental sculpture embodying two linear measures (Aegean of 5C BC) and the fragment of a frieze of an Athenian temple. In the show-cases are temporary displays of individual facets of ancient art. To the W are the *Petrie Room*, featuring Egyptian pre-dynastic objects, mainly from Sir Flinders Petrie's excavations; the *Chester Room*, with scarabs, beads, seals, papyri, etc; and the *Egyptian Dynastic Gallery*, which includes pottery, bronzes, jewellery, faience, glass and ivories, mostly from excavated sites. The Egyptian Sculpture Gallery (Griffith Gallery) contains the •Shrine of Taharqa from Kawa (7C BC) adorned with bas-relief; finds from the Oxford excavations in Nubia; reliefs, stelae and sculpture; mummy cases and funerary equipment; sculpture and wall-paintings from Tell el Amarna; masks and Coptic textiles.

From here a passage leads to the *Marshall Room* with coloured Worcester porcelain (17501–83).

North of the Randolph Gallery, the MEDIEVAL ROOM contains the 9C •'Alfred Jewel' found in 1693 near Athelney in Somerset, where Alfred spent the winter of 878 in hiding; it bears the inscription 'Aelfred mec heht Gewyrcan' (Alfred had me made) and may be the handle of an 'aestel' or pointer for following lines of illuminated MSS. Also displayed are the similar 'Minster Lovell Jewel'; local pottery;

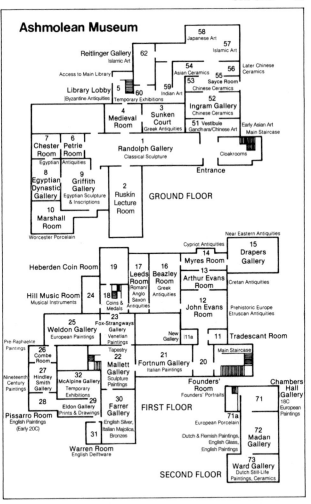

Ashmolean Museum

GROUND FLOOR

- 58 Japanese Art
- 57 Islamic Art
- 62 Reitlinger Gallery — Islamic Art
- Access to Main Library
- 54 Asian Ceramics
- 56 Later Chinese Ceramics
- 55 Sayce Room
- 53 Chinese Ceramics
- 5 Library Lobby (Byzantine Antiquities)
- 60 Temporary Exhibitions
- 59 Indian Art
- 52 Ingram Gallery — Chinese Ceramics
- 4 Medieval Room
- 3 Sunken Court — Greek Antiquities
- 51 Vestibule — Gandhara/Chinese Art
- Early Asian Art — Main Staircase
- 7 Chester Room — Egyptian Antiquities
- 6 Petrie Room
- 1 Randolph Gallery — Classical Sculpture
- Cloakrooms
- Entrance
- 8 Egyptian Dynastic Gallery
- 9 Griffith Gallery — Egyptian Sculpture & Inscriptions
- 2 Ruskin Lecture Room
- 10 Marshall Room — Worcester Porcelain

FIRST FLOOR

- Near Eastern Antiquities
- Cypriot Antiquities
- 15 Drapers Gallery
- 14 Myres Room
- 19
- Heberden Coin Room
- 17 Leeds Room — Roman/Anglo Saxon Antiquities
- 16 Beazley Room — Greek Antiquities
- 13 Arthur Evans Room — Cretan Antiquities
- Hill Music Room — Musical Instruments
- 24
- 18 Coins & Medals
- 12 John Evans Room — Prehistoric Europe Etruscan Antiquities
- 25 Weldon Gallery — European Paintings
- 23 Fox-Strangways Gallery — Venetian Paintings
- New Gallery — 11a
- 11 Tradescant Room
- Pre-Raphaelite Paintings
- 26 Combe Room
- 22 Mallett Gallery — Tapestry
- 21 Fortnum Gallery — Italian Paintings
- Main Staircase
- 20
- 27 Hindley Smith Gallery — Nineteenth Century Paintings
- 32 McAlpine Gallery — Temporary Exhibitions
- Sculpture Paintings
- Founders' Room — Founders' Portraits
- Chambers Hall Gallery — 18C European Paintings
- 71
- 28
- 29 Eldon Gallery — Prints & Drawings
- 30 Farrer Gallery
- Pissarro Room — English Paintings (Early 20C)
- 31
- 71a — European Porcelain
- **SECOND FLOOR**
- Warren Room — English Delftware
- English Silver, Italian Majolica, Bronzes
- 72 Madan Gallery — Dutch & Flemish Paintings, English Glass, English Paintings
- 73 Ward Gallery — Dutch Still-Life Paintings, Ceramics

brooches; medieval tiles; the ancient Odda stone, the foundation stone of 1056 of the Saxon chapel at Deerhurst; and objects of historical interest. Accessible from the Medieval Room, the SUNKEN COURT, containing large numbers of Greek vases, is open to students on request.

Opposite the main entrance is the **Department of Eastern Art**. In the *Vestibule* are examples of Gandhara sculpture, artefacts from prehistoric Asia, and early Chinese bronze. The *Ingram Gallery* of Chinese ceramics (400 BC–14C AD) contains also pottery tomb figures (AD 618–906), and a Sung gilt bronze Bodhisattva and 16C cast iron heads. The following rooms to right and left show Chinese porcelains 14–20C, and Chinese decorative arts. The end room is devoted mainly to Japanese ceramics and other decorative arts. The *Screen Gallery* (left) houses Japanese fine arts, and leads into the Tibetan Room and into the *Gerald Reitlinger Gallery* of Islamic Art. Beyond is the *Eric North Room* on the right (exhibitions here are usually changed monthly), and on the left stone, metal and terracotta works of India and South East Asia are displayed in two adjacent rooms.

First Floor. The small *Founders' Room* contains portraits of the Tradescants and of Elias Ashmole; in the corridor is a display illustrating the early history of the Museum. A few steps down lead to the DEPARTMENT OF ANTIQUITIES, the many superb finds arranged for expert study rather than aesthetic appreciation. The TRADESCANT ROOM, perhaps the most entertaining in the museum, exhibits objects from the original collections, and historical relics such as Guy Fawkes' lantern, Bradshaw's hat, Powhatan's mantle, etc. Displayed in the JOHN EVANS ROOM are gold ornaments and other objects of the European prehistoric periods with a large alcove for Italic and Etruscan antiquities. The Cretan collection in the ARTHUR EVANS ROOM, principally from the excavations of Sir Arthur Evans at Knossos, is of special importance, and includes Minoan seals, Linear B tablets, pottery, jewellery, and objects from the Diktaean Cave and the Cycladic Islands. Beyond is the *Myres Room* of Cypriot antiquities, with seals, jewellery, sculpture, etc; to the right is the *Drapers' Gallery* of finds from the Near East including 'Luristan Bronzes' and objects from Jericho. To the left the BEAZLEY ROOM is devoted to Greek antiquities including silverware, Geometric, orientalising, black- and red-figure pottery (note especially those with scenes of men at work: a shoemaker, potters in their workshop, and a helmet maker), bronzes, terracottas, gems and jewellery. The LEEDS ROOM houses finds from the Roman Empire and Europe during the Dark Ages, with particular reference to Britain. A staircase descends to the Byzantine Lobby.

The Hill Music Room contains Italian and English stringed instruments (16–18C) including 'Le Messie' by Stradivarius. The *Heberden Coin Room* contains rich collections of Greek, Roman, Oriental, medieval English and European, and modern coins, and medals, a selection from all periods being on exhibition. Students may consult the main part of the collection by appointment only.

The DEPARTMENT OF WESTERN ART occupies the remainder of the upper floors. Beyond the Founder's Room (see above) is the FORTNUM GALLERY, containing the well-known Fortnum collection of Renaissance bronzes, as well as a remarkably representative collection of Italian •Paintings of the 13–17C (see also below): *Orcagna*, Birth of the Virgin; *Bronzino*, Portrait of Giovomo de' Medici as a boy; *Giacani Pacchiarotti*, Virgin and Child; *Christofano Allori*, Portrait; *Andrea Solario*, Ecce Homo; *Davide Ghirlandaio*, Saints; *Uccello*, Hunt in a Forest; *Lorenzo di Credi*, Madonna and Child; *Vittorio Crivelli*, St. Catherine of Alexandria; *Andrea Vanni*, Virgin and Child; *Fra Filippo Lippi*, Meeting of Saints; *Ghirlandaio* (attrib.), Portrait of Young Man; *Piero di Cosimo*, Forest Fire; *Pinturicchio*, Virgin and Child; cartoons by *Raphael* and *Sodoma*.

At the end is the *Mallett Gallery* with tapestries and sculpture including a bust of Cromwell, and of Marlborough by *Rysbrack*. Here also are *Van Dyck*, Deposition, and *Paolo de Matteis*, Choice of Hercules.

The FOX-STRANGWAYS GALLERY contains Italian paintings,

mostly of the Venetian school: *Giov. Bellini*, St. Jerome; *Veronese*, Holy Family; *Giorgione*, The Tallard Madonna; *Montagna*, Virgin and Child; *Tintoretto*, Resurrection, and some unusual works by *Jacopo Bassano*. The WELDON GALLERY beyond is devoted to Italian painters of the 17C, but including Frenchmen working in Italy (*Poussin* and *Claude*), and baroque sculpture in silver, bronze, and marble, and a collection of 13–18C rings.

In the *Combe Room* of Pre-Raphaelite paintings are works by *Rossetti*, *Millais*, and *Arthur Hughes*.

The HINDLEY-SMITH GALLERY displays English and French works of the last hundred years. *Courbet*, *Corot*, and *Pissarro* are well represented, and there are works by *Toulouse-Lautrec*, *Matisse*, *Van Gogh*, *Manet*, *Monet*, *Bonnard*, and *Picasso*. The sculpture is by *Rodin*, *Degas* and *Daumier*. In the *Pissarro Room* are paintings from the 20C English School. Beyond this is the ELDON GALLERY, with a changing selection from the rich collection of drawings, watercolours and prints.

A vestibule at the far end containing drawings by *Samuel Palmer* gives access to the *Fine Art Library* and reference collection of prints (adm to ticket-holders or on application to the attendant), and to the small *Warren Room* with English Delft ware.

In the FARRER GALLERY are the Fortnum ceramics, mainly Hispano-Moresque, Turkish and Italian, and collections of silver, including works by Huguenot craftsmen working in London (c 1705–50; *Lamerie*, *Platel*, and the *Courtaulds*); also some examples of Italian sculpture, including works by the *Della Robbia*. Among the smaller works of art here are ivories and plaquettes; Limoges enamel (13–16C) including a reliquary depicting the Martyrdom and Burial of St. Thomas Becket in champlevé enamel; and a fine display of timepieces (16–17C).

The Farrer Gallery leads back into the Mallett Gallery, from which a staircase showing examples of tapestry and needlework leads to the Second Floor.

The **Second Floor** contains the *Chambers Hall Gallery*, devoted to European paintings and sculpture of the 18C, including *Tiepolo*, *Guardi*, *Canaletto*, *Reynolds*, *Gainsborough*, *Hogarth*, *Batoni* and *Panini*, and *Roubiliac*; the *Madan Gallery* of Dutch and Flemish works of the 17C (works by *Rubens*, *Van Dyck*, *Van Goyen*, *Ruisdael*, *David Teniers the Younger*, and some English painting of the 19C, including *Constable* and *Palmer*) and the Marshall Collection of 17–18C glass; and the *Ward Gallery* of Dutch 17–18C paintings of flowers and still-life.

The *Cast Gallery* (Mon–Fri 10–4, Sat 10–1) lies to the north of the Museum, approached from St. John's St. It contains over 250 casts of Greek and Graeco-Roman statuary, arranged in historical sequence.

BEAUMONT STREET, laid out in 1828 and built of Bath stone, is spacious and gracious, although the Vict-Gothic Randolph Hotel (left) is hardly in keeping with the rest. Immediately beyond it is the *Playhouse* (sympathetically designed by Sir Edward Maufe, 1938) belonging to the university and used both by the amateur Oxford University Dramatic Society (OUDS) and by professional companies. Facing the junction of Beaumont St and Walton St (right) is **Worcester College** (Pl.A7), founded in 1714 on a site originally occupied by

Gloucester College (1283), which provided a centre for monks of the Benedictine order studying at Oxford, each parent abbey being responsible for its own 'house' (cf Magdalene College, Cambridge, p 147). The Dissolution in 1539 brought the college to an end; it was later re-established as *Gloucester Hall*, partly dependent on St. John's College, which by then owned the site. The present foundation was made possible through the benefaction of a wealthy Worcestershire landowner, Sir Thomas Cookes. The outcome of this history is visually very pleasing, medieval picturesqueness and 18C elegance sharing the front quadrangle in perfect harmony. The comparative remoteness of the college from the centre of Oxford, from which it was even more isolated before Beaumont St was opened, earned it the soubriquet 'Botany Bay'.

The entrance front and N (right) side of the first quadrangle are 18C. Hawksmoor may have had a hand in their design. Building proceeded very slowly and was not completed until 1791. Both Hall and Chapel are in the entrance block; the *Hall* (left) was decorated by Wyatt 1776–84, and although redecorated (by Burges, who did the Chapel) in 1877, has now been returned to its original style, with an entrance screen of columns, cool colours, and delicate plasterwork on the immensely high ceiling. There are few portraits; the whole effect is particularly light and airy, and is in strong contrast to the *Chapel* (to the right of the entrance). This also was designed by Wyatt, and like the Hall has a screen of columns, but was completely redecorated by Burges in 1864 in the High Victorian manner, though the wealth of ornament and rich colours can hardly be seen in the gloom created by the crude heaviness of the stained-glass windows.

The N (right) side of the quadrangle and Provost's Lodgings are mid-18C, with a few medieval buildings wedged in between, and modern additions beyond. The S (left) side consists of the *medieval houses of Gloucester College; the arms of the abbeys which maintained them can be seen over some of the doors (Glastonbury, Malmesbury, St. Augustine's Canterbury, Pershore), though not all are in their original positions. The W side, opposite the entrance, is open to the beautiful *gardens with lake and playing fields beyond, which are one of the greatest charms of this particularly attractive college. They are reached through a passage (left). On the S and E sides of the garden are the Nuffield Block (1939) and New Building (1961, by Sir Hugh Casson). The Sainsbury Building (named after its principal benefactor) rises romantically from the edge of the lake in a picturesque pattern of columns and triangles, somewhat reminiscent of a Babylonian ziggurat (1983, by Richard MacCormac, Peter Jamieson, and David Prichard). Its main approach is off Worcester Place.

FAMOUS MEMBERS: Gloucester Hall: Richard Lovelace, Cavalier poet, 1618–57; Worcester College: Thomas de Quincey, essayist and author of 'Confessions of an Opium Eater', 1785–1859.

Along Walton St beyond Worcester (left) is *Ruskin College* (Pl.A7), in William and Mary style, 1912, founded in 1899 by Walter Vrooman and Charles Beard, American admirers of John Ruskin, to enable working men to study history, sociology, and economics in the academic atmosphere of Oxford. It has no official connection with the University.

Further on is the famous *Oxford University Press* (Pl.A5), one of the most prestigious publishing houses in the world. It was moved from the Clarendon Building (see p 72) to this part of Oxford, known as Jericho, in the 1820s; its learned publications still bear the imprint 'Clarendon Press', and it is still controlled by the University, whose Delegates still conduct their meetings in the Clarendon Buildings.

Opposite, up Little Clarendon St, are the smart new *University Offices* (Pl.A5) built round Wellington Sq (Sir Leslie Martin, 1969–73). At the far end of Walton St, where it becomes Kingston St, a turn left (Walton Well Rd) leads to the canal, the Thames, and *Port Meadow,* (see p 97 for details).

Worcester St, to the right as you leave Worcester College, passes the Gloucester Green Bus Station and car parks and leads to **Nuffield College** (Pl.C1), whose massive tower (housing books) and slender copper spire are a conspicuous Oxford landmark. The main entrance is in New Rd (left); only the quadrangles may be visited. The college was endowed by Lord Nuffield in 1937 for postgraduate studies, particularly in sociology and associated subjects, and was the first to admit both men and women. Its founder was known to refer to it as 'that bloody Kremlin, where left-wingers study at my expense'. It is on the site of the old Oxford Canal basin, and although designed in 1939 was not actually built until after the war. It is in traditional Cotswold materials and style, with gabled roof-line and mullioned windows; the quadrangles, on two levels, are enlivened with ornamental pools, in the upper of which is an abstract sculpture by Hugh Dalwood (1962). The small *Chapel is up a stairway (left) in the lower quad; the windows, that on the N side showing the Five Wounds of Christ, and the candlesticks were designed by John Piper, and the striking reredos (a Crucifixion) by John Hoskins. The Library (no adm) has an amusing collection of Gillray cartoons (1809) of the Life of Cobbett, with captions taken from 'The Political Register'; the reading-room walls are decorated with paintings of the Four Seasons.

The huge grassy mound on the S side of New Rd is all there is to be seen of the *Castle,* built by Robert d'Oilly in 1071, whose site is now occupied by the County Hall and Assize Court (Vict-Norman, 1841), modern Education Offices, and Oxford prison, within whose precincts stands the massive ruined tower of the old castle. The castle itself has little history. During the struggle for the throne between Stephen and Matilda she was besieged here in 1142, eventually escaping through the snow camouflaged in white, as the romantic story goes. It may have been the birthplace of her grandson, Richard I (born 1157). It was already in ruins in the early 1300s.

Further up New Rd on the opposite side is **St. Peter's College** (Pl.C1, C2), a pleasing if rather confusing collection of buildings reached through small flowery gardens from Bulwarks Lane. Its foundation, in 1928, was inspired by F.J. Chavasse, Bp of Liverpool, to provide places for men of limited means and those wishing to be ordained in the Church of England; the project was actually carried out by his son C.M. Chavasse (later Bp of Rochester) who was the first Master. Initially it was a Private Hall, St Peter's House, and received full collegiate status in 1961. It is now a mixed college with no restrictions on entry. It stands on the site of Trellick's Inn (afterwards New Inn Hall), one of Oxford's oldest medieval halls, and three houses already there were incorporated into the new foundation: Hannington Hall (1832 but much altered), the old rectory (Georgian), and Canal House (1827) which was formerly the offices of the Canal Company. At the same time the church of St. Peter-le-Bailey (1874, but with some materials and monuments from the former medieval church along the road) became the college *Chapel.* The themes of the glass in the E window (John Hayward, 1964) are: the personality of St. Peter; the history of the college; C.M. Chavasse. He is accompanied by his cigarette holder, his pet tortoise and squirrel, his Military Cross, his 'tin leg', and the Olympic symbol which recalls his part in the 1908

Games. His father is commemorated in a large bronze relief on the
N wall.

The earliest buildings specially designed for St. Peter's were a series of
neo-Georgian staircases built in the 1930s, and the Besse staircase (1952, by
Kenneth Stevens). Residential blocks, the Latner and the Matthews Buildings,
were added in the early 1970s (also by Kenneth Stevens). The former Oxford
Central Girls School, facing on to New Inn Hall St, has also been converted for
college use, and the area behind it re-landscaped as an extension of the
Hannington Quadrangle.

   Opposite St. Peter's, across New Inn Hall St, is the restored gateway of St.
Mary's College, dissolved under Elizabeth I, an Augustinian house where
Erasmus stayed in 1498–99 while preparing his Greek Testament. The site is
now occupied by Frewin Hall and belongs to Brasenose College.

   The area S and W of New Rd and the Castle was once the site of several
religious houses, Osney Abbey, Rewley Abbey, and the Franciscan house of
which Roger Bacon was a member (see p 50); there is a tablet to him in the
wall of The Terrace at the junction of Turn Again and Old Greyfriar St (Pl.C4).
All this is now recalled only in some remaining street names: Osney Lane,
Paradise St, Blackfriars Rd, Friar's Wharf, Abbey Place, etc. The railway long
ago cut across the old abbey sites, and between it and the city centre there has
recently arisen a huge development of ring roads, houses, shops and car parks.
The entrance to the multi-storey car park, seen from a raised walkway off Roger
Bacon Lane, is topped by a splendid geodesic sphere looking like a vast glass
football.

At Bonn Sq, New Rd becomes Queen St, which leads up to Carfax.

4   North and North-East of the Martyrs' Memorial

The distances covered in this section are considerable. The earlier
part of the route can easily be done on foot, but beyond about St.
Anne's all but the most energetic will need transport. There are
frequent buses along the Woodstock and Banbury roads and it is
possible to park a car in St. Giles for a short period, and for longer
in the more outlying areas. Much of Oxford's post-war building is
included in this itinerary; for anyone at all interested in modern
developments the extra effort involved in following the route is well
worth while.

   Unlike the three previous routes this one begins not at Carfax, but
at the S end of ST. GILES, a wide thoroughfare lined with trees,
many of which flower in May and June, giving a foretaste of North
Oxford's riot of springtime blossom. From medieval times a great
two-day fair has been held here at the feast of St. Giles (Mon and
Tues following the first Sun in September); the road is closed and all
traffic diverted. On the E (right) side is the Martyrs' Memorial (see
p 79) and shortly N of it is the entrance to St. John's College.

St. John's College (Pl.A8) was founded in 1555 by Sir Thomas
White, a rich clothier and former Lord Mayor of London, on the site
of the old Cistercian College of St. Bernard founded by Abp Chichele
in 1437 and closed at the Dissolution. The object was to 'strengthen
the orthodox faith' and the statutes were strongly religious in
character. White was a Merchant Taylor and a number of places
were reserved for boys from the Merchant Taylors' School. The
college is dedicated to St. John the Baptist, patron saint of tailors.

Shortly after the founder's death the Fellows acquired estates which included the Manor of Walton, now the residential area of North Oxford and thus a source of great wealth. Elizabeth I visited the college in 1567, welcomed with a Latin speech by young Edmund Campion, later executed, in 1581, for his alleged complicity in a Roman Catholic plot against the Queen. Royal visits were also paid by James I (who was entertained by a play which went on till 1 am), by Charles I and by Charles II (see below). In the 18C St. John's was still staunchly Jacobite in its loyalties. Its most distinguished President was William Laud (1611–21), who afterwards became Abp of Canterbury and one of Charles I's chief advisers. A controversially High Churchman, he suffered execution at the hands of the Puritan faction in 1645. He was a great benefactor of the college, and is buried in the chapel between the founder and his successor as President, William Juxon (who was also later Abp of Canterbury, and as Bp of London ministered to Charles I in his last moments on the scaffold).

The oldest part of the college is FRONT QUAD, the remains of St. Bernard's College. The attic rooms with dormer windows were added in the early 17C to relieve overcrowding. Over the gateway is the original statue of St. Bernard flanked by the two founders, Abp Chichele and Sir Thomas White; on the inner side is a statue of the patron saint by Eric Gill (1936). The buildings to the N, designed by G.G. Scott the Younger in 1881, blend well with the old.

On the N side of Front Quad are both Chapel and Hall. The *Chapel*, though dating from 1530, has been altered many times, and is now almost wholly Victorian (Blore, 1843; reredos and E window by Kempe, 1892). Only the Baylie Chapel (N side) built in 1662, retains its original appearance; it has a plasterwork fan-vault and contains some interesting monuments, and late 15C altar frontal and vestments. (The college has a large collection of frontals and vestments, witness to its Catholic traditions).

The *Hall* (open 2–4), built in mid 16C, was largely remodelled inside in mid 18C. Above the plaster-panelled ceiling of 1730 the original timber roof survives; the Portland stone screen with gallery above is by James Gibbs (1742). Over the handsome marble fireplace (William Townesend 1731) hangs an 18C scagliola (imitation marble) picture of St. John the Baptist, looking unusually young and cheerful, a copy after Raphael by Lamberto Gorio, brought to England in 1759. There is another picture by Gorio in the Old Library (see below), a small coloured drawing of his master F.E. Hugford (1696–1771), who perfected the technique of scagliola.

Opposite the main gateway a handsome portal and fan-vaulted passage lead through an even handsomer portal into *CANTERBURY QUAD, built in 1631–36 by Laud when Abp of Canterbury and Chancellor of the University. Lined by arcades and richly decorated on the E and W sides in the classical manner, it presents an interesting spectrum of architectural styles, the N and S sides being in the more traditional and restrained Oxford Jacobean-Gothic. The bronze statues opposite and over the doorway are, respectively, of Charles I and Henrietta Maria (by Le Sueur, 1633; cf Earl of Pembroke outside the Bodleian, p 73). The King and Queen opened the new buildings, and were also entertained with a play in the Hall. The S side was actually built as the library about 30 years before Laud extended it; some of the stone used came from the monastic buildings of Gloucester College (see Worcester College, p 84). The *Old Library* (adm on written application only) is a splendid room, with a ceiling of carved beams and 16C bookcases and benches. Here are displayed a number of college treasures: Laud's crook and the staff he carried on his way to the scaffold, his skullcap and his diary; a painting on wood of Charles I and his queen, and a portrait of the King in which his features are deliniated in minutely-written psalms. When Charles II visited St. John's he asked for this picture of his father, but later, on offering the hospitable Fellows whatever they wished and their choosing the picture, graciously returned it. Here also are the founder's chest (cf the Divinity School and Merton College Old Library) and a portrait of Dr William Paddy, physician to James I, and a great benefactor of the college.

To the S of the Front Quad (right) is DOLPHIN QUAD, partly late 18C, partly mid 20C by Sir Edward Maufe. This abuts on to a narrow passage and the Dolphin Gate to Trinity College (see p 77). The quad to the N (left) is mostly 19C and 20C work, by far the most striking building being that on the E side, a series of interlocking polygons creating a honeycomb effect, topped by polygonal lanterns (Architects Copartnership, 1958–60). N again is the Sir Thomas White Building (Arup Associates, 1974). The college also has postgraduate accommodation in Pusey Lane and Leckford Rd. The *gardens, laid out in the 18C, are among the most beautiful in this city of beautiful gardens.

FAMOUS MEMBERS: Edmund Campion, Jesuit martyr, 1540–81; Abp Laud, 1573–1645 and Abp Juxon, 1582–1663 (see above for both); James Shirley, playwright and poet, 1596–1666; A.E. Housman, poet, 1859–1936; Gilbert Murray, classical historian and champion of international understanding, 1866–1957; Philip Larkin, poet, 1922–1985.

Going N (right) from St John's along the E (right) side of St. Giles one passes some of the handsomest Georgian houses in Oxford. Where the road forks into Woodstock Rd (left) and Banbury Rd (right) is *Queen Elizabeth House*, a centre for the study of Commonwealth affairs, set up in 1954 and maintained jointly by the University and the Government, and beyond, on the 'Keble Road Triangle', the towering buildings of the *Department of Engineering*, and the Nuclear Physics and other laboratories. In the fork itself is St. Giles Church, mostly 12C and 13C, a still point between rivers of traffic.

On the W (left) side of St. Giles, almost opposite St. John's, is the Taylor Institution (see pp 79–80). Beyond it is *Blackfriars*, established in the 1920s for Dominican monks studying in Oxford; the spacious chapel, in Perp style, is welcoming and serene. Next door is **St. Cross College** (Pl. A8), which has now taken over the buildings originally occupied by *Pusey House*, a High Anglican theological centre founded in 1884; its name commemorates Edward Pusey, one of the leaders of the Tractarian Movement (see History, p 13, and Pusey House Gardens p 110). There is still a small group of clergymen in residence, who maintain the chapel services and the important theological library, and provide pastoral care to graduates and undergraduates of the university. St. Cross College takes its name from its first home, near St. Cross Church (see p 96). It is a small graduate college, founded in 1965, and many of its senior members hold university posts. It encourages a wide diversity of studies and interests. The pleasant Gothic-style buildings were designed by Temple Moore, and completed in the early 1920s.

In Pusey St is *Regents Park College*, a training centre for the Baptist ministry, established in London in the 19C and moved to Oxford in 1938. It is not a college proper, but a Permanent Private Hall of the University, as is *St. Benet's*, further up St. Giles, set up in 1847 as an Oxford centre for Benedictines from Ampleforth. In Pusey Lane (left, off Pusey St) is the Oriental Institute (1958–60).

Continuing left up Woodstock Rd one soon comes to the vast pile of St. Aloysius Roman Catholic Church (1873–75), then to the entrance to **Somerville College** (Pl.A5; grounds open daily 2–5.30, chapel and hall by arrangement at the Porter's Lodge), founded in 1879 for women students, who for long had to brave the opposition of the more conservative elements in the university (for details of the women's education movement see History, pp 14–16). It still admits only women. Unlike Lady Margaret Hall, founded a year earlier for Church of England girls, Somerville was deliberately undenominational (the chapel was not built till 1935; see below). Beginning as Somerville Hall and named after Mary Somerville, a distinguished mathematician (died 1872), its title was changed to 'College' in 1894. It became a fully independent self-governing body in 1926, soon after women were admitted as members of the university. It has always had a formidable reputation for academic excellence, and the roll of its past members now outstanding in academic and public life is impressive indeed. It seems a far cry from Ruskin's patronising comment in a birthday book of 1881: 'So glad to be old enough to be let come and have tea at Somerville, and to watch the girlies play at ball'.

The buildings are somewhat confusing. The first quadrangle (*Darbishire*) is one of the newest, built in 1933 by Morley Horder. Of Bladon stone and of two storeys only and to a comfortably domestic uniform design, it is in marked contrast to the second (*Middle*) quad, which is dominated on the left by the sheer yellow brick cliff of St. Aloysius Church, and on the right by rather aggressively Vict-Gothic ranges designed by Sir T.G. Jackson (1881) and Walter Cave (1895) as extensions to Walton House, the college's first residence. Through the arch (S) is the third (*Garden*) quad, again with buildings of various dates and styles, mostly red brick neo-Queen Anne, set pleasantly round spacious treed lawns. Immediately E (left) through the arch on the first floor is the *Hall*, beautifully panelled and hung with portraits.

On the W side is the library (Basil Champneys, 1903), on the S the startling Wolfson Block (Arup Associates, 1959), and Vaughan, Margery Fry-Elizabeth Nuffield houses providing both graduate and undergraduate accommodation. Standing alone and lonely is the undenominational *Chapel* (1935), as austere within as without. The sculptures in the grounds are by Wendy Taylor, Sam Werthmann, and Polly Ionides.

FAMOUS MEMBERS: Rose Macaulay, novelist, 1889–1958; Dorothy L. Sayers, novelist and religious writer, 1893–1957; Barbara Ward (Lady Jackson) DBE, author and economist, 1914–81; Indira Gandhi, prime minister of India, 1917–84; and many distinguished scholars and political figures still living.

Immediately N of Somerville is the Radcliffe Infirmary, built in the late 18C with funds bequeathed by Dr Radcliffe (see University College, p 62 and Radcliffe Camera, p 74), a dignified stone edifice in classical style, round which has grown up a collection of heterogeneous 19C and 20C accretions. It is a part of the great teaching hospital, the John Radcliffe Hospital in Headington, and fittingly the *Radcliffe Observatory* (Pl.A5) immediately adjacent has become the centre-piece of **Green College** (Pl. A3), a graduate society established in 1979 to encourage the development of clinical medicine and related subjects having links with social sciences and industry. Originally to be called Radcliffe College, it was renamed after its principal benefactors, Dr and Mrs Cecil Green of Dallas, Texas. The beautiful Observatory was built in the 1770s (again with funds from Dr Radcliffe) and mostly designed by James Wyatt. It has long single-storey wings with alternating windows and arched niches, and at the centre a second storey topped by a polygonal tower, inspired by the Temple of the Winds in Athens, and decorated with reliefs of the winds and their Greek names. Above is a copper-covered globe supported by lead figures of Atlas and Hercules.

Opposite is **St. Anne's College** (Pl.A3; grounds open daily). It was founded in 1879 as the Society of Oxford Home Students, for women studying in Oxford but not living in college; it gradually acquired a number of hostels, and eventually few students actually lived at home, but there were no college buildings until the 1930s. It became St. Anne's Society in 1942 and received full collegiate status in 1952. Men are now admitted. Perhaps because of its rather informal background, its reputation was one of sociability and versatility, which its present appearance somehow seems to reflect. It is one of the very few colleges to announce its name at the main gate.

The buildings are of considerable variety, yet together make up a very harmonious group and provide accommodation to suit differing tastes. Until the 1930s the site, between the Woodstock and Banbury roads, was occupied by Victorian houses with large gardens, used as hostels. These have been left in situ, and their modern neighbours have grown around them; the gardens likewise have been allowed to preserve their domestic intimacy; there are no quadrangles as such.

The *Founder's Gatehouse* (1966 by Howell, Killick, Partridge and Amis, who also designed Wolfson and Rayne buildings) is an evocation in modern terms of the traditional towered college gateway. To the S (right) is the *Dining Hall* (Gerald Banks, 1959), whose N and E sides are almost entirely of glass lined with wood slats, which allows a good view of the interior. An E-facing wall is decorated with a vast abstract mural (Stefan Knapp). The glass cupola above makes a pleasing contribution to the skyline.

N (left) are the older college buildings, Hartland House (by Giles Gilbert Scott, 1938), extended in 1951 and 1972), housing library, common rooms and study-rooms. Ahead are the new residential blocks, Wolfson, 1964, and Rayne, 1968.

N across Bevington Rd is **St. Antony's College**, which also announces its name (Pl.A3; open Mon–Sat 2–5; visitors should call at the Porter's Lodge), a graduate college for international and regional studies specialising in modern history and the social sciences. It was founded in 1950 on the benefaction of Antonin Besse, a French shipping magnate, who also gave generous benefactions shared by various of the less well-off colleges (see History, p 16). The Main Building occupies the site of a former Anglican convent, the chapel of which is now the Library (J.L. Pearson, 1891). The Hilda Besse Building (1968–70) is by Howell, Killick, Partridge and Amis. In the entrance hall is a bronze statue of St. Antony of Padua by Mestrovic, and in the 2nd Floor Common Rooms are busts of the founder and his wife by Oscar Nemon.

At the other end of Bevington Rd, across Banbury Rd, is *Wycliffe Hall*, an evangelical Church of England theological college. About 5 minutes walk N is **St. Hugh's College** (Pl.A1), founded for women as St. Hugh's Hall in 1886 by Elizabeth Wordsworth, Principal of Lady Margaret Hall, and daughter of the Bp of Lincoln, after whose predecessor, St. Hugh of Lincoln, the Hall was named. It became a college in 1911 and was incorporated by Royal Charter in 1926. Originally occupying various houses in Norham Rd and Gardens it moved to its present site in 1916. During the Second World War it was requisitioned as a military hospital. Men are now admitted as Fellows, and to junior research fellowships.

The buildings (seen by arrangement with the Domestic Bursar) face S with their backs to St. Margaret's Rd. They are neo-Georgian, red brick and bow-windowed. The Library (W), built in 1936, is named after the first Principal, Miss C.A.E. Moberley; the *Hall* (E) was extended in 1958; it contains some interesting portraits. Above the front entrance is the small *Chapel* where Miss B.E. Gwyer, a former Principal, is commemorated outside by a bust (by *Miriam Coatman*) and inside by an engraved glass panel (1976, by *Laurence Whistler*).

The Kenyon New Building (1966), by David Roberts, won an architectural award. The bold new Wolfson Building (1968) in very red red brick is also by David Roberts (cf Magdalen, Sacher Building, and much work at Cambridge).

The colourful terraced gardens (open during daylight hours exc August, Christmas and Easter) were partly the creation of Miss Annie M.A.H. Rogers (d 1937) a pioneer of women's education in Oxford, and a famous Oxford 'character'.

Just S of St. Hugh's, across Banbury Rd, Bardwell Rd leads past the famous Dragon School (for boys aged 8–13), then becomes Chadlington Rd; at the end of this turn right for ***Wolfson College** (see Pl.A2, about half a mile, grounds open daily, quadrangles and buildings by prior arrangement only). Beginning life in 1965 as Iffley College, a society for graduates reading for advanced degrees, it became Wolfson College in 1966, when benefactions from the Wolfson and Ford Foundations made large-scale development possible. The majority of members are scientists or mathematicians, and the first President was the philosopher Sir Isaiah Berlin.

Modern Oxford at its best: Wolfson College

The college occupies a spacious well-treed site beside the Cherwell; it has its own small marina, and a footbridge over the river leads to open water-meadows and a pleasant riverside path. The low white concrete buildings banded with grey panels, by Powell and Moya (cf Brasenose and Christ Church, and the Cripps Building of St. John's College, Cambridge) have won a number of architectural awards. They provide accommodation ranging from small family houses to bed-sitting room units, large common and study rooms, library, and a wood-panelled dining-hall with pyramid-shaped roof.

Returning to the Dragon School one can reach Lady Margaret Hall either by cutting through Dragon School Lane (beside the school; cyclists and pedestrians only) and Fyfield Rd, or by returning to Banbury Rd and turning left down Norham Gardens opposite St. Anne's (about 10 minutes walk from this point), passing the Department of Education en route.

Lady Margaret Hall ('L.M.H.'; Pl.B1; open daily exc August, Christmas and Easter; visitors to the Hall and Chapel should call at the Porter's Lodge) was founded for Church of England girls in 1878, amid the controversy surrounding women's education (see History, pp 14–16) and owed much to the championship of Dr E.S. Talbot, Warden of Keble College, after whom one of the buildings is named, and who at a great age dedicated the chapel in 1933. The college itself is named after Lady Margaret Beaufort (died 1509) 'a scholar, a gentlewoman, and a saint', founder of St. John's and Christ's Colleges, Cambridge, and of professorships in Divinity at both universities. It grew rapidly both in numbers and reputation, and was incorporated by Royal Charter in 1926. Men are now admitted.

The first students were accommodated in the brick villa which still stands S of the entrance gate. In 1881 this was extended by Basil Champneys (cf Newnham College, Cambridge) in the Georgian style which set the pattern for most of the college's future development, so that although the buildings are of many different dates they form together a mellow and integrated whole. The only exceptions are the residential blocks of 1972, five-storey towers of bright red brick and glass.

The handsome entrance leads into Wolfson Quad; to the E (right) are the residential blocks of Wordsworth (1886), Talbot (1910), and Toynbee (1915); to the S (left) is Lodge (1926); all are by Sir Reginald Blomfield. Opposite (N) is the Library (by Raymond Erith) built only in 1957, but in perfect agreement with its older neighbours. It is named after Lynda Grier, a former Principal. A passage opposite the entrance leads to a second quadrangle with the Deneke Building E (right), housing the large dining-hall, and the Chapel, both by Sir Giles Gilbert Scott, 1931–33. The *Chapel* (access through the Deneke Building) is in the Byzantine style, and contains a painting of the Flagellation of Christ attributed to *Taddeo Gaddi* (14C, Florentine), a beautiful triptych by *Burne-Jones* (1863) and handsome carved stalls. The gardens are exceptionally spacious and peaceful; to the E a long path near the river leads to the college landing stage and punts.

On the N side of L.M.H. a gateway leads out into Benson Pl and Norham Rd, a short way up which (right) is *Maison Française*. Founded in 1946 as a centre of Anglo-French cultural studies and friendship, it moved from Woodstock Rd to its present elegant home in 1963. In front is a sculpture, 'Flore', by *Maillol*.

The *University Park* (the Parks), with numerous playing-fields including the University Cricket Ground, tennis courts and croquet lawns, lies immediately S. During the Civil War Charles I's artillery was encamped here; during the Second World War parts were used for vegetable-growing in the voluntary 'Dig for Victory' campaign. The Parks are criss-crossed by footpaths and bounded on the E side by the Cherwell, which can be crossed either by Rainbow Bridge, beyond which the path leads to Marston, or in the SE corner near the men's bathing place *Parson's Pleasure*. Here the river divides, and paths lead either along the bank (Cherwell Water Walks) or between the two streams (Mesopotamia) to emerge (about 1m.) into Marston Rd.

On the W side of the Parks, in Parks Rd about 3 minutes walk from the end of Norham Gardens, is **Keble College** (Pl.A6) founded in 1870 as a memorial to the Revd John Keble (1792–1866), one of the leaders of the Oxford Tractarian Movement (see History, p 13), to provide 'persons desirous of academical education and willing to live economically, with a college wherein sober living and high culture of the mind may be combined with Christian training based upon the principles of the Church of England'. Membership of the College was restricted to members of the Church of England. Money for the foundation was raised by public subscription, the Chapel, Hall and Library being given entirely by the Gibbs family of Tyntesfield, Somerset, enthusiastic Tractarians. Initially it was governed by a council and Warden who appointed tutors; Fellows were elected in 1930, and it became fully independent and of equal status with the older colleges in 1952, when religious tests were finally abandoned. Its past members include many famous church leaders, bishops and archbishops.

The original buildings (1868–82) are all by William Butterfield, himself a High Churchman and much associated with the Camden Society (Cambridge equivalent of the Tractarians). They are in his characteristic style, asymmetrical Gothic, red brick diversified with polychrome patterns and stone dressings (it has been described as 'The Fair Isle Jersey'). The rooms open off corridors instead of staircases as is traditional in the older colleges. *Liddon Quad* (right of the entrance) is dominated by the vast *Chapel, whose soaring interior is a riot of colour and decoration, with more polychrome brickwork, carved stonework, a floor of encaustic tiles laid in patterns of increasing elaboration as they approach the altar, and above the blind arcading mosaic panels of biblical scenes, inspired by the design of the upper chapel in the basilica of St. Francis at Assisi. These and the stained glass are by A. Gibbs. The nave seats face E, a departure from the usual college chapel arrangement of stalls. In 1892 a small side chapel by J.T. Micklethwaite was added to house Holman Hunt's famous picture 'The Light of the World', presented by Mrs Combe, widow of the Superintendent of the Oxford University Press; Butterfield would not allow it to be hung in the chapel, 'a place of Worship, not a gallery'.

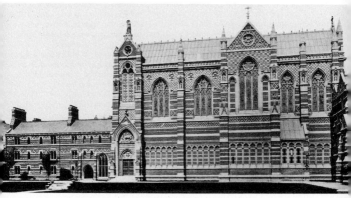

High Victorian Gothic at Keble College

On the S (left) side of Liddon Quad is the *Library* (no adm, but glass doors afford a glimpse inside). The furnishings are by Butterfield, and it possesses a valuable collection of illuminated MSS and early printed books bequeathed by Canon Charles Brooke. Beyond it is the *Hall*, containing portraits of Keble and many other saintly-faced men associated with the college, and a huge painting 'A Tale from Boccaccio' by G.F. Watts (1817–1904), on indefinite loan from the Tate Gallery. S (left) again is *Pusey Quad* and the Warden's Lodging, and W (on to Blackhall and Museum Rds) are award-winning buildings (1970) by Ahrends, Burton and Koralek; they face inwards, yellow brick with slit windows to the outer side, glass to the inner (cf Queen's College, Florey Building, p 62).

Almost opposite Keble is the **University Museum** (Pl.A6; open Mon–Sat 12–5), built in 1855 to meet the growing need for scientific facilities. The object was to assemble 'all the materials explanatory of the organic beings placed upon the globe'; lecture rooms and laboratories were also provided. It is perhaps more interesting to the general visitor for its architecture than its exhibits, spectacular and curious as some of these, especially the skeletons, are. The moving spirit in its inception was Dr *Henry Acland* (later Regius Professor of Medicine). John Ruskin, his close friend and Slade Professor of Fine Art, had a strong influence on the choice of Italian neo-Gothic for the design (by Benjamin Woodward, of the Dublin firm of Sir Thomas Deane, Son and Woodward), and took a great interest in every stage of the building.

It is of red and brown stone, with steeply pitched roof and central tower; the window arches carry tracery and are richly decorated with carved natural objects. The cathedral-like •interior is constructed of cast-iron and glass, with a lofty central 'nave' and side 'aisles' which carry, above, an arcaded gallery whose pillars are each of different stone, a practical geology lesson. The ubiquitous decoration also serves an instructional purpose, all the flowers, fruit, foliage and animals, whether in iron or stone, being faithful copies of nature. The stone-carvers included the Irish O'Shea brothers, whose fiery tempers were legendary; on the mouldings of the outer portal can still be seen the mutilated remains of their caricatures of Oxford worthies, alternating with the heads of parrots and owls, which they were subsequently made to obliterate.

The small octagonal building (right) is a copy of the Abbot's Kitchen at Glastonbury; it was the original Chemistry Laboratory. Next to it is the Radcliffe Science Library (Sir Thomas Jackson 1901 and Sir Hubert Worthington 1934), whose underground extension is beneath the Museum forecourt. Behind is the *Pitt-Rivers Museum of Ethnology and Pre-History* (open Mon–Sat 2–4) built in 1885 to house the collection of General A.H. Lane-Fox Pitt-Rivers.

Round this nucleus has grown up the great complex of the Science Area, extending to the bottom of South Parks Rd. Although some buildings date from the late 19C and early 20C, the great majority belong to the post-Second World War years, the architectural partnerships mainly responsible being *Lanchester and Lodge*, and *Ramsey, Murray, White and Ward*. Characteristically of Oxford, flowering trees are planted along all the fronts and roadways.

On the S side of South Parks Rd is *Rhodes House* (Pl.A6) built in 1929 (Sir Herbert Baker) as the HQ of the Rhodes Trust and centre for Rhodes Scholars and Commonwealth, American and African studies. It houses the appropriate department of the Bodleian Library. It is a Cotswold-style building, entered through a massive pillared portico and copper-domed rotunda topped by a bronze bird copied from the carved stone birds found at Zimbabwe. In the circular vestibule are memorials to Rhodes Scholars of all nationalities who fell in the First and Second World Wars.

Beyond Rhodes House, in Mansfield Rd (right; closed to through traffic), opposite the modern *Institute of Virology* (Tinsley), is **Mansfield College** (Pl.B5/7). Founded in 1838 as a theological college for the Congregational (now United Reformed) Church, it moved to Oxford in 1886; since 1955 it has been a Permanent Private Hall of the University, and its members now read a variety of subjects. The buildings, set round very spacious lawns, are in the Gothic style (Basil Champneys, 1887–89). In the chapel (right) is a series of statues, and stained-glass windows relating to famous dissenters such as Cromwell,

A Cathedral of Science: the iron and glass 'nave' of the roof of the University Museum

Milton, Hampden, William Penn (the American window), and one to Margery Fry. The Library (opposite the entrance; no adm) has interesting timberwork and a ceiling of painted panels.

Further on past Savile Rd is **Manchester College** (Pl.B7) also founded as a Nonconformist (Unitarian) training college. Beginning in Manchester in 1786, it moved several times before settling in Oxford in 1889. In addition to ministerial training, it now offers degree courses in a number of subjects. The Vict-Gothic buildings are by Thomas Worthington, and his son Percy designed the Arlosh Hall (1915). In the Chapel are windows by *Burne-Jones* and *Morris*.

At the bottom of South Parks Rd a path straight ahead leads to the Cherwell and Parson's Pleasure bathing pool. To the right is the impressive white concrete building, partly mounted on stilts, of the *Departments of Zoology and Psychology* (1965–70 by Sir Leslie Martin, who also designed the new pathology block in the Science Area). Opposite this is **Linacre College** (Pl.B5), modestly housed in early 19C buildings formerly Cherwell Edge, a Roman Catholic convent. Founded in 1926 as a society for graduates, mostly of other universities, wishing to study at Oxford, and named after Thomas Linacre (Renaissance scholar and physician, d 1524; see also All Souls College p 66) it became a college in 1965. The modern residential block beside it blends well with the other buildings.

St. Cross Rd runs S between college playing fields to the junction with Manor Rd (left, about a quarter of a mile). Just before the junction, on the left, are the striking *English Faculty* and *Law Libraries*, by Sir Leslie Martin, 1964. (The *Institute of Economics and Statistics*, round the corner in Manor Rd, is part of the same complex.) Opposite (right) are two residential buildings of Balliol College, the second also by Sir Leslie Martin. On the right in Manor Rd stands Holywell Manor (early 15C but radically altered in 1926). At the end of this road is **St. Catherine's College** (Pl.B8). Beginning in 1868 as a society for non-collegiate students (cf St. Anne's), both under-graduate and graduate, it became a college in 1963. The buildings, furniture, and gardens were all designed by the Danish architect Arne Jacobsen (1960–64); it is the only Oxford college to have this complete unity of conception.

The plan is strictly geometrical throughout. Built of specially-made small yellow bricks, it is a long rectangle running N and S, with residential accommodation along each side, common rooms and huge *Hall* (tapestries at both ends designed by Tom Phillips) across the N end, and beyond the central circular lawn separate blocks for lecture rooms and the library, named respectively after the Bernard Sunley Trust and the Wolfson Foundation, two of the college's principal benefactors. Between them rises a tall thin campanile; near by is *Epstein's* bronze bust of Einstein. Both library and rooms have windows to floor level, affording the occupants little privacy. The gardens between the buildings are set with rows of parallel walls imprisoning small trees and shrubs. Outside the rectangle, on the E side, are water gardens, with a sculpture by *Barbara Hepworth*, and the Music Room, an interesting double hexagon design. To the original buildings, two new ones have been added on the N side: the Alan Bullock Building and the Mary Sunley Building, both designed by Jacobsen's associate Kund Holcher. Beyond, across a meadow, flows the Cherwell.

As its chapel the college uses *St. Cross Church* (12–13C) in St. Cross Rd. About 5 minutes walk further on are Holywell St, leading to the Broad, and Longwall St, leading to the High.

ENVIRONS OF OXFORD

The Immediate Vicinity

For those who have time and want a change from intensive sightseeing, there are a number of places, many within walking distance of the centre, which are pleasant to visit.

South Side

A path beside the Thames, accessible near Folly Bridge, leads downstream to Abingdon, passing a number of locks and weirs, and beyond Sandford winding through quiet watermeadows, with Radley College (boys' public school) away to the W and the beautiful park and woods of Nuneham Courtenay across the river (E). At *Iffley* (about 1½m.) is one of three locks built on the Thames in 1632 (rebuilt in 1923). The others are at Sandford and the Swift Ditch. Over the river, which can be crossed here, is the village, an oasis of peace in spite of urban development and heavy traffic all round. In the main street, opposite the stone-built, thatched old school, is the former Dame School, inscribed 'Mrs Sarah Nowells School 1822'. The Norman *Parish Church is one of the finest in England. All the doorways are richly carved, as are some of the windows and the tower arches inside. The top stage of the tower, with its vigorous carvings, is a 1975 restoration. In the churchyard is a font-bowl of unknown date, and an extremely ancient yew tree.

Immediately E of Iffley is *Cowley* (about 1m.), with the vast motor manufacturing works developed from the Morris Motors started so modestly just before the First World War by Lord Nuffield.

SW of Oxford is *Boar's Hill*, a semi-rural residential area at the top of which (Old Boar's Hill) is *Jarn's Mound*, a wild garden and wood made by the archaeologist Sir Arthur Evans (d 1941). The mound itself, approached up very steep steps, provides a splendid view of the city.

West Side

Immediately W of the town the Thames flows through *Port Meadow*. This rather desolate expanse, frequently flooded, belongs to the Freemen of Oxford, who from the time of Edward the Confessor (d 1066) have enjoyed the right of free pasture here; once a year grazing animals are rounded up by a posse of Freemen led by the Sheriff, who is also Curator of the Meadow, and a nominal fine imposed on the owners. It can be reached from Walton Well Road (Pl.A5) by a bridge over the canal, from which paths lead to *Wolvercote* (about 1½m.) or, more pleasantly, straight ahead and then across and beside the river.

A path left (about ½m. from the bridge) leads to *Binsey*, a tiny village set round a wide green. The small 12–13C church is ½m. beyond; in the churchyard is a holy well associated with the legend of St. Frideswide. The path beside the river continues to *Godstow Lock* (about 2½m.) with the remains of a Benedictine nunnery, where Fair Rosamund, mistress of Henry II, was educated, and where she was buried after her death at Woodstock (possibly at the hands of the jealous Queen).

Opposite is the famous *Trout Inn*, with a riverside terrace. The

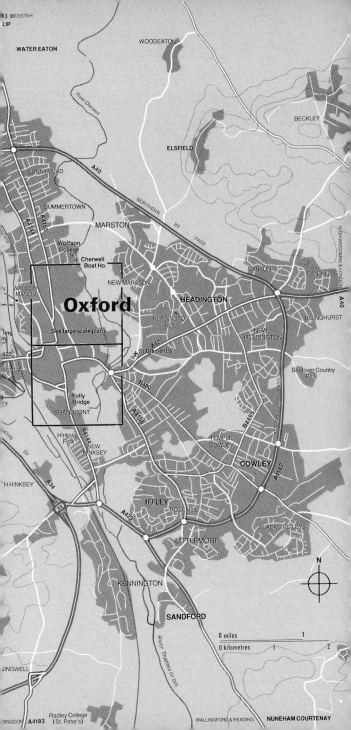

towpath continues to Eynsham and beyond.

From here a narrow road leads (about 1m.) to *Wytham* (pron Wit'm) a completely unspoilt village of stone and thatch cottages; in the inn car park is a circular dovecot. Village and beautiful woods belong to the University (access to the woods only by permit from the secretary to the University Chest). To the SW is the country described in Matthew Arnold's 'Scholar Gipsy': *Bablock Hythe, Fyfield*, and *Cumnor Hill* (now a residential suburb). In Cumnor church is a contemporary statue of Elizabeth I and a memorial to Amy Robsart (see also the church of St. Mary the Virgin, p 65).

East Side

S of Headington is *Shotover Country Park* (about 4m.), a large area of open common and woodland good for picnics and walks, with views of Oxford from the very steep approach road.

North Side

Elsfield village (about 4m.) was the home from 1920 until his death in 1940 of Lord Tweedsmuir, distinguished as a scholar, statesman, and Governor General of Canada, but best known as John Buchan, author of 'The Thirty-Nine Steps' and numerous other exciting books. *Water Eaton* (little more than a manor-house and chapel) and *Islip* are attractive places on the Cherwell, and can be reached by boat.

Further Afield

Oxford, at the very centre of the southern half of England and with excellent train, coach, and bus services, is an ideal base from which to explore an area particularly rich in interesting places, pleasing villages, and historic houses. Moreover, although the immediately surrounding countryside, the basin of the river Thames, is far from exciting, within a short distance there are welcome and delightful changes of scenery: to the north-west the limestone Cotswolds, to the south the chalk uplands of the Berkshire Downs, to the south-east the folding hills, valleys, and beechwoods of the Chilterns.

A comprehensive guide would be out of place in this book (consult *Blue Guide England* for exhaustive coverage), and no attempt has been made to detail every pretty village or stately home within reach. The places described in the following pages are a selection only, and are all within about twenty miles of the city. Although arranged in areas, the diverse opening times of houses may well make it impossible to explore any one region thoroughly on the same day. Opening times, and public transport (if available), should always be checked in advance at the Information Office.

Mileages in brackets after a place-name indicate the distance from Oxford.

South Side

The Thames flows south from Oxford; its course is punctuated by many attractive villages and small towns. The whole area, though mainly agricultural, is also thickly populated and has disconcerting pockets of development more urban than rural in character. S and E rise hills, the Berkshire Downs and the Chilterns.

TOWARDS HENLEY-ON-THAMES AND READING

Leave Oxford by Folly Bridge, Abingdon Road, A4144, and A423.

Nuneham Courtenay (5m.) is a neat little estate village, described in *Buildings of England* as 'a Georgian version of ribbon development'. Lord Harcourt moved to Nuneham from the family seat at Stanton Harcourt (see p 113) in 1756, choosing the site for its riverside setting and distant views of Oxford. The house, designed by Stiff Leadbitter, was originally a small Palladian villa, but was much enlarged subsequently, first in 1781 (by 'Capability' Brown) and again in 1832 and 1904. It is now a conference centre. Brown's plans for the grounds entailed the demolition of the old village (1766). A new village was built along each side of the road, and a new church in classical style on a hill in the park (perhaps not very convenient for worshippers, but a pleasing eye-catcher, as intended). It is partly the work of 'Athenian' Stuart, who also contributed to the interior decorations of the house. The Jacobean conduit head from Carfax is also in the park, which Horace Walpole described in 1780 as the most beautiful in the world. Brown's landscape succumbed to changes in fashion in the 1830s, and during the Second World War fell into total disorder, but restoration is now in progress; there is a good view of the park from a boat on the river, or from the footpath on the far bank (open 2–5.30 a few days in late August).

Clifton Hampden (turn right off A423 on to B4015 just S of Nuneham Courtenay park) is a pretty village on the river.

Sutton Courtenay, about 3m. W, although overshadowed by the cooling towers of Didcot power station, is also a very charming village set along a green, and close to the river. Almost opposite the church is a stone-built Norman hall-house (1190–1200) with a black and white timbered house attached (private).

Dorchester (8m.) lies on the W bank of the river Thame, which joins the Thames just S of the little town. In Roman times, as its name suggests, Dorchester was a military station; later it developed into an important Saxon settlement, and after the conversion of Wessex to Christianity in the mid 7C, the missionary centre of southern England, and the seat of the bishops of Wessex and later of Mercia. Following the Norman Conquest the see was transferred to Lincoln (1072) and Dorchester's importance declined. Today its claim to fame rests largely on the medieval abbey which serves as the parish church.

Augustinian canons founded a priory here in 1140, replacing the Saxon cathedral, of which no trace remains, with a Norman church completed c 1180. The nave and W end of the choir survive, but the rest of the church was rebuilt: the S nave aisle, and the S and N choir aisles in the early Dec period (c 1280–1320) and the •East end, which is the glory of the church, in the late Dec period (c 1340). *The great E window*, filling the whole wall, is fully traceried, without the usual mullions (though with a massive central buttress). The tracery is richly carved, and decorated with standing figures at the intersections. Some 14C glass remains; the rest is 19C. A panel in the third tier, right-hand side, shows St. Birinus preaching to King Cynegils. *The N window* is a Tree of Jesse, the standing figures representing the ancestors of Christ, the angel Gabriel, and the Three Wise Men. The S window has figures of saints and monks carrying the bier of St. Birinus. Below it are the piscina and sedilia, with carved canopies of exceptional glory, beneath which are small circular stained glass windows, a most unusual feature. The E end was restored in memory of Sir Winston Churchill, by the American Friends of the Abbey (see also below).

In the S nave aisle, above the raised altar, are fragments, much restored, of 14C wall paintings. On the corbel of one of the pillars are carvings of monks falling asleep, perhaps a warning of temptation. The lead font (c 1170) is decorated with figures of the apostles. A memorial slab in the floor commemorates a lady 'whose artless beauty, innocence of mind, and gentle manners once obtained her the love and esteem of all who knew her. But when Nerves were too delicately spun to bear the rude Shakes and Joltings which we must meet with in this transitory world, Nature gave way, She sunk and died, a martyr to excessive sensibility' (1799).

In the S choir aisle are other interesting monuments, including the vigorous effigy of a knight of 'a most determined countenance' (1280) and a conjectural reconstruction of the shrine of St. Birinus (1964).

Some alteration was made to the church in the early 17C (W tower and round transept arches), and the whole was heavily restored in the mid 19C, by William Butterfield, whose work aroused a storm of controversy, and by Sir George Gilbert Scott.

Dorchester is linked to the United States through the enthusiasm of a Bostonian lady, Edith Stedman, who founded the American Friends of the Abbey. Her portrait head is carved on the buttress at the SW corner of the church (left, round the corner, as you approach the door). On the site of the abbey cloisters (N side) is an 'Anglo-American' garden, where a cross recalls the benefactors. There is also a plaque dedicated to American airmen killed in the Second World War, and various memorial seats and trees, one of which was planted in memory of President Kennedy.

Of the monastic buildings the only possible survivor is the Old School House just W of the abbey, which may have been the guest house. It was converted into a school c 1654, and now houses the *Abbey Museum*, in which is an interesting pictorial history of the town (open 10.30–12.30 and 2–6 Tues–Sat and BH; 2–6 Sun, May–September).

There are some attractive 17C and 18C houses along the main street. Footpaths lead across fields to the Thames, and (over a footbridge at Day's Lock) to Little Wittenham and the Clumps, venerable beech plantations on the site of an ancient hill fort. They are at present (1986) closed to the public, being considered unsafe, but the long views from the hilltop of the Thames Valley and Berkshire Downs are well worth the climb.

Shortly after Dorchester, in Shillingford, two alternative routes diverge.

Straight ahead the A423 continues towards Henley. On the W (left) side is *Benson RAF Airfield*, during the Second World War an important bomber base. In the village is a *Veteran Cycle Museum* (open by appt only, tel. Wallingford 38414, Easter–end September). After some 5m. the road crosses a spur of the Chiltern Hills. It is a typical chalk landscape: grassy slopes dotted with hawthorns and yews, hedges festooned with traveller's joy, deep valleys and thick beechwoods. A maze of lanes lead to small villages of flint and brick, many of them set round a green, and the whole area is crisscrossed with easily followed footpaths.

From Nettlebed the road drops down again towards the Thames

Valley; about 7m. NE is **Stonor Park**, for 900 years the seat of the
Stonor family (Lord Camoys). Turn left on to B480 4m. S of Nettlebed;
Stonor is then about another 4m. (from Oxford 23m.).

HISTORY: The house, set in a charming fold of the hills, is
predominantly Georgian in appearance, except for the obviously
Tudor entrance gable (facing S), yet this conceals a very much older
building. The original house, built c 1300 by Sir John de Stonore (or
Stonor), consisted of hall, solar, and chapel. The hall and solar have
been incorporated into the present house and much altered in the
process; the chapel, however, which was a separate building, is still
recognizably medieval, although drastically altered in the then
fashionable 'Gothick' style in 1757 (cf Milton Manor, p 108). During
the 14C additions were made by the Stonors: a new solar, hall, and
buttery were built, W of the old hall, and a separate kitchen beyond
that; a new building, possibly for priests' accommodation, connected
house with chapel. In Tudor times, probably starting in about 1534,
the house was further enlarged to become a sizeable E-shaped
mansion built of brick, which was used also to cover much of the
timber and stone of the former buildings.

The Stonors, however, resolutely refused to take the Oath of
Supremacy demanded by Henry VIII, and at the Reformation stuck
doggedly to the old religion. Consequently their fortunes, which had
grown steadily, now declined. Stonor became a centre of Roman
Catholicism, and a refuge for priests, including Edmund Campion,
who had his book, *Decem Rationes* (Ten Reasons), printed in a secret
room in the roof. (He was eventually tried for treason and cruelly
executed.)

In the greater tolerance of the 18C, the Stonors were able to emerge
from the obscurity in which they had been forced to live. They again
modernized their Tudor house: windows were sashed, the pointed
gables were cut back and attic dormer windows were inserted; the
interior, and that of the chapel, was 'Gothicized'. After the Catholic
Emancipation Act of 1829, when it once more became possible for
Roman Catholics to hold office, Thomas Stonor immediately became
MP for Oxford. He also claimed, and got, the ancient barony of
Camoys, which he had inherited through his Biddulph grandmother.

TOUR: A tour of Stonor starts at the *chapel*, one of only three in England where
the Roman mass has been continuously celebrated. Built on the site of an
ancient stone circle, it incorporates a large stone in the base of its SE corner.
The brick tower is of 1416–17, a very early use of brick in England. The interior,
as we have seen, was made 'Gothick' in 1757. Gallery and altar rails were
added between 1796 and 1800. The chapel was restored in 1959–60 and
redecorated in its 18C colours. Although it is a private chapel, Roman Catholics
from the surrounding district also attend mass here.

Visitors enter the house by the front door. The *entrance hall*, part of what
was formerly the 'new' Tudor hall, is now Georgian, with a Gothic bridge. This
hall occupies the· place where the high table stood, opposite the musicians'
gallery. In the main hall on the right, the banqueting table is Tudor. The next
two rooms, drawing room and dining room, were created by Thomas Stonor,
Lord Camoys, in 1834. In the *drawing room* a portrait by Kneller of Thomas
Stonor (1667–1724) hangs over the fireplace; there are Italian bronzes, and a
fine pair of fire dogs by Algardi. In the *dining room* the most remarkable feature
is the wallpaper of c 1816 showing the important buildings of Paris *arranged
next to each other*. In the study is a late 17C pair of Venetian globes by Mario
Coronelli, complete with ornate stands of the same date.

The extraordinary shell-shaped bed and the wooden shell chairs in *Francis
Stonor's Bedroom* were bought by Francis Stonor (1829–81) in Paris. *The library*,

occupying the site of the solar built in the 14C, contains a large and important collection of Roman Catholic books, many of them illegally printed or imported. The grand table is from Sawston Hall, near Cambridge, as are the portraits of James II and of Mary Tudor, the latter being the first picture painted of her as queen. In *Lady Camoy's Bedroom* the 17C bed-hangings are crewel work on linen. There is a Chippendale chest of drawers and a wardrobe by Hepplewhite. Of course the furniture mentioned in this and all the other rooms—also pictures and *objets d'art*—is a tiny fraction of the whole collection. A long but by no means exhaustive list is given with the guidebook obtainable in the hall.

The Gothic bridge and a narrow flight of stairs lead to the *Edmund Campion Room*, where his life—and death—are vividly illustrated. Not for the squeamish.

Visitors leave the house through the remains of the 13–14C hall. On the N side, climbing up the hill, is a pleasant walled garden, broken up with lines of shrubs and trees. In the E half is a sundial circled with flower beds, and two ponds, and in the NE corner a summerhouse. (House and grounds open 2–5.30 Wed, Thurs, and Sun, and Sat in August, April–end September, also BH Mons 11–5.30; fee.)

The main road A423 continues to **Henley-on-Thames** (23m.) one of the most attractive of Thames-side towns. The wealth of handsome Georgian houses and inns are reminders of its importance as a coaching stop between London and Oxford in the 18C. It was also an important centre of river transport, and today the river, now used for sport and pleasure, still plays a major role in the life of the town. The first boat race between Oxford and Cambridge was rowed here in 1829 (see also p 20), and in 1839 the first rowing regatta was held with the object of 'producing the most beneficial results to the town'. It succeeded; Henley Royal Regatta (first week in July) is one of the premier events in both the rowing and the social calendars. During regatta week the whole place is 'en fête'. Near the bridge is the headquarters of the famous Leander Rowing Club. There are numerous facilities for boat hire and for river trips, which provide good views of the many pleasing houses and gardens along the waterside, and of the beautiful country beyond.

A handsome bridge of 1786, decorated with masks of Thames and Isis (by Mrs Damer) leads directly into the wide main street (Hart St); on either side are 18C inns, The Anchor (left) white stuccoed, the Red Lion (right) mellow red brick. Immediately beyond is the large Dec parish church. Facing the churchyard are two groups of almshouses, founded in the 16C and 17C, but both rebuilt mid 19C, and the ancient Chantry House (c 1400), an interesting example of medieval domestic building (open 10–12 Wed, Thurs, Sat). Hart St is lined with Georgian-fronted houses, many much older in origin, and is closed at the top end by the pretty Queen Anne style Town Hall (actually 1900).

The alternative route at Shillingford is to turn right on to the Reading road, A329. At *Shillingford bridge* (about ½m.) the river flows between wide grassy lawns and past a large white hotel set in colourful gardens, the whole making an exceptionally beautiful picture.

Wallingford (12m.) is a charming and typical riverside town, predominantly Georgian in appearance, but with a number of gabled and timbered houses of the 16C and 17C, and a small colonnaded Town Hall of 1670. It received its first charter, from Henry II, in 1155, two years after the signing of the Treaty of Wallingford, which ended the civil war between Stephen and his cousin Matilda and her son Henry; during the war Matilda used the castle as a stronghold (ruins open 10–6 daily, April–October). Near by is the elegant bridge, partly medieval, but extensively rebuilt in 1809. The eminent jurist Sir William Blackstone (1723–80; see also All Souls College) lived at

Castle Priory in Thames St (open by appt; tel 37551). He is buried in St. Peter's church.

Down river (continue on A329) are the small pretty towns of *Streatley* and, on the opposite bank, *Goring*, where there is a profusion of locks, weirs, and backwaters, on one of which stands the mainly Norman parish church. The ancient Icknield Way crosses the Thames here.

2m. S of Streatley is *Basildon Park* (NT) a classical mansion of 1776 recently restored, and containing a fine collection of pictures and furniture (open 2–6 Wed–Sat, also Sun and BH Mon 12–6, April–October; fee). About 1m. beyond is the *Childe-Beale Wildlife Trust* and headquarters of the World Pheasant Association. Here, in a setting of woods, river, and small lakes, scattered with statuary and fountains, are an interesting collection of birds and various rare breeds of sheep, goats, and cattle (open 10–6 daily except Fri April–September; small fee).

Pangbourne, another pleasant little town, was the home from 1924 until his death in 1932 of Kenneth Grahame, author of the children's classic *The Wind in the Willows*. He lived in Church Cottage (no adm.). The river is crossed by a pretty white-painted toll bridge, and there is a large expanse of open recreation ground and a footpath alongside. On the hill above the town is Pangbourne College, formerly a training school for the Merchant Marine, but no longer exclusively devoted to nautical education.

A few miles S of Pangbourne the road enters the sprawling outskirts of Reading.

ABINGDON AND WANTAGE AREAS

Leave Oxford by Park End St (past the railway station) and Botley Rd A420. For the *Abingdon* area join the bypass A34, turn left after about 3m. on A4183. The A34 can also be reached via Folly Bridge and Abingdon Rd. For the *Wantage* area leave A420 6m. S of Oxford on A338.

Abingdon (6m.) owes its existence to the abbey, founded in the late 7C. At the time of Domesday (1086) the 'town' consisted of 'ten traders before the gates' (Pevsner). After its foundation the abbey was twice destroyed by the Danes before being re-established by St. Ethelwold in the 10C. It was completed c 1170, the abbey church being 370ft long. From the 10C to the 16C it was much visited by royalty: Edward the Confessor (whose queen, Edith, in a letter that still exists, complained of the 'vehement' cold); Queen Matilda, who escaped from Oxford Castle in the snow in 1142 and with a few knights followed the frozen river to take refuge here (see p 85); King John, who came to 'cool off' after being forced to sign Magna Carta at Runnymede (1215). His pious son, Henry III, was a frequent visitor; Richard III also came, and granted benefits to the town, which consequently sent a contingent to fight for him at Bosworth Field (1485). The last was Henry VIII, who spent three months here to avoid an outbreak of the plague. Notwithstanding this, Abingdon was one of the first of the larger abbeys to be dissolved at his command in 1538.

There was no love lost between abbey and town, the former owning all the markets and fairs and imposing numerous tiresome restrictions. Furthermore, the town had a fine church of its own, so that when the abbey was dissolved the townsfolk lifted not a finger to save it; consequently there is very little left of the abbey buildings.

Thames Valley charm: Abingdon

The Abbey remains: Of the vast complex of buildings that comprised the abbey at the height of its fame, all that are now left are the main gate flanked by St. Nicholas' Church and St. John's Hospital, the granary, checker and undercroft, and the Tudor long gallery. Everything else—abbey, church, cloister, chapter house, refectory, infirmary, abbot's lodgings, royal apartments, etc.—have disappeared; indeed although the site of the abbey church and cloister is known, the locations of the other buildings (whose one-time existence is well attested) are somewhat conjectural.

Visitors today start at one of the cottages in Thames St, facing the old mill stream, from there passing straight into part of the old *abbey granary* (probably 12C). This building is thought at one time to have stretched along much of the mill stream frontage, and later included also malthouse, brewhouse, and bakehouse. (The mill stream itself was dug in the 10C). In the granary is an interesting group of exhibits. Visitors then go round into the *Checker Hall*, but before entering, notice the remarkable 13C chimney of the Checker itself, considered to be the finest 13C chimney in all England. In the Checker Hall, the clerks of the Checker, or counting-house, may have been accommodated. After the Dissolution it was turned into a dwelling by the new owner, William Blacknall. It is now used as a theatre.

From here one passes by an old staircase into the upper part of the Checker, and thence into the *Tudor Long Gallery*. Originally only the N (left) side would have been a 'long gallery', the S side being divided into several rooms. After the Dissolution, the Checker, together with the Long Gallery and the ground floor under it, were used as part of a brewery until 1895. The ground floor of the gallery was much altered during the intervening centuries, doors and windows being opened up indiscriminately, and its original plan is not clear, but in recent years considerable restoration has been carried out. The Long Gallery is now best seen from the attractive garden that has lately been created beside the mill stream.

The *Checker Undercroft*, a handsome rib-vaulted chamber of the 13C with a contemporary fireplace, is the last room to be visited in this part of the remaining buildings. Next come the main gateway, St. Nicholas' Church, and St. John's Hospital (turn left at the top of Checker Walk). This is a common grouping of buildings at the entrance to a monastery: the gatehouse flanked by a small church and a hospital for the sick and poor dedicated to St. John the Baptist. This particular group dates from the 12C, with alterations and rebuilding in the 15C.

Gatehouse: the large central arch had wooden gates which were closed at night, as well as the door in the smaller N arch. The arch on the S side is on the site of the porter's lodge. The gatehouse was completely rebuilt in the 15C. Some time after the Dissolution the porter's lodge was turned into a house for the sergeant-at-mace, responsible for the prisoners in the room over the gate, until in the early 19C the prisoners were moved to the new county gaol, on the riverbank, which has now itself become an arts and leisure centre. In a niche over the central arch of the gatehouse is a 15C statue of the Virgin Mary, patron saint of the abbey. The head is a 19C replacement. (Abbey remains open 2–6 daily, April–September; 2–dusk Tues–Sun October–March. Closed Good Friday; fee.)

St. Nicholas' Church: built in the 12C for travellers, and for occupants of abbey property. Originally it was a small rectangular church with lancet windows. The river Stert, which ran and still runs under the nave, was the abbey boundary. In the 15C new large windows were inserted and a tower built.

St. John's Hospital: best viewed from the garden on the S side, once a courtyard through which the open river Stert ran, and which was enclosed by a wall on the W side, separating it from the street. On its S side were almshouses, while part of the E range (now the Roysse Room) was the large Common Hall for the sick and poor, and probably formed part of the almonry. St. John's Hospital, run by lay brothers and sisters, formed the N range and contained a large dormitory. The hospital was founded in the early 12C. Like St. Nicholas' Church, it was given new windows in the 15C, and then, or shortly afterwards, began to be used as courtrooms. A new large room was built over the former hospital ward in the 18C, and the whole building is now the guildhall. In 1563 John Roysse helped to re-house the old grammar school in the Common Hall. The present S range of the courtyard was built in 1810.

Across Stert St in Market Square stands the splendid *County Hall*, built in 1678–82 by Christopher Wren's master mason Christopher Kempster, and described by Celia Fiennes as the finest in England. The arcaded ground floor is open and was formerly used as a market; the upper floor has very large arched windows and its hipped and balustraded roof is topped by a cupola. Once a courtroom, this floor is now a museum, largely devoted to local history (open 2–5 daily, closed some BH; small fee).

From the County Hall, East St. Helen's St, with many attractive Tudor and Georgian houses, leads to *St. Helen's Church*. The 13C spire is much older than the rest of the church, which was largely rebuilt, in noble proportions, in the 15C Perp style. On the panelled roof of the inner N aisle are paintings dating from 1390 (in the process of restoration 1986). The pulpit is Jacobean.

In the churchyard are three sets of almshouses: in the centre Christ's Hospital or Long Alley Almshouses (1446 but much renewed), with an unusual wooden cloister walk (the Governor's Hall seen by appt); on the right Twitty's Almshouses (1707), and on the left Brick Alley Almshouses (1718). Just beyond the church and almshouses is the river, across which is a large expanse of open meadow and footpaths. This pleasant place can be reached via Bridge St and the handsome bridge, built in 1416 but extensively renovated in 1927.

Milton Manor (about 14m.; take A34 and at S end of Abingdon bypass turn left for Milton) consists of a Carolean house with 18C wings, together with outbuildings and walled garden, added 100 years later. At the same time the grounds were landscaped, and three ponds created from a tributary of the Thames.

The Carolean house was built for Paul Calton in 1663, and apart from the 18C sash windows looked very much as it does now. It was a square house, each side the same in external appearance too, and indeed even now the back (W) side is the same as the front, that is, three storeys of five bays separated by wide pilasters decorated with fleurs-de-lis. There is a tradition, supported by some evidence, that the house was designed by Inigo Jones, though built after his death; it undoubtedly shows his influence.

In 1764 the Manor House was acquired by Bryant Barrett, a Roman Catholic, who made the Georgian alterations and additions. The present owner is a direct descendant. Inside, he repanelled the whole house, while the new library and chapel were both done in the then highly fashionable 'Strawberry Hill Gothick' style, popularised by Horace Walpole.

TOUR: The first room shown is the hall, with a superb 17C fireplace elaborately carved in red pine. There is also a 16C monks' settle, probably from Abingdon Abbey, which serves as a table as well as a seat.

The *drawing room* has its original 17C oak-and-bay-leaf carved ceiling, and an 18C fireplace surmounted by another elaborately carved 17C overmantel. The room contains among much else of interest a pianola (in working order) specially made by the German firm of Steck for Princess Beatrice, the youngest daughter of Queen Victoria. Then comes the dining room, with Georgian panelling and elegant Georgian alcoves, all in their original colour.

In the passage between here and the Gothick library is a remarkable collection of teapots, of all shapes, sizes, and origins. At the top of the sturdy 17C staircase is a portrait by Kneller of two of the daughters of the 1st Duke of Marlborough: Henrietta, who became the 2nd Duchess in her own right, and Anne, from whom the present Princess of Wales is directly descended.

The *Chinese Bedroom* comes next, so called on account of its Chinese wallpaper. The furniture here is mainly 18C and 19C Dutch marquetry. In the dressing room next door the Chinese wallpaper is continued; the marquetry bed is 18C Dutch.

The flamboyant *Gothick chapel* (cf the chapel at Stonor, p 103) contains some notable medieval stained glass, and some Flemish glass of the 17C and 18C. Here too are the vestments of Bishop Challoner, the friend of Barrett and the first priest to celebrate mass in the chapel. Cardinal Hume, Archbishop of Westminster, has done so in recent times.

Beyond the stable block is the pleasant walled garden, intersected with box-hedged paths and flower borders, with a small pool and statue at the centre. (House and garden open 2–5.30 Sat, Sun, and BH, Easter–late October; fee.)

Didcot (17m., on A4130) is a busy railway junction; the old locomotive sheds house the *Didcot Railway Centre*, a living museum dedicated to the history of the Great Western Railway. On 'steamdays' there are demonstrations of all the activities of a steam locomotive depot and free rides for visitors (open Sat, Sun, and BH early March–late October, and much more frequently late July–early September; fee. Steamdays 1st and last Sun and BH April–October, also Sun and Wed in August, and for special events at various other times).

Wantage (15m.) is just below the north-facing slope of the Berkshire Downs, along the edge of which the ancient Ridgeway track runs from Avebury (W) to Goring-on-Thames (E). Its course is punctuated by prehistoric burial mounds and hill forts. Below Uffington Castle hill fort (about 6m. W of Wantage) a figure of a horse cut into the hillside gives the valley its name: '*The Vale of White Horse*'.

2½m. E of Wantage is **Ardington House**, a sophisticated and urbane house set, surprisingly, in a totally rural village. Built c 1720, it is of red and grey brick, perfectly balanced and of excellent proportions, in the low-key English Baroque style. The builders were very probably members of the Strong family, master masons who worked under Wren for several of his city churches, including St. Paul's, and under Vanbrugh at Blenheim. The owner was Edward Clarke, whose extravagance forced him to sell two other properties belonging to his wife, and most of the Ardington estate, to pay for his new house. It still retains almost exactly its original appearance. In 1833 it was bought by a Robert Vernon, who had made a fortune selling horses to the British Army during the Napoleonic wars. He added the wooden loggia with Doric columns on the S side and made a few other alterations, but the stone rendering with which he covered some of the brickwork has been removed (1980) by the present owners, who also added (1961) the harmonious kitchen wing on the E side.

Inside, the most striking feature is the 'imperial' staircase, rising as two, left and right, in the entrance hall, and continuing as one to the floor above. It is possibly unique in England. The dining room retains its original 18C panelling.

In the garden are some exceptionally fine cedar trees. (House and garden open 2.30–4.30 Thurs and BH, May–September; guided tours, usually by the owners; fee.)

South West Side

Leave Oxford by Park End St (past the railway station), Botley Rd, and A420. This road leads through the Vale of White Horse, flat country, but with the line of the Berkshire Downs on the southern skyline.

Pusey House Gardens (13m., turn left on B4508 about 12m. from Oxford). The house (not open to visitors) is a rather severe 18C mansion of grey stone, and was once the home of Dr Edward Bouverie-Pusey, the famous 19C Anglican scholar and divine, who was a champion of the Oxford Movement (see p 13). The gardens are the creation of the present owners, who bought the property in 1935, although obviously many of the magnificent trees are much older than this, some indeed probably as old as the house itself.

The entrance, through an archway, gives on to a great expanse of lawns, across which a sinuous lake, crossed by a pretty 'Chinese' bridge, runs the full width of the garden. On each side are herbaceous borders; to the W (right) is Lady Emily's Garden, a warm brick-walled retreat giving shelter to a rich profusion of shrubs, roses, and herbaceous plants. Just beyond is a small classical temple, erected in memory of a previous owner in the mid 18C.

Across the lawns are shrubberies, the Main Shrubbery to the W, smaller ones—the East Pleasure Garden and Compton's Glade—to the E. At the E end of the lake are water gardens, as rich in scents as in visual pleasures. The official guide book contains full and detailed information on the plants and trees to be found in all parts of the garden (open 2–6 Tues, Wed, Thurs, Sat and Sun, also BH, early April–late October; fee).

Faringdon (17m.) is a small town with an attractive old centre, formed by the wide Market Place, which runs uphill from the colonnaded 17C Town Hall (now the public library) to the large handsome church, set against a background of trees in the park of Faringdon House. The church (probably locked) is predominantly Transitional Norman; the S door (13C) is decorated with scrollwork and dragons' heads. There is much rich carving inside the church, notably the sedilia, piscina, and capitals, and a variety of 14–16C memorial brasses. The Market Place itself is lined with Georgian-fronted houses and inns; open market stalls add a cheerful touch of colour.

E of the town, clearly seen from the road (A420) is *Lord Berner's Folly*, a battlemented brick tower 140ft high. Built in 1935, it is perhaps the last of its kind in England.

At *Great Coxwell* (2m. SW of Faringdon) is a magnificent early 13C tithe barn (NT), said by William Morris to be 'as noble as a cathedral'. It is stone-built, and the Cotswold stone tiled roof is supported on oak timbers hardly altered over the last 700 years (open daily at reasonable hours; entry free).

Buscot Park (21m., NT) is 3m. W of Faringdon on A417. It houses a notable collection of pictures of dates from 14C–20C, beautiful furniture, and other treasures.

HISTORY: The house was built shortly before 1780 by Edward Loveden Townsend, probably acting as his own architect. After several changes of ownership it was bought in 1889 by the financier, Alexander Henderson, afterwards 1st Lord Faringdon. He built on a large portico, a W wing, and an ornamental balustrade, and made a number of changes to the interior. Lord Faringdon's eldest son pre-deceased him, so that at his death in 1934 he was succeeded by his grandson. The 2nd Lord Faringdon promptly removed his grandfather's additions, restoring the house to its original exterior appearance. The pictures seen at Buscot today are the combined collections of the 1st and 2nd Lords, the bulk of them the purchases of the latter. They had quite different tastes, which contributes to the catholicity of the collection. The present Lord Faringdon, nephew of the 2nd Lord Faringdon, continues the policy of enriching it.

The treasures of Buscot are too numerous to describe in detail. The following account of the rooms and their contents merely touches on some of the highlights.

TOUR: The Hall has panels and trompe l'oeil trophies painted by Laurence Hobdell in 1950. The furniture is 'Egyptian' Regency style, designed by Thomas Hope c 1807. Over the chimneypiece is a glazed terracotta panel, probably from the workshop of Andrea della Robbia (late 15C).

The *Sitting Room* also contains Regency furniture, and is hung with portraits, including three by Reynolds. Over the chimneypiece is a landscape by Gainsborough.

The *Staircase Hall* contains one of Buscot's outstanding pictures, Murillo's 'Triumph of the Eucharist'. There is a small collection of Old Master drawings, among them studies of hands by Lely, and three pictures by Rembrandt.

The pictures in the *Normanton Room*, which takes its name from the state bed (originally at Normanton Park in Rutland), are in complete contrast, being the work of 20C artists, such as Peter Greenham, Jane Dowling, John Ward, Allan and Emilie Gwynne-Jones, and Graham Sutherland.

Again in complete contrast is the *Pre-Raphaelite Room*; this contains, as well as pictures by Pre-Raphaelites such as Rossetti and Millais, works by a variety of 19C artists, including Etty, Leighton, and Watts. The furniture is late 18C.

The main staircase leads down to the principal reception rooms. First the *Drawing Room*, which still has its original 18C plasterwork ceiling (possibly by Joseph Rose the younger) and white marble chimneypiece. The pictures are Italian, and include Mola's 'St. Jerome' and Palma Vecchio's 'Marriage of St. Catherine'. The tondos on each side of this are by a follower of Leonardo da Vinci (left) and from the workshop of Botticelli (right). The room is further enriched by ceramics and objets d'art from Italy, Germany, Spain, France, and China.

The *Saloon* also retains its 18C plasterwork ceiling and frieze, its original mahogany doors, and early 19C white marble chimneypiece. The rest of the decorations, including the gold silk wall hangings, date from the 1890s, and are contemporary with the large paintings 'The Legend of the Briar Rose' (The Sleeping Beauty) by Burne-Jones, which dominate the room. The beautiful furniture is again late 18C, and there is a varied collection of ceramics.

The *Dining Room* has a plasterwork ceiling and frieze, of modern workmanship, but in the 1770s style of James Wyatt. The mahogany table and chairs are respectively of Sheraton and Robert Adam design. Here hang landscapes, by Richard Wilson (d 1782) and George Lambers (d 1765), one of the earliest English painters of natural landscapes.

The *Music Room*, with a plasterwork ceiling (modern) in the style of Robert Adam, contains the jewel of Buscot's picture collection, Rembrandt's portrait of (?) Clement de Jongh, c 1650. Over the fireplace is a portrait by Rubens, c 1606. The furniture is mostly of Sheraton and Chippendale design, and the mirrors between the windows in Robert Adam style.

The *Garden* well matches the house. The most popular part with visitors is the water-garden to the NE of the house, laid out by Harold Peto for the 1st Lord Faringdon, who wished to link the house with the large lake created by Townsend. It is formal and Italianate in character, a chain of canals and stairways flanked for much of their length by box hedges, and enclosed by woods. Water trickles past ordered clumps of water-lilies to the huge lake, in which there is an island covered with trees dominated by a Scots pine and a group of oaks. On the right other paths run down, roughly parallel, between avenues of poplar and oak, and yet other paths cross at right angles. Statues and urns are dotted about, but in no haphazard fashion.

On the other, W, side of the house the old kitchen gardens, with their extraordinary concentric circular brick walls, fully ten feet high and enclosing a vast area, are being developed partly as a nursery and partly as an area of plants, shrubs and trees.

The 'small' lake (28 acres in extent) that one passes on approaching or leaving the park was the creation of R.T. Campbell, who had acquired the estate in 1859 and was a man of ambitious ideas. The lake formed part of a drainage and irrigation system in connection with the production of sugar beet and alcohol. Alas, these and other schemes foundered on the rock of over-capitalization, and by the time of Campbell's death in 1887 the estate was hopelessly mortgaged. Shortly afterwards, happily, Alexander Henderson stepped in (open 2–6 Wed, Thurs, Fri, also 2nd and 4th Sat and Sun in each month, April–end September. Closed BH Mon; fee).

Lechlade. (23m.), about 3m. W of Buscot, is a small town definitely Cotswold in character, although the hills are still several miles away, and it lies in fact at the confluence of four rivers, the Coln, the Leach, the Cole, and the Thames. The profusion of water gives the setting great charm. At St. John's Lock is a Victorian statue of Old Father Thames; originally made for the Crystal Palace, it was subsequently moved to the source of the Thames near Cirencester, but moved again, for greater safety, to its present site. In the Market Place is a large Perp church, built, as so many others in this area, on a generous scale in the late 15C, when the Cotswolds flourished on the wool trade. The chancel roof has ten bosses carved with angels holding instruments of the Passion, and another depicting a medieval wrestler. Near the church is the New Inn, built in the early 18C in red brick; most of the surrounding houses are 18C or early 19C, in a very pleasing variety of grey Cotswold stone and mellow brick.

Kelmscott, 3m. E of Lechlade, down a narrow 'no through road' off B4449, is famed for its association with William Morris, leader of the Arts and Crafts movement, who owned the Manor from 1871 until his death in 1896, and is buried in the churchyard. His low ridge-shaped stone tomb, designed by his friend and associate Philip Webb, is near the hedge to the right of the entrance gate, behind a small bay tree. The house, at the far end of the village, was restored in the 1960s as a monument to his work as an artist, designer, writer, decorator, craftsman, and printer (open 1st Wed of every month, April–September, or by written appointment). On the way to the house is a pair of cottages built in 1902 by Jane Morris in memory of her husband; they were designed by Philip Webb, and carry a decorative plaque also designed by him. Many of the Pre-Raphaelite artists and writers visited, or even for a time lived at, Kelmscott, though not all of them regarded it, as did Morris, as 'heaven on earth'; Rossetti described it as 'the doziest dump of old grey beehives'. It is indeed extremely quiet. The village gave its name to Morris's Kelmscott Press at Hammersmith.

North and north-west of Lechlade rise the Cotswold Hills. There are many attractive stone-built villages and small towns, some with magnificent Perp 'wool' churches, notably *Fairford,* whose church retains its original set of 15C stained glass windows. *Bibury* is picturesquely set on the river Coln; the early 17C weavers' cottages known as Arlington Row (NT) must be among the most photographed houses in England.

North-West and North Sides

The country north-west and north of Oxford takes its character from the Cotswold Hills, of whose beautiful grey or golden limestone the small towns and villages, handsome houses and attractive cottages in the vicinity are for the most part built. The hills are higher to the north-west. Here is scenery typical of limestone country, rather treeless uplands, with shallow valleys watered by clear smooth-flowing rivers, fields divided by drystone walls, or low hedges thickly entangled with traveller's joy, the sheen of whose silver-plumed seed-heads brightens the autumn and winter landscape.

To the north, where the hills begin to peter out, the country is gently undulating, the fields very large, and dotted with clumps of woodland: good fox-hunting terrain. But the buildings still proclaim the Cotswold influence.

NORTH-WEST: THE COTSWOLDS AND WINDRUSH VALLEY

Leave Oxford by Woodstock Road; at the roundabout about 4m. N turn left on to A40.

Stanton Harcourt Manor (9m.; turn left on to B4449 and go through Eynsham) is the original seat of the Harcourt family, who moved to Nuneham Courtenay in 1750 (see p 101).

In the middle of the 12C Isabel de Camville married Robert de Harcourt, and received as a wedding gift from Queen Adeliza, second wife of Henry I, the manor (or estate) of Stanton, which from then until now has been known as Stanton Harcourt. Although it has passed through many vicissitudes the present house, formed from the original gatehouse, is occupied still by descendants of the Harcourts.

The original house, one of the earliest unfortified manor houses of England, built over the years 1380–1470, formed three sides of a square. The W side contained the servants' quarters and the offices, including the Great Kitchen (1380), still standing and open to visitors. The N side, containing hall, parlours, and chapel, has disappeared except for the NE corner ('Pope's Tower', 1470). The E side, containing the family bedrooms, has gone completely. The present rose garden is on the site of the inner courtyard and the croquet lawn on that of the outer, which was reached through the gatehouse, the porter's lodge (1540) forming the centre of the entrance front of the present house. The arch of the original gateway can still be seen from the village street.

Pope's Tower is so called because in 1717–18, during a time when the big house had been abandoned, the tower was lent to Alexander Pope while he was working on his verse translation of Homer's Iliad. Pope himself recorded this on a pane of glass, which may now be seen in the library of the house. The ground floor was the chapel of the original manor house.

The *Great Kitchen* is part of the oldest buildings here. It is square, with an octagonal roof. The smoke from both the open fireplace and the ovens was collected in the cone of the roof 70ft above, and let out by opening the wooden louvres according to the direction of the wind. Centuries of smoke have blackened the wall above the ovens, to the left of the entrance door. There was originally a well in the middle of the floor, but this has since been filled in. The only other medieval kitchen remotely like this one is the Abbot's Kitchen at Glastonbury, which is, however, much later in date (see also under University Museum, p 94).

Inside the house visitors can see the entrance hall, the library and dining room added c 1860, and the garden hall and drawing room added in 1953, which all blend harmoniously. There are numerous fine pictures (including a comparative rarity: a *landscape* by Rubens), and interesting exhibits, among them a fragment of the standard of Henry Tudor carried by Robert Harcourt at the battle of Bosworth, (1485).

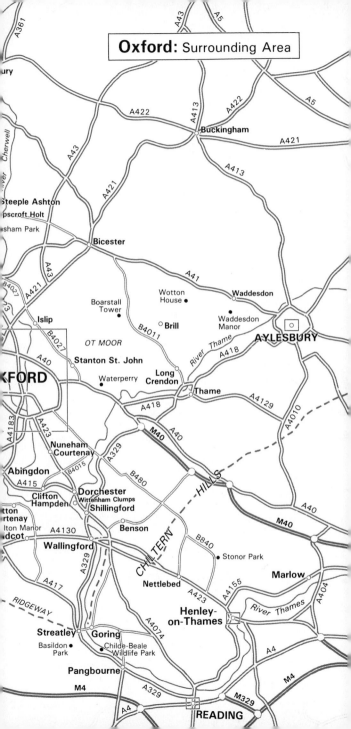

Oxford: Surrounding Area

The garden as it now exists was largely the creation after 1948 of Viscountess Harcourt—there is a gazebo at its edge erected in her memory in 1963. The garden and the old medieval stonework complement one another perfectly. Within the area enclosed by the old buildings the garden is formal, with lavender beds, rose beds, and herbaceous borders; then as one passes through a stone arch a grassy path goes curving off between shrubs and trees. Everywhere there is water: moat, stew, Park Pool, Lady Pool and the Great Fish Pond or 'Church Pool'. This last was in days gone by accessible from the churchyard by a flight of steps, and provided fish for the whole manor, the fish being bred in the stew-ponds, of which the 'Lady Pool'—the subject of a romantic legend—was the largest. (House and garden open 2–6 a few days in each month April—September; fee.)

The church of Stanton Harcourt is just over the garden wall (but one has to go round to get to it). It is partly Norman, and repays a visit, as it contains much of interest, including the Harcourt chapel, in the SE corner of which is the tomb and effigy of the Robert Harcourt who bore the standard at Bosworth. The tattered remains of it hang over the tomb—a moving sight. A detailed description of the church is to be found in the guidebook, and also on handboards, available there.

Witney (14m.; turn right off A40 on to B4022) is a small town of great charm; its prosperity since the 18C, reflected in its predominantly Georgian domestic architecture, is founded on the manufacture of blankets, which are still made here in the well-designed buildings in Mill St, beside the river Windrush, whose waters once powered the looms. The centre of the town is Market Square, with a small 18C Town Hall (one room over an open ground floor) two Georgian hotels, and a buttercross of timber and Cotswold stone (c 1600) topped by a cupola and clock turret (1683). To the S the road is divided into two by a long green, running up to the church, which has a particularly grand early 13C central tower and spire, embellished with carvings of crouching beasts. The church is largely of the 13C, though with later additions, notably a number of richly decorated chantry chapels and windows of the Dec period. On the left of the church is a group of almshouses, originally built for the widows of blanket makers in 1724, but rebuilt in high Vict Gothic style in 1868. Some of the houses along the green are much older than they look; several were used by Oxford colleges as retreats from outbreaks of the plague.

In the long High St and its continuation Bridge St, are many interesting or beautiful old buildings. One of the oldest is Staple Hall (early 14C) speculatively connected with the contemporary Exeter College (see p 75); one of the most beautiful is Blanket Hall, built, in the baroque style, in 1721 for the weighing and measuring of blankets. Its pediment carries a clock, and its roof a cupola and bell turret.

In Church Lane, just E of the town, is *Cogges Farm Open Air Museum*, which tells the 1000-year history of Cogges Village, and reconstructs the life of a working farm of the Edwardian period (open 10.30–5.30 daily Easter–end October; closes 4.30 in October; fee).

The valley of the river Windrush above (W) of Witney is both scenically beautiful, and punctuated by a series of beautiful villages. As the main road A40 runs along the ridge well above the river, the valley, reached by narrow tortuous lanes, is for the most part peaceful and unspoilt.

Minster Lovell (about 4m. W of Witney on B4047) makes a very pretty picture, with its houses of local stone, some thatched, and an ancient inn, all beside the river, where ducks swim, adding to its photogenic attractions. The 14C church, across the river, up a hill, and down a long unmade road, still retains some of its medieval glass; the alabaster tomb chest, with the effigy of a knight, may be that of William Lovell (d 1455) or his son John (d 1465). The manor belonged to the Lovell family from the 12C, and the ruins of their vast hall-house lie immediately behind the church. Although there was, no doubt, a house on the site from earlier times, the house whose remains we see now was built c 1431–42 by William Lovell. Set round three sides of a courtyard, facing the river, its central block comprised the great hall, chapel, and solar; there was a series of five living rooms on the W side, and kitchens, domestic offices, and stables on the E. Across a field, in a farmyard, is a large circular dovecot.

In the Wars of the Roses (1455–85) the Lovells belonged to the Yorkist faction, and after the battle of Bosworth Field (1485) their estates were confiscated by the Crown. The property was bought in 1602 by Sir Edward Coke, whose descendant Thomas Coke, Earl of Leicester, dismantled the house in 1747—hence its present state of dereliction. It is now in the care of English Heritage (open 9.30–6.30 Mon–Sat, 2–6.30 Sun; closes at 4 in winter; fee).

Swinbrook, about 2m. W of Minster Lovell, was in the 1920s the home of the eccentric Lord Redesdale and his large family, of which four daughters, Nancy, Diana, Jessica and Unity Mitford, achieved fame (or notoriety) in their different ways. Their family life at Swinbrook is amusingly portrayed in some of Nancy and Jessica Mitford's books. There are monuments to the Redesdales in the church, and Nancy and Unity are buried in the churchyard (just W of the porch). Also in the church is a spectacular monument to five generations of the Fettiplace family, two sets of three life-size reclining figures (early and late 17C).

At *Widford*, which consists of a few houses only, the tiny 13C church stands all alone in a field. It is built on the site of a Roman villa, of which a fragment of mosaic flooring remains in the chancel. Also in the chancel are traces of 14C wall paintings.

Burford (23m.; just N of A40) is a small town evidently and understandably very popular with visitors. Its long High St, partly tree-lined, runs downhill from the main road to the river. Hills rise beyond, a backdrop for the vista of picturesque houses, inns, and church.

In the middle ages Burford was one of the principal centres of the Cotswold wool trade, and was described in the 16C as 'a very great market town replenished with much people'. Until the early 19C, when the present main road was built and bypassed the town, Burford lay on the road to London, and drew wealth from its many inns even after its prosperity from the wool trade declined in the 17C. The houses, some timbered, some of stone, are of all dates between 14C and 18C. Even the Georgian brick-fronted Bull Hotel is in fact much older at the back than its facade suggests.

At the bottom of the hill near the river is the church; although Norman in origin only fragments remain from that period. There was vigorous rebuilding in both the 13C and 15C, and a restoration in the 1870s so vigorous that it prompted William Morris to found the Society for the Preservation of Ancient Buildings.

The history of the town is told in the *Tolsey Museum* (High St, open 2.30–5.30 daily Easter–end October; small fee).

NORTH SIDE: TOWARDS CHIPPING NORTON

Leave Oxford by Woodstock Road and A34.

Woodstock (8m.) is a small, handsome town mainly Georgian in character; buildings of the local stone and of mellow brick harmonize pleasantly in the wide, spacious streets. Its quiet, dignified appearance gives little hint of the spectacular palace and park which are its immediate neighbours, and which, attracting as they do, huge numbers of visitors from all over the world, must inevitably dominate the town for much of the year.

Set in the Forest of Wychwood, Woodstock was a royal manor from Saxon times. Henry I built a palace, or hunting lodge, here; this was later much enlarged. Somewhere in the vicinity was the secret retreat, or 'bower', of Fair Rosamund, mistress of Henry II (see also Godstow Lock, p 97). Elizabeth I was imprisoned in the palace gatehouse for a time by her sister Mary Tudor. Royalty visited frequently until the Civil War, when the palace was besieged and badly damaged. It was finally demolished in 1710, to make way for its infinitely more grandiose successor.

The High St, becoming Park St, begins at the Town Hall (1766 by Sir William Chambers; the ground floor, originally open arches, was enclosed in 1898). On the right is the church, until the 18C a small chapel of ease, the parish church being at Bladon (see below). It has a tower of 1785 in classical style; otherwise it is almost entirely Victorian. Opposite is Fletcher's House, the Oxfordshire County Museum (open 10–5 Mon–Fri, 10–6 Sat, 2–6 Sun; closes one hour earlier, and all day Mon, October–April). A little further on is the large and famous Bear Hotel. At the end of Park St a magnificent triumphal arch leads into the park of **Blenheim Palace**.

HISTORY: Blenheim was built from 1705 for the 1st Duke of Marlborough, who had been presented by his grateful monarch, Queen Anne, with the royal manor of Woodstock and the promise of sufficient funds—or so it was thought—for the building of a great palace, a national monument in celebration of the Duke's famous victory of the previous year over the French and Bavarians near the village of Blenheim, on the banks of the Danube. The Duke called in as architect John Vanbrugh, a model of whose work at Castle Howard in Yorkshire he had seen and admired. Vanbrugh was wise enough, in view of his comparative inexperience with large-scale buildings, to employ as his assistant, both at Castle Howard and at Blenheim, Nicholas Hawksmoor, who had been thoroughly trained at the Office of Works and was to all intents and purposes a professional architect. The grand conceptions were Vanbrugh's, their translation into practice was largely Hawksmoor's. The original estimate for Blenheim was £100,000; the final cost, twenty years on, when the Duke had been dead three years, Vanbrugh had departed, and Hawksmoor had gone and later returned, came to the huge sum for those days of £300,000.

The park is the work of 'Capability' Brown, who in the 1760s transformed the insignificant stream of the river Glyme into the vast lake we see today, making better sense of Vanbrugh's colossal bridge, or viaduct, originally designed to be surmounted by towers and arcading and thus to be considerably larger even than it is now. Brown's lawns swept right up to the palace, but in 1908–30 the 9th Duke employed Duchene to make formal gardens E and W of the palace, and to formalise the N forecourt, thus providing a less abrupt transition from park to palace.

Grandiose baroque: the Marlborough monument, Blenheim Palace chapel

At the top of the hill across the valley to the N, over the Great Bridge, stands the Column of Victory by Lord Herbert; it is surmounted by a lead statue of the 1st Duke, the whole, including the statue, being 134ft high. It was completed in 1730. At the base, on the side facing the palace, is a long inscription by Lord Bolingbroke; on the other three sides are incised the Acts of Parliament whereby the estates had been bestowed on the family of the Duchess and allowed to descend through the female line. Sadly the fine avenue of elms leading up to the column have all perished from Dutch Elm Disease.

TOUR OF THE PALACE: Inside the palace, small groups are conducted by expert guides through a series of immensely impressive rooms, containing an almost overwhelming array of portraits, tapestries, furnishings, porcelain, clocks, and memorabilia. The tour, being all on one level, is particularly well suited to the disabled, the steps up to the front entrance being provided with ramps. Crossing the E (or Kitchen) Court, visitors pass through an archway into the N (or Great) Court, looking back to admire the stone carvings on top of the columns on either side of the archway. These are by Grinling Gibbons, and show lions, emblems of Britain, savaging cocks, emblems of France. Visitors then cross the Great Court, surmount the steps, and walk through the main door of Blenheim Palace into the *Great Hall*. This is no less than 67ft high. The painting by Sir James Thornhill on the ceiling depicts Marlborough showing Britannia the battle plan of Blenheim. Also specially noteworthy here are the Grinling Gibbons stone carvings, including the coat-of-arms of Queen Anne over the huge arch, and perhaps the elaborate brass locks of the entrance door (copied from some locks found in Warsaw), and their enormous coroneted key.

Next comes the suite of apartments to the W, once occupied by Marlborough's domestic chaplain, in one of which Sir Winston Churchill (1874–1965) was born. The rooms are given over to photographs and other Churchill memorabilia, while recordings from some of his famous speeches may be heard.

In the Green Drawing Room, the Red Drawing Room, and the Green Writing Room, the ceilings are all by Nicholas Hawksmoor. In the first of these rooms are notable portraits, including one by Romney of the 4th Duke, who employed Brown to re-organise the park. Here too is a particularly fine French clock, of which there are a large number throughout the palace. Much of the furniture, too, is French, acquired from royal palaces after the French Revolution.

The *Red Drawing Room* has two contrasting portraits at opposite ends of the room: that to the right is of the 4th Duke and his family by Reynolds, while to the left is one of the 9th Duke and his wife, Consuelo (née Vanderbilt), by Sargent.

The next room, the *Green Writing Room*, contains the famous tapestry showing Marlborough receiving the surrender of the French commander, Marshal Tallard, at Blenheim.

The *Saloon* is the state dining room, used by the family once a year, on Christmas Day. The walls and ceiling are painted by Laguerre (who has included himself among the characters portrayed), and the marble doorcases designed by Gibbons.

After the Saloon come the three staterooms; the walls of all three are hung with tapestries of Marlborough's campaigns. In the *First Stateroom* there is a portrait over the chimneypiece of the 9th Duchess by Duran, painted when she was seventeen. The cradle to the right is that in which she rocked her son, the 10th Duke; it was given to her by her mother, who saw its original in Venice and admired it so much that she had it copied. In the centre of the room is the actual *note written by Marlborough to his wife asking her to let the Queen know that the battle at Blenheim had been won; he wrote it on the back of a tavern bill, the only piece of paper to hand.

In the *Second Stateroom* hangs a large portrait of Louis XIV, by Mignard. Among several valuable pieces here are some examples of 12C Persian pottery. The Third Stateroom has some splendid specimens of Boule furniture.

The last room visited in the main part of the palace is the *Library*, with a beautiful Hawksmoor ceiling, which he himself considered the best he ever did. The room is 183ft long, and is estimated to house some 10,000 books, largely collected by the 9th Duke. At one end of the room is a statue of Queen Anne, by Rysbrack; at the other is a Willis organ.

From the end of the library visitors are directed to the *chapel*, where the immense and elaborate tomb of Marlborough and his Duchess, by Rysbrack, adorns one of the walls. At the nearby shop tickets may be obtained to visit the private apartments, on the E side of the palace. Tours take half-an-hour, and are full of interest.

The servants at Blenheim used to sleep in what came to be called The Heights, to either side of the Great Hall, maids to one side, footmen to the other. These rooms were well named, since the servants had to climb 132 steps to reach them.

The Garden and Park include the formal gardens, the Grand Cascade at the W end of the lake, the Temple of Diana, the walled kitchen garden, and the garden centre, which may easily be reached by the narrow-gauge railway. There is also a nature trail, an adventure playground, a miniature railway, and motor-launch trips on the lake, as well as a gift shop, and a licensed restaurant and self-service cafeteria. (Park open 9–5 daily throughout the year. Palace and Gardens open 11–6 daily mid March–end October; fee.)

The parish church of Blenheim is at *Bladon*, a village on the far side of the park. In the churchyard Sir Winston and Lady Churchill lie buried.

Ditchley Park (13m.; turn left off A34 in Over Kiddington) is one of the finest 18C mansions in Oxfordshire, built from 1722 for Lord George Henry Lee, 2nd Earl of Lichfield, to replace the 16C house here which had belonged to the Lee family since 1583. This family was possibly connected with the Lees of Virginia, USA. The house was designed by James Gibbs, in a restrained Palladian style which is in interesting contrast to the flamboyant Baroque of Vanbrugh's Blenheim. Many of the interiors are by William Kent and Henry Flitcroft, and there are decorations by the famous Italian artists Artari, Vassalli, and Serena. The grounds were landscaped by 'Capability' Brown in the 1770s.

During the Second World War Ditchley was frequently used as a retreat by Sir Winston Churchill, and as a venue for Anglo-American conferences. After the war it became a permanent centre for Anglo-American study courses and conferences, under the auspices of the Ditchley Foundation. It is very seldom open to the public (about two weeks in late July and early August), but rewarding to visit if opportunity arises.

Chipping Norton (20m.) is a busy market town, whose large and splendid Dec and Perp church is evidence of its prosperity in the great days of the Cotswold wool trade. The main street is attractively set on two levels. On the western outskirts of the town is the Bliss Valley Tweed Mill; this was built in the 1870s, to resemble a country mansion, and its tall chimney, designed in the form of a Tuscan column, and rising from a domed tower, is a striking landmark. The mill closed in 1980, and its future is at present (1986) in doubt.

NORTH SIDE: TOWARDS BANBURY

Leave Oxford by Banbury Road and A423.

Rousham Park (12m.; turn right at Hopcrofts Holt and right again in about 1m.) is an unusually splendid and intact example of the work of William Kent, 'the father of English landscape gardening'.

The original house was built c 1635 for Sir Robert Dormer, shortly before the Civil War, in which Sir Robert was taken prisoner at the battle of Edgehill (1642). During the war Rousham played no part, except from time to time as a billet for Royalist troops; after the war Sir Robert returned to live an uneventful life at Rousham. In about 1738 his grandson, Gen. James Dormer, employed William Kent to remodel the house and lay out the gardens. It is still the home of the Cottrell-Dormer family. (Gen. James Dormer, one of seven brothers, none of whom left heirs, died in 1743, when Rousham passed into the possession of his cousin, Sir Charles Cottrell, who took the name of Cottrell-Dormer.)

The **gardens** are the chief feature of Rousham, representing the first phase of English landscape gardening and remaining virtually unaltered to the present day. They are unique in England, and therefore in the world. 'Unlike the later "total landscape", relating house and garden, Rousham depends on movement through the garden for effect'. The gardens turn their back on the house, so to speak, to flow out into the surrounding countryside, while they themselves form a landscape within a landscape, revealing a series of delightful surprises.

The visitor to Rousham should if possible walk round the gardens first, before entering the house, and follow the route suggested in the leaflet provided; the route is, incidentally, easily accessible to wheel chairs; what few steps there are can easily be avoided. At the far end of the bowling green, running northward from the house, is the dramatic sculpture by P. Scheemaker of a lion attacking a horse (1740). This is the focal point of the near view; but then the eye is carried beyond it, across the valley to Kent's arresting 'Eye-Catcher', a three-arched artificial ruin standing on rising ground in the middle of a field, in the distance. This extends the limit of the gardens far beyond their true limit, which is the river Cherwell. Also beyond their true limit, but beside the river, is Kent's 'Temple of the Mill', in rustic Gothick.

Returning to the 'landscape within a landscape', we next find, on either side of the bowling green's northern edge, two small white arbours by Kent, with seats. From the left-hand one of these a path leads by a wooded glade to another sculpture by Scheemaker, the *'Dying Gladiator'*, flanked by herms (squared pillars topped with heads), below which is Kent's 'praeneste', or arcade, in stone, with seats and niches, overlooking the river Cherwell across a concave slope.

From the end of the praeneste the path descends to Venus' Vale, the main feature of which is an octagonal pond, half covered with water lilies; above the pond is a cascade surmounted by a statue of Venus; other statues surround the glade. Set into the stone of the cascade is an inscription mourning the death of Ringwood, 'an OTTER-HOUND of extraordinary Sagacity', in four verses, the first of which sets the tone of the rest:

> Tyrant of the Cherwell's Flood
> Come not near this sacred Gloom,
>   Nor, with thy insulting Brood,
>   Dare pollute my *RINGWOOD'S* Tomb.

A lower cascade below the octagonal pond marks the end of Venus's Vale.

From the pond the 'Watery Walk' leads on through woods. The wide path is so named because in the middle of it runs a shallow rill of clear water. Half-way through the wood it runs through another, but small, octagonal pool beside which is a distinctly uninviting 'cold bath', evidently not now used for this, or any, purpose.

At the far end of the wood is the Temple of Echo, built by Townesend of Oxford to Kent's design; below it another concave slope runs down past a statue of Apollo to the river. After this the chunky 13C Heyford Bridge closes off this part of the gardens.

Returning along the valley floor we pass Kent's boathouse. Above, on the right, is the 'Praeneste', flanked by handsome urns and containing seven garden seats. Next, also just above the river, is a 'natural theatre' (which once had a 40ft-high fountain); statues of Greek gods stand about. This 'theatre' is part of the garden planned by Charles Bridgeman in the 1720s, before Kent took over; Bridgeman's plan for Rousham is now in the Bodleian Library in Oxford.

Beyond this two more concave slopes run down to the river, the first from the end of the bowling green, the second from the 'pyramid', a building containing another view-seat. At the end of this riverside section of the walk is a secluded 'Classic Seat', for four people, whence a short but fairly steep ascent leads to the walled gardens, one a vegetable garden and the other, larger, consisting of lawns, fruit trees, and extensive borders, with a central fountain. Beyond, to the E of the house, is a formal rose garden, in which stands a pigeon house dating from 1685, which still has its potency (revolving ladder).

Kent's remodelling of the 17C house, originally built on an H plan, with mullioned windows and possibly gables, transformed it into 'something vaguely resembling an early Tudor palace in free Gothic Style'. Rather unfortunate additions, and alterations to the windows, were made in the 1860s.

Inside the house Kent made few structural changes, but many to the fittings and decorations. Exceptions are the oak door of the entrance hall, with holes to enable Sir Robert Dormer, the first Dormer owner, to fire on any advancing Parliamentarians, and the Oak Chamber, which still has its Jacobean panelling and contains an elaborately carved Elizabethan bed; burn marks made by candles can be seen on the headboard. The staircase is also Jacobean. But the library and drawing room have been transformed. The 17C kitchen became the Painted Parlour, an exquisite 18C room decorated by Kent in the grand manner although he kept the original shape. The carved brackets on the walls were specially designed to display Gen. Dormer's collection of Italian bronzes; they also adorn the overmantles of the three false doors. (Kent complained that 'Gen. Dormer is bronze-mad'.) The room seen today is just as Kent designed it, except that the furniture is about the room instead of round the walls, and the walls, and ceiling background, are green instead of white.

The *pièce de résistance* is the Great Parlour, remodelled by Thomas Roberts of Oxford in 1764, although Kent's chimneypiece and magnificent ceiling are retained. The dining room, by contrast, is a large typically Victorian room, with interesting portraits. It has a fine set of dining chairs, probably designed by Kent, and side-tables by Chippendale. But perhaps its best feature is the view from the window, over the bowling green across the valley to Kent's 'Temple of the Mill' and the 'Eye-Catcher', a view hardly altered in the long years between then and now. (Open: house 2–4.30 Wed, Sun, and BH, April–September; gardens 10–4.30 daily; fee.)

Immediately N of Rousham is *Steeple Aston*, a large attractive village with a 14–15C church which surprisingly contains a huge baroque monument of 1714 to Sir Francis (Judge) Page and his wife. Dressed in full legal regalia and periwig he reclines beside his wife, who wears only the most informal déshabille.

Great Tew, hidden away down narrow lanes about 5m. NW, must once have been the quintessential picturesque English village. Built round two greens, thatched cottages of golden stone nestle among trees, with mansion and church on the hill above. The village was refurbished and prettified as part of a grand landscape design in the early 1800s, when the estate was bought by Matthew Robinson Boulton, son of the famous engineer. Now, sadly, half the houses are dilapidated or even in ruins, and the isolated church stands in a wilderness of weeds.

East and North-East Sides

The landscape east and north-east of Oxford is pleasantly rural, for the most part low-lying, but diversified by isolated hills, outliers of the Chilterns, which, rising abruptly from the plain, give the impression of greater height than they actually have, and afford wide views of the surrounding countryside.

The places described below are in the area bounded to the south-west by the Oxford–London roads A40 and M40, and to the north-east by the Aylesbury–Bicester road A41. In between are no major roads, and to find the way a detailed map is essential. For this reason only a general indication of each place's location is given.

Leave Oxford by Magdalen Bridge and Headington Road. At Headington roundabout, the junction with A40, go straight on.

Stanton St. John (5m.) is a pleasant village whose church has a grand EE and Dec chancel, and pews with unusual double-sided poppyheads, carved with humans or grotesques back-to-back. Opposite the church is a very handsome 16–17C L-shaped house. To the N lies Ot Moor, a large tract of ancient common land which is the habitat of many rare species of plants, insects, and butterflies, and the object of much conservationist attention.

Waterperry Horticultural Centre (8m.), just to the E, is a combination of ornamental gardens, nursery gardens, training school in practical gardening for professionals and amateurs alike, and garden sales centre. It is both the fulfilment and the continuation of the work of Miss Beatrix Havergal, who moved here in 1932 with £350 and six students; her aim was to educate women in all aspects of horticulture, both decorative and utilitarian, hence the enormous variety of plants grown here: flowering trees, shrubs, herbaceous and alpine flowers, fruit trees, soft fruits, and exotics grown in glasshouses. Plants are available to buy as well as to admire. (Open daily: 10–5.30 (6 on Sat and Sun) April–September; 10–4 October–March. Fee for adm to ornamental garden.)

Brill (12m.) is a large spacious village set on a hill top, nearly 700ft above sea level. There are spectacular views. Houses and cottages, mostly of mellow brick, and many decorated with contrasting brick diaper patterns, are set round a wide green and a square.

2m. W is *Boarstall Tower and Duck Decoy* (NT). The tower was the gatehouse of a 14C fortified manor, the rest of which has disappeared (open 2–6 Wed May–September, by written appointment only). The duck decoy, one of the few surviving in England, is now used for scientific purposes; the ducks caught are ringed and released. In the past they were killed and sent to market. The lake on which the decoy 'pipes' are set is surrounded by a large area of woodland, with nature trails (accessible to wheelchairs). Open 10–5 Sat, Sun, and BH, 2–5 Wed, Easter–late August. Decoying demonstrations twice daily, except Wed; fee.

3m. NE of Brill is **Wotton House** (14m.), a stately mansion of 1704, designed on exactly the same lines as Buckingham House, London (now Buckingham Palace, and much altered), with the main house flanked by two service 'pavilions'. The architect is unknown, but may have been John Keene, Sir James Thornhill, or even Sir Christopher Wren himself. After a fire in 1802 Wotton was completely remodelled inside by Sir John Soane, who also altered the relative proportions of the floors and windows to bring the exterior appearance of the house more into keeping with that of its pavilions. The interior is one of Soane's masterpieces. The proportions of the exceptionally light and cheerful rooms are superb, with vistas not only from room to room, but also from room through room to the country outside. The hall and arched passages give an Italian (or Spanish) impression; the staircase, rising at one side of the hall, has a beautiful wrought-iron balustrade.

Both house and grounds fell into a sad state of dereliction after the Second World War, and at one stage were sentenced to demolition. Their rescue and loving restoration (by the present owner) are a triumph (open Wed afternoons August–end September; guided tours at 2 and 3; fee).

5m. S of Brill, on B4011, is the large and attractive village of *Long*

Crendon (18m.), also set on a hill and with distant views. Near the church is Long Crendon Courthouse (NT), a 14C partly half-timbered building, probably first used as a woolstore; manorial courts were held here from the reign of Henry V (early 15C). The upper floor only is open to visitors (2–6 Wed, 11–6 Sat, Sun, and BH, April–end September; small fee.)

Waddesdon Manor: French château in the English countryside

Waddesdon Manor (24m., NT) lies about 6m. NW of Aylesbury, on the Bicester road A41. It was built 1874–89 for Baron Ferdinand de Rothschild largely to house his priceless collection of (predominantly 18C) art treasures. Most of these, enriched by the collections of his successors, are still on display here. The house was designed by a French architect, Gabriele Hippolyte Destailler, in the French Renaissance style, and incorporates features inspired by Blois, Chambord, and other châteaux. The grounds were also designed by a Frenchman, the landscape artist Lainé. The whole might have been lifted straight from the Loire valley, and is a surprising denizen of this quiet corner of the very English Buckinghamshire countryside. (Open: house 2–6 Wed–Sun, 11–6 Good Fri and BH, late March–late October; grounds same days and dates, but open from 1pm, and 11.30 Sun; fee.)

CAMBRIDGE

The City of Cambridge   Cambridge University

Practical Information

Transport

BY CAR, from London: A1, A1(M), A505, A10, or M11. About 1¼ hrs, longer at busy times.

BRITISH RAIL: Railway station in Station Rd, off Hills Rd, (1¼m. from the city centre, 8 minutes by frequent bus service). Trains to and from London (Liverpool St) about every hour during the day (approximate time 65 minutes), or alternatively London (King's Cross), slightly less frequently (approximate time 85 minutes). Tel 311999. London timetable tel. 359602.

BUS AND COACH SERVICES: Bus and Coach Station *Drummer St.* There is an excellent service of local and long distance buses and coaches (operated mostly by Cambus, United Counties, or Premier Travel). London: Express motorway service half-hourly at peak times, hourly at other times, journey time approximately a little under 2 hours; stopping service to N and E London and West End hourly, journey time approximately 2¾ hrs. Regular service to Heathrow (about 2¼ hrs) and to Oxford (about 2½–3 hrs). Connections to all parts. All enquiries tel. 355554.

A Park and Ride service operates on Saturday from the southern side of the city (Cattle Market, Cherry Hinton Rd).

Parking: Car parks are shown on the map. The more central ones are often full after about 9.30 am. There is some limited street parking in the centre (meters).

Main Post Office: St. Andrew's St, tel. 351212.

Information Office: Wheeler St, Cambridge, CB2 3QB, tel. 322640. Open March–October: Mon–Fri 9–6, Sat 9–5. November–February: Mon–Fri 9–5.30, Sat 9–5. May–September: Sun and BH 10.30–3.30.

Accommodation of all kinds is plentiful, but should always be booked in advance if possible, especially in the peak summer period during May Week (mid June) and during the July festivals, when rooms can be very hard to find. The Information Office will help.

Theatres: Arts Theatre, Peas Hill, tel. 355246; ADC Theatre, Park St, tel. 352001 (University Amateur Dramatic Club, and other amateur groups).

A music and drama festival and a folk festival are held in July.

There are numerous concerts and recitals all the year round.

Cinemas: Arts, Market Passage, tel. 352001; Victoria, 1 and 2, Market Square, tel. 352677; ABC 1 and 2, St. Andrew's St, tel. 354572.

Brass Rubbing: The Wesley Church Library, King St. Open Tues–Sat 10–5, also Mon in July and August.

Boating is a popular recreation in summer and a good way of seeing the 'Backs' or getting to Grantchester. Rowing boats, punts, and canoes can be hired at Quayside (off Bridge St) and Mill Lane for the Backs, and at Mill Lane, upper river, for Grantchester (about 2 hours there and back). Motor boats can be hired below Jesus Lock, and in summer there are regular motor-launch excursions. For advice to novices in the art of punting see p 40. At Cambridge you stand on the flat end of the boat to punt.

Bathing: In the *river* at Sheep's Green. *Swimming pools*: Jesus Green, open air; Parkside Pool, off Gonville Place, indoor and heated (open all the year round); Abbey Pool, open air and heated (summer only; off Newmarket Rd, on the edge of Coldham's Common).

Sightseeing

At present (1986) most of the colleges are normally open all day; their chapels also are usually open. Halls are often closed unless the staff are about (mid morning and early afternoon). Staircases and working libraries are **never** accessible to sightseers unless special arrangements for a particular purpose are made in advance in writing. Visitors are courteously asked to be quiet, and not to walk on the grass. Cambridge lawns are sacred to the feet of resident Fellows.

Where opening times are restricted or permanently fixed details are given under the appropriate entry. An increasing number of colleges close during the summer examination period (early May–mid June); some also close for holidays in August and at Christmas and Easter.

From Easter to October there are guided tours of the colleges, starting from the Information Centre in Wheeler St, morning and afternoon Mon–Sat and Sun morning in the season (April/May–October/November); Sat afternoon only December–March. There are special arrangements and regulations for large groups.

History

Cambridge, on the southern edge of the Fens, has a definitely East Anglian character, compounded of wide skies, flat expanses—it is nowhere more than 50ft above sea level—and light reflected by the waters of river, brooks, channels, and winter-flooded fields. And often an icy east wind blows 'straight from the steppes of Russia'.

Excavations on the higher ground north of the river (Castle Hill area) have revealed evidence of Belgic settlements pre-dating the arrival of the Romans in c AD 43. The Romans established a camp here, and round it and on the south side of the river (Market Hill area) there gradually grew up a prosperous town, for the Cam was navigable from this point northward to the sea, while to the south and west Roman roads linked it with the rest of the country.

Early names for the river were Rhee and, more frequently, Granta

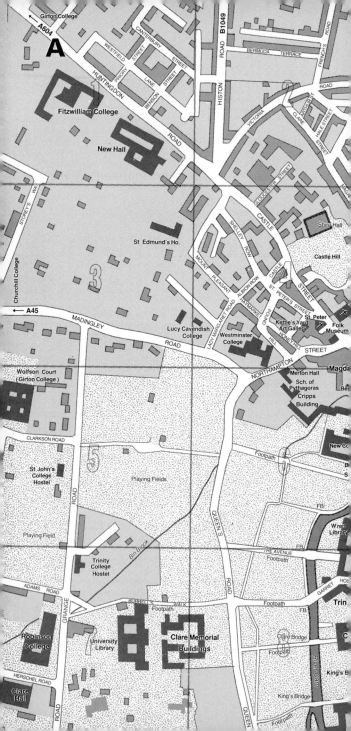

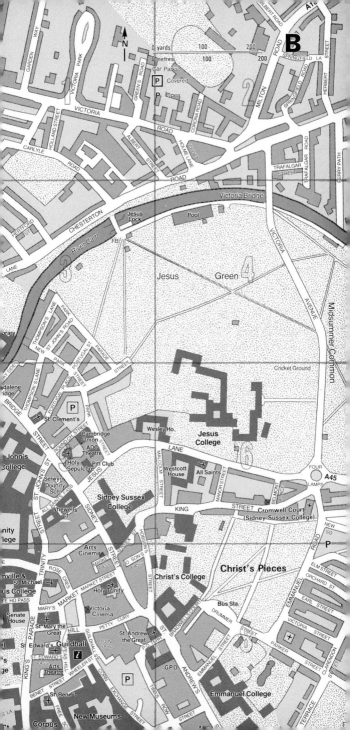

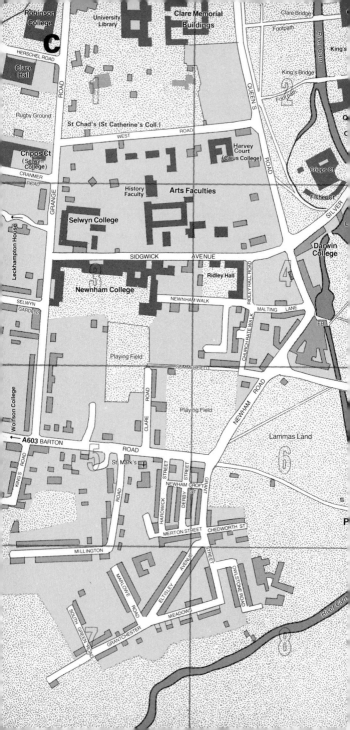

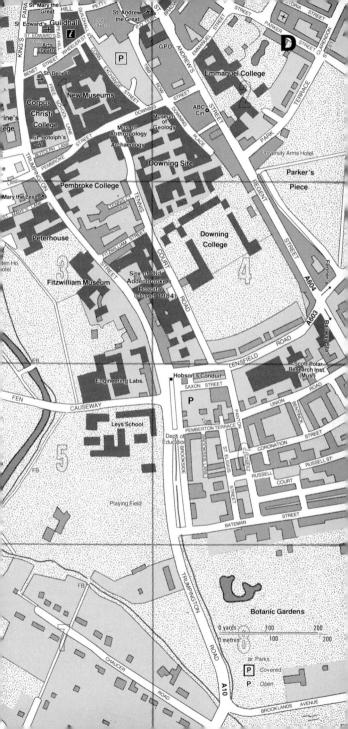

(now usually applied to the two branches above Cambridge), whence derived the town's Saxon name of Grantabrycge (Granta-bridge). Through a number of variations this eventually developed into Cambridge, from which (and not the other way round) the river took its present name.

Soon after the Conquest the Normans built the castle (1068) of which now only the mound remains, and made Cambridge their base of operations against Saxons holding out, under Hereward the Wake's leadership, in the fastnesses of the fens. It became the chief centre of their authority in the area. Churches were built, religious houses established (Barnwell Priory, St. Radegund's, and various friaries, and some time in the 12C the defences were strengthened by the construction of the King's Ditch. This artificial 'moat' enclosed the south and east sides of the town, and followed roughly the line of Mill Lane, Pembroke St, Lion Yard, Hobson St and Park Parade, where it rejoined the river.

Cambridge flourished as a commercial centre, and the great annual fair held on Stourbridge Common, east of the town, attracted traders not only from all over England, but from the Continent as well. The dues from this fair were, in 1211, granted by King John to the leper hospital maintained by the monks of Barnwell Priory. After the Dissolution Henry VIII granted them to the town; from then on the conduct and revenues of the fair became one of the many points of dispute between the town and university authorities. It was the great event of the Cambridge year, formally visited by both Mayor and Vice-Chancellor with their several entourages, and it flourished until well into the 19C.

Scholars began to arrive in Cambridge very early in the 13C, and as at Oxford the university soon acquired a position of pre-eminence and authority over the town which was to be for centuries the source of endless conflict. The university's encroachments caused much damage to the town's prosperity; land alongside the river, where there had previously been busy wharves and warehouses, was acquired for college buildings, and areas of pasture taken over as recreation grounds for the students.

A matter of common concern was the frequent outbreaks of plague, which attacked citizens and scholars alike. Miasma from the fens was regarded as the cause, but the true source of infection was the water supply from the polluted river, and the filthy King's Ditch, used as an open sewer and as a repository for the town's rubbish. Dr Perne of Peterhouse realised this truth when he wrote, in 1574, 'Our synnes is the principall cause . The other cause I conjecture is the corruption of the King's Ditch'. He suggested a scheme (in fact mooted by Matthew Parker of Corpus Christi some years earlier) for a fresh water supply which would also flush out the ditch, and this was eventually carried out in 1610, in a rare instance of co-operation between town and university (see p 171 for details).

Little changed in Cambridge until the 19C, when enclosure of open fields made expansion possible beyond the former town boundaries. The railway arrived in 1845, and thereafter river trade declined. But with the development of scientific studies in the university and the building of research laboratories new science-based industries grew up to supply their needs, and such industries, later widely diversified, became an important source of employment and prosperity in Cambridge. In the 20C the town grew to envelop many surrounding villages, and has now a population of about 90,000. In 1951 it was granted the status of city.

Happily the expansion has taken place round the perimeter, so that the many open spaces in the centre, which are such a distinctive and attractive part of the Cambridge scene, remain as from time immemorial common pasture land. Horses graze on Coe Fen and Lammas Land, and cattle browse on Midsummer Common. 'Rus in urbe' indeed.

CAMBRIDGE UNIVERSITY has 26 colleges, of which two are for graduates: Darwin, and Wolfson (which admits a few mature students as undergraduates). Three were founded for women: Girton, New Hall, and Newnham. Girton now admits men also. All the former men's colleges except Magdalene now admit women. There are five Approved Societies or Foundations, primarily for graduates: Clare Hall, Homerton College, Hughes Hall, Lucy Cavendish College (women only) and St. Edmund's House. The last two accept a few mature undergraduate students.

There are about 9500 undergraduates in the university.

Historic Cambridge is an easy place to explore; about a mile long, and half a mile wide, all within walking distance. It is bounded to the west by the river; the colleges and university buildings lie mostly beside and between two roughly parallel roads running south to north—*Regent St*, which becomes first *St. Andrew's St* then *Sidney St*, and *Trumpington St*, which continues as *King's Parade*, *Trinity St* and *St. John's St*. These long roads converge at *Bridge St* and cross the river at *Magdalene Bridge*. Here the river takes a sweeping eastward bend, so forming, with the big expanses of open commonland on its righthand bank, the northern boundary of the old city. In finding the way about both the city and individual colleges it is useful to keep this north-south pattern of river and roads firmly in mind.

Market Hill, Cambridge: in the background St. Mary the Great and (left) the pinnacles of King's College Chapel

Most of the modern university and college developments are immediately across the river to the west, along *Queen's Rd* and *Grange Rd*. Even here the distances are not very great. It is only to visit the few colleges which lie to the north-west beyond Magdalene Bridge that transport is really needed.

Market Hill is a convenient point from which to start explorations.

1   North of Market Hill

MARKET HILL (Pl.B7) and its immediate environs are the civic and shopping centre of Cambridge. Though it does in fact slope slightly down from W to E, the word 'hill' is used here, as elsewhere in Cambridge, to denote an open space. It is the scene of a colourful market. On the S side (to the left going up the hill) is the Guildhall, below which (left) Guildhall St, with a sculpture, 'Talos', by Michael Ayrton, leads to the multi-storey car park, and to Wheeler St, in which is the *Tourist Information Office*.

Past the turn to Guildhall St is the curiously named *Petty Cury* (pedestrians only) and *Lion Yard*, formerly the 'yard' of the Red Lion Inn, now a covered shopping precinct, in whose central square a large red lion mounted on a white pole looks down benignly on shoppers and on visitors to the public library.

On the N side (right), on the corner of St. Mary's St and Rose Crescent, is *Bacon's tobacco shop*, celebrated by the scholar and parodist Charles Calverley (d 1884); his bust and the appropriate verses appear on a wall plaque. Above the Guildhall (left) in Peas Hill, is *St. Edward's Church* (Pl.B7; entrance in St. Edward's Passage, where there are some picturesque old houses and, on the N side of the church, a large fig tree).

Only the base of the tower remains of the original church, built in 1175. The rest was rebuilt in the Dec style, c 1400. The pale, slender piers of the nave, and lofty pointed arches, make the interior particularly attractive and spacious. The chancel aisles were added in 1446 to serve as chapels for Trinity Hall (N side) and Clare College (S side), whose members had previously worshipped in St. John Zachary, demolished when King's College was built. The living is in the gift of Trinity Hall, and carries the designation of 'chaplaincy'. Many alterations were made in the mid 19C (E window by Sir George Gilbert Scott) and the font was given by the Cambridge Camden Society (the 'Ecclesiologists', see History, p 14). In the late 1940s new windows were installed in the nave aisles (designed by Sir Albert Richardson), those on the S side commemorating Hugh Latimer and Thomas Bilney, leading figures in the early Reformation; the original pulpit, from which they preached, was also reinstated. At the W end of the S aisle is a tablet to F.D. Maurice (1802–72) theologian and social reformer, who founded the Working Men's College, and the first college for women (Queen's College, London). He was chaplain in the last year of his life.

Just beyond St. Edward's is the *Arts Theatre*, built and presented to Cambridge by the economist John Maynard Keynes (d 1946). It has special links with the church.

On the upper (W) side of Market Hill is **St. Mary the Great** ('Great St. Mary's'), the university church and principal parish church of Cambridge. In the past it was used, as was normal, for many secular purposes for which a large meeting place was needed. The university held disputations here, and it was used for degree-giving ceremonies until the Senate House was built in 1730.

Although there has been a church on the site at least since the 12C, the present building dates from the late 15C–early 16C; two kings, Richard III and Henry VII, and many eminent statesmen and ecclesiastics, contributed to its cost. Henry VII also gave the timber for the roof, which, skilfully preserved in the 18C by James Essex, can still be seen in its Tudor magnificence. St. Mary's has the lofty simplicity of the late Perp style; the characteristic adornments of the period—wall-paintings, carvings, and stained-glass windows—were mostly removed, as being idolatrous, during the Reformation. Many leading reformers preached here, some of whom later died at the stake during Mary Tudor's efforts to restore the old faith. The bodies of the German theologians Bucer and Fagius, buried here and in St. Michael's respectively, were exhumed and burned on Market Hill, and both churches were cleansed of their presence in an elaborate ceremony. When Elizabeth I came to the throne their ashes were given reverent reburial. (Brass floor plate in the chancel, S side.)

In the 17C galleries were built to accommodate the large congregations which gathered on special occasions or to hear the university sermon (attendance at which was compulsory for undergraduates), and an enormous three-decker pulpit, designed by James Essex, and nicknamed 'Golgotha', was installed at the W end. Its woodwork was used to make vestry and side chapel screens when both it and some of the galleries were removed during the vigorous alterations carried out in the 19C, largely influenced by the tenets of the Camden Society (see History, p 14).

The entrance is through the S porch; ahead to the left is the font (1632), Gothic in design, Renaissance in decoration. Near it hangs the vicar's mace, which with the carved Madonna and Child, and the processional cross and candle-holders (in the N aisle), are the work of a local craftsman, Loughnan Pendred. Behind is the *tower*, which can be climbed for a splendid view (usually open; small fee). The great organ at the W end was built for the church of St. James's Piccadilly, London, by Bernard Schmidt ('Father Smith') and bought by the university in 1692. In the floor near the W end of the N aisle (left) is a slab commemorating the death of Andrew Skinner in '1710–11', the double date caused by the discrepancy between the legal and the historical year at that time. At the E end of the aisle is the hearse cloth of Henry VII, used when his requiems were sung. The *pulpit*, on the N side of the chancel steps, can be pulled out on rails into the middle of the nave; it is one of the few movable pulpits in England. Behind the *high altar* is a spectacular gilded wood-sculpture of Christ in Majesty (Alan Durst, 1960). Most of the *windows* date from the 19C restoration. Those in the aisle carry the arms of the original benefactors, royalties on the N side (left), clerics on the S (right). In the clerestory are apostles, prophets, and martyrs, some of them with the faces of prominent Victorian divines. The chimes of the *tower clock* (1793), installed by the Rev. J. Jowett of Trinity Hall, and possibly composed by a musician named William Crotch (then an undergraduate), were subsequently widely copied, and are now familiar everywhere as the chimes of Big Ben beside the Houses of Parliament.

About 30 yards down Trinity St (right) is the small Dec church of *St. Michael*, built in the early 14C by Hervey de Stanton (d 1327), who is buried in the chancel. It was long used as a chapel for Michaelhouse, also founded by de Stanton (see Trinity College, p 141). Now no longer needed for worship, the main body of the church has been converted into a meeting room, though the Founder's Chapel is intact (approached through old churchyard, now St. Michael's Court of Caius College; key at Great St. Mary's), and is occasionally used for services.

Almost opposite Great. St Mary's, across King's Parade, is the ***Senate House** (Pl.B7; no adm unless open for use), designed by James Gibbs (who was also then working on St. Martin-in-the-Fields, London, and on the Radcliffe Camera, Oxford), as part of a plan which envisaged an exactly matching building opposite, and a linking N–S range between, intended to house George I's recent gift of some 30,000 books. This was the occasion for the famous verses:

> The King, observing with judicious eyes
> The state of both his Universities
> To one he sent a regiment. For why?
> That learned body wanted loyalty.
> To t'other he sent books, as well discerning
> How much that loyal body wanted learning.

Only the Senate House ever materialised; built between 1722 and 1730 in the Palladian style, it consists of one long room with ante-room and galleries. The plasterwork ceiling is by Artari and Bagutti, and the handsome woodwork by the James Essexes, father and son. There are statues of the Duke of Somerset (Rysbrack) and Pitt (Nollekens). All university ceremonies and large gatherings take place here. Congregations are held three times a term, at which degrees may be conferred, while the most splendid occasion is the summer General Admissions, when honorary degrees are bestowed, and a procession of richly robed university dignitaries, led by Esquire Bedells carrying maces, wends its way right round and into the building.

Immediately behind the Senate House are the *Old Schools* (entrance in Trinity Lane, but no adm for visitors), dating from between 1350 and 1476. They were the first university (as opposed to college) buildings, and provided a Divinity School, meeting rooms, a chapel, and accommodation for the growing library. In the intervening centuries they have undergone such radical alterations that little of the medieval structure is now visible, except on the SW side; this, with its handsome gateway, was originally the Old Court of King's College (1457–76), sold to the university in 1829 when King's New Court was built. The Palladian range on the E side, facing King's Parade, was built in the 1750s (by Stephen Wright); again it was the only part to be completed of a much grander grandiose scheme. The Old Schools now house university offices and the Law Faculty.

Directly across Senate House Passage is **Gonville and Caius College** (Pl.B7; usually known as Caius, pron 'Keys'). It was founded as Gonville Hall in 1348 by Edmund Gonville, a Norfolk parson, on the site where Corpus Christi is now. Gonville died in 1351, entrusting his college to William Bateman, Bp of Norwich, who moved it in 1353 to its present position next to Trinity Hall, which he himself had just founded. He renamed it the 'Hall of the Annunciation of the Blessed Virgin Mary', and the Annunciation is still shown on the college seal. In 1557 the college, which was not prospering, was refounded by another Norwich man, John Caius (the latinised form of Keys) who became Master in the following year. He had been a student at Gonville Hall in 1529, and afterwards a Fellow, before going to Italy to study medicine. He was for a time Professor of Greek Philosophy in Padua; on returning to England he achieved great renown as a doctor and was court physician in turn to Edward VI, Mary Tudor, and Elizabeth I. Although imbued with the New Learning, Caius had a great respect for tradition, and retained not only Gonville's old buildings, but also his name in the title of the new foundation. In 1565, at 4 am on 5 May (sunrise by the old calendar, and judged to be an auspicious hour) the first stones were laid of his new Caius Court. He ordained that for health reasons it should be of three sides only, to admit sunlight and fresh air (a pattern followed by a number of later colleges); he also laid down strict rules on cleanliness and behaviour. A true Elizabethan, he delighted in 'conceits' and embellished his buildings with many symbolic 'devices' (including a column carrying 66 sundials) most of which have now disappeared. His grandest device, however, in part remains. This is the 'academic path' he designed for his students, leading from the Gate of Humility (originally at the Trinity St entrance, now in the Master's garden), along a narrow passage to the Gate of Virtue, the other side of which was the Gate of Wisdom, on the E side of Caius Court. Finally the Gate of Honour (S side of Caius Court) took the successful scholar to the Schools. These gates are among the earliest and most interesting Italian Renaissance style buildings in the country. The Gate of Honour with its six sundials was restored in 1958 to celebrate the 400th anniversary of the refounding of the college.

Caius died in 1573, after some years of increasingly unhappy relations with his own Fellows and with other college Masters, which culminated in 1572 with a raid on his rooms and the destruction of the Catholic vestments and the vessels he had carefully preserved.

The medical tradition of the college, established even before the time of Caius himself, still survives. Until the 19C there were also strong traditional links with the county of the founders; it was 1852 before a Master was elected who did not come from the diocese of Norwich. Caius men wear blue gowns faced with black. This distinctive pattern was adopted in 1837.

Alfred Waterhouse in flamboyant mood: Caius College, the south front of Tree Court

The main entrance leads into TREE COURT, originally dating from the early 17C, when benefactions from the Master, Thomas Legge, and a distinguished medical Fellow Dr Perse (who also founded the Perse Grammar School), financed an expansion of the college. It was entirely rebuilt 1868–70 by Alfred Waterhouse in flamboyant French chateau style, all towers, pinnacles, turrets and ornamental flourishes.

Niches on the outer side carry busts of benefactors and famous members. Opposite the gatehouse the Gate of Virtue leads into CAIUS COURT (1565–67), unpretentious and domestic-looking, except for the resplendent *Gate of Honour* (left).

On the N side (right) is the *Chapel*; built before 1375, it was greatly altered in 1637, when the E end was extended, the wood-panelled ceiling with its cherubs and rays of light installed, and Dr Caius's monument moved from over his grave to the N wall (left), where there is also a monument to Dr Perse (1615).

On the S side is a similar monument to Dr Legge (1607) and near it, behind a hinged panel above the stalls, the old piscina of the 14C chapel. In 1716 the exterior was faced in stone and the E end again rebuilt. Finally, in 1870 Waterhouse added the apse, decorated with mosaics (by Salviati) portraying 'scenes of instruction'. The beautiful altar frontal, the cross and candlesticks (1958, by Gerald Benney) commemorate the quatercentenary of the refounding.

A passage W (left) of the chapel leads into GONVILLE COURT. Although the oldest, it was 'classicised' in 1754 by the then Master, Sir James Burrough (cf Peterhouse). On the W (left) side is the *Hall*, rebuilt in 1853 by Anthony Salvin. It has a handsome hammerbeam roof, and a gallery with the Royal Arms above. Behind the dais, in a curtained glass case, is the flag flown at the South Pole in 1912 by Scott's last expedition, of which Edward Wilson (an exhibitioner of Caius) was medical officer, and a member of the small party which perished with Scott on their return journey to base. Portraits of distinguished Caians include those of Dr Caius, Bp Cosin, Sir Thomas Gresham and Professor Sir John Seeley.

In 1903 the college expanded across Trinity St with ST. MICHAEL'S COURT (by Sir Aston Webb, designer of Admiralty Arch in London), enlarged by Murray Easton in 1934. Across the river off Queen's Road is *Harvey Court*, built in 1961 (see p 176).

FAMOUS MEMBERS: Thomas Gresham, founder of the Royal Exchange in London, 1519–79; William Harvey, physician and discoverer of the circulation of the blood, 1578–1657; Jeremy Taylor, theologian and divine, 1613–67; William Wilkins, architect, 1778–1839; John Venn, logician, inventor of Venn diagram, 1834–1923; Edward Wilson, Antarctic explorer, member of Scott's last expedition, 1872–1912; J.E. Flecker, poet, 1884–1915, and Nobel prizewinners Sir Charles Sherrington, physiologist, 1857–1952, Max Born, physicist, 1882–1970, *Sir James Chadwick*, physicist, 1891–1974, and many others still living.

At the bottom of Senate House Passage, to the left is **Clare College** (Pl.A8), founded as University Hall in 1326 by Richard de Badew, then Chancellor of the University, and refounded in 1338 by Elizabeth de Clare, grand-daughter of Edward I. The name was then changed to Clare Hall, and became Clare College only in 1856. Its elegant simplicity and the beauty of its setting make Clare one of the most immediately attractive and romantic looking of colleges at either Oxford or Cambridge.

Its largely uniform appearance is due to its complete rebuilding in the 17C. This was predominantly the work of John Westley and of the famous Grumbold family, between them responsible for many fine Cambridge buildings. It is a most interesting example of English Renaissance architecture, Gothic heavily overlaid with Italianate Classical, although many of the more Gothic elements, such as battlements and pointed windows, were further 'classicised' in the 18C. Begun in 1638, the great court was not complete until 1707, partly because of the long interruption caused by the Civil War (the Parliamentarians seized the building materials to refortify the castle; however Cromwell did, honourably if belatedly, pay for them).

The handsome Baroque gateway, whose fan-vaulting is some of the last to be done in England, is approached down a long path between lawns; on the N side is the *Chapel*, entered through a passage at the upper right side of the court. It replaces a Tudor Chapel (members of the college previously worshipped in St. Edward's church, see p 134), and is a purely classical building designed by Sir James Burrough in 1762, and completed after his death by James Essex. A feature of the ante-chapel is the high timber lantern, the only one of its kind in Oxford or Cambridge. The spacious interior has a barrel-vaulted plasterwork ceiling and contemporary panelling, furnishings, and altar-piece (an Annunciation, by Cipriani). On the N side (left) are modern stained-glass windows, commemorating two Fellows—Hugh Latimer, one of the 'Oxford Martyrs' (see History, 12), and Nicholas Ferrar, founder in 1625 of the Little Gidding religious community, whose small church appears in the picture. His earlier support of pioneering ventures in Virginia led in the 18C to a considerable American connection with the college. In the S side window the founder, de Badew, offers his college to the Virgin and Child.

The *Hall* (up the steps in the centre of the N side) dates from 1688, though the ceiling and the woodwork above the dais are late 19C. Its portraits include a number of 18C statesmen, and one of Lord Cornwallis, whose surrender at Yorktown in 1781 marked the end of the American War of Independence. Over the doorway of the Small Hall, across the passage, is a 15C stone panel carved with the college arms, sole survivor of the medieval buildings.

The gateway on the W side leads to the river and to *Clare Bridge*, built in 1638 by Thomas Grumbold, and the oldest surviving in Cambridge. It is beautifully carved and surmounted by fourteen stone balls, one of which has a segment missing. There are various explanations for this, ranging from an undergraduate wager to a 'fault' in the stone. Through the wrought-iron gates (*Thomas Warren*, 1714) an avenue leads past the Fellows' Garden (right, open Mon–Fri 2–4.45, but a good view at any time from the path) to another gateway (also 1714) and Queen's Road. Across this are the college's *Memorial Buildings* (see p 178). Clare also has an undergraduate hostel below Castle Hill (see p 179).

FAMOUS MEMBERS: Hugh Latimer, 1485?–1555; Nicholas Ferrar, 1592–1637; Lord Cornwallis, English Commander-in-Chief in the American War of Independence, afterwards Governor-General of India, 1738–1805.

Immediately N of Clare is **Trinity Hall** (Pl.A8), the only old college to retain that designation, although its original title was in fact 'The College of the Scholars of the Holy Trinity of Norwich'. It was founded in 1350 by the Bp of Norwich, William Bateman, who the following year also refounded Gonville Hall (see above, p136). The two colleges, by his express intention, had 'a league of amity and support' which long continued. As well as being an eminent churchman Bateman was a leading authority on canon and civil law, and his college was founded to provide men trained in law, who could replenish the ranks of the profession decimated by the Black Death of 1345–47. It remained a college of lawyers, specialising after the Reformation (when canon law was abolished) in civil law, until well into the 19C; most of its Fellows had large legal practices, many in London, where Trinity Hall established and controlled *Doctors Commons*, a centre for those engaged in civil law, which existed until 1856. The consequent coming and going between Cambridge and London probably influenced the Fellows of Trinity Hall, who in the 17C made financial provision for the improvement of roads leading into Cambridge. With monies from their bequests milestones were also set up. These bore the college insignia, and one can be seen in Trumpington Rd (W side) almost opposite Brooklands Av. Although studies are now diversified the strong traditional connection with the law remains. The college also has a formidable reputation on the river, dating from the 1880s and 1890s.

The entrance, in Trinity Lane, leads into the principal court. Although the buildings are among the oldest in Cambridge, its appearance is of 18C, the original medieval fabric having been refaced in stone and 'classicised', during the Mastership of Sir Nathaniel Lloyd, by Sir James Burrough and James Essex, and the upper (E) side rebuilt after a fire in 1852, by Salvin. On the lower S side (left) is the *Chapel*, 15C but completely remodelled c 1730. The piscina is the only visible relic of the old building, as at Caius tidied away behind a hinged panel (S side). The roof, splendidly renovated, is decorated with heraldic emblems, a guide to which hangs on the left inside the ante-chapel screen.

In the archway opposite the main gate is the entrance to the *Hall*, again of the 18C, though over the panelling behind the dais a Norman window from one of the houses on the site in Bateman's time is a reminder of the college's antiquity. There is the usual impressive array of portraits.

Through the archway are the charming gardens giving on to the river, and right the *Old Library*, an attractive Elizabethan brick building with crow-step gables. Inside it remains practically unaltered, and retains the old arrangement of sloped reading desks, benches, and chained books (cf Merton College and the Bodleian Library, Oxford).

In the 19C and 20C the college expanded on both S and N sides. Built into the gatehouse facing Garret Hostel Lane (N) is the 14C gateway, which originally formed part of the Porter's Lodge on the S side where South Court is now. In the 1960s and 1970s further accommodation was built in Huntingdon Rd, between Fitzwilliam and the playing fields, and at Thompson's Lane in the 1980s.

FAMOUS MEMBERS: Sir John Paston, of the 'Paston Letters', 1442–79 (also Peterhouse); Stephen Gardiner, Bp of Winchester, famed for persecution of Protestants under Mary Tudor, 1483–1555; Lord Howard of Effingham, admiral, and commander of the English fleet against the Spanish Armada, 1536–1624; Robert Herrick, poet, 1591–1674 (a block of the new flats in Huntingdon Rd bears his name); Lord Chesterfield, statesman, wit, letter-writer, 1694–1773; Richard Fitzwilliam, founder of the Fitzwilliam Museum, 1745–1816; Bulwer Lytton, novelist and statesman, 1803–73; F.D. Maurice, theologian and social reformer, 1805–72 (see also St. Edward's church, p 134). Leslie Stephen, man of letters, agnostic, mountaineer, father of Virginia Woolf and Vanessa Bell, 1832–1904; *J.B. Priestley*, novelist, playwright, critic and broadcaster, 1894–1984.

Beyond the corner of Garret Hostel Lane, Trinity Lane turns sharply right and rejoins Trinity St, where there are some pleasant bow-fronted shops and 18C houses. Shortly on the left is ***Trinity College** (Pl.B5), largest and grandest of the Cambridge colleges, and in many ways comparable with Oxford's largest and grandest—Christ Church.

Henry VIII founded Trinity College in 1546, as one of his last acts, to this end taking over two existing colleges, King's Hall and Michaelhouse, and enriching them with valuable endowments of money and property, much of it derived from the newly-suppressed monasteries. King's Hall already had a long royal connection, having been established by Edward II in 1317, as a training-ground for public servants, and continuing, with some fluctuations of fortune, to enjoy the royal patronage of his successors. Initially it drew its scholars principally from the choristers of the Chapel Royal, hence their designation as 'King's Childer', a name also given to the lane that formerly ran past the college. Michaelhouse was a more modest establishment. Its founder, in 1324, was Hervey de Stanton, Chief

Justice and Chancellor of the Exchequer to Edward II, who also built St. Michael's church (see p 135), and it never enjoyed the same wealth and prestige as its neighbours.

The present magnificent appearance of Trinity is largely due to Thomas Neville, appointed Master by Elizabeth I in 1593 (see below). Subsequent Masters and eminent members down the centuries have added to the splendour both of its buildings and of its reputation as a centre of academic distinction, and the home of scientific enquiry and liberal-minded ideas.

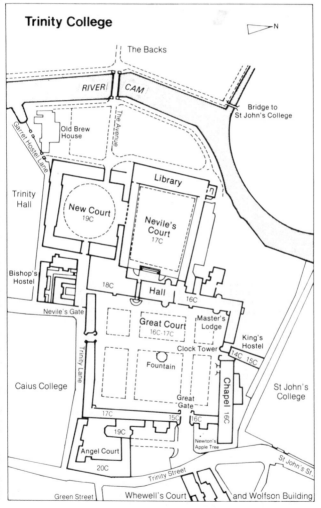

Trinity College

The Backs

RIVER CAM

Bridge to
St John's College

Old Brew
House

The Avenue

Garret Hostel Lane

Library

Trinity
Hall

New Court
19C

Nevile's
Court
17C

Bishop's
Hostel

18C

Hall

16C

Nevile's Gate

Great Court
16C-17C

Master's
Lodge

King's
Hostel

14C 15C

Clock Tower

Trinity Lane

Fountain

Caius College

Chapel 16C

St John's
College

Great
Gate

17C

15C 16C

19C

Newton's
Apple Tree

Angel Court

20C

St John's St.

Trinity Street

Green Street

Whewell's Court

and Wolfson Building

The Trinity gown is dark blue. The boat club is known as 'First and Third Trinity'.

The Great Gate lies back from Trinity St across a cobbled forecourt with to the left the entrance to Angel Court (1959), and to the right a small lawn on which grows an apple tree directly descended from Isaac Newton's tree at Woolsthorpe Manor, which first set him thinking about 'the notion of gravitation'. Newton was one of Trinity's most famous members; the rooms where he lived and wrote his 'Principia Mathematica' are to the right of the Great Gate (staircase E, no adm).

The impressive turreted brick *Gatehouse*, dating from the 1490s, belonged to King's Hall; it bears the name of Edward III and royal coats of arms. It also carries outside a statue of Henry VIII and inside statues of James I, his wife Anne and son Charles (Charles I). All these were put up by Nevile, c 1615, except that of James I, which is a recent replacement. Henry VIII grasps not a sceptre but a chair-leg—an undergraduate joke which has now become a hallowed tradition.

•GREAT COURT is the largest in Cambridge or Oxford (approx 340ft × 288ft). It was created by Thomas Nevile between 1597 and 1615, replacing the jumble of miscellaneous buildings and open spaces belonging to Michaelhouse (of which virtually nothing is left) and King's Hall. Its predominantly Tudor-Gothic style has survived numerous restorations. Nevile retained from earlier buildings only the Great Gate, part of the Master's Lodge, and on the N side (right) the Chapel (1555–67) and *King Edward's Tower* (1428). This had been a gatehouse of King's Hall; Nevile moved it to its present position, and installed the statue of Edward III (wearing Elizabethan armour, and impaling three crowns on his sword), and a clock (replaced in 1726 by the present one, which strikes the hour twice). Behind the tower is *King's Hostel*, another relic of King's Hall.

The *Chapel* (usually open; choral services Sun 9 and 6.15, Tue and Wed 6.15), largely the gift of Mary Tudor, was mainly constructed of materials acquired through the demolition of Ramsey Abbey and the Franciscan friary which stood where Sidney Sussex College is now. Outside a simple Perp style building, inside its appearance is mainly of the 18C, when the highly controversial Master of the time, Richard Bentley, put in the screen, panelling, and magnificent canopied reredos. His tomb-slab is on the N (left) side of the altar rails, but does not record his Mastership, of which he was deprived but which he never relinquished.

In the ante-chapel are statues of great Trinity men, including Francis Bacon, Lord Macaulay, Tennyson (with his pipe, partly concealed in laurel leaves), all 19C, and one of •Newton (by Roubiliac, 1755) which inspired Wordsworth's famous lines: 'The marble index of a mind for ever/Voyaging through strange seas of thought, alone'. There are also numerous wall-monuments. Sorrowfully impressive in their seeming endlessness are the names of the 1000 sons of the college killed in the two World Wars, those of the first at each side of the altar, those of the second in the ante-chapel.

Near the centre of the court is the beautiful canopied fountain (1610). Its water was supplied from a pipeline laid by the Franciscans in the early 14C from springs over a mile away across the river (Conduit Head Rd, beyond Churchill College). On the S side is *Queen's Gate* (1597) with a statue of Nevile's royal patron Elizabeth I. The W side of the court is dominated by the large *Hall* (open Mon–Sat, 10–12, entrance to the right in the passage up steps). Paid for by Nevile, and built by the famous Cambridge master-mason Ralph Symonds, it is closely modelled on the Middle Temple in London. The style is again Perp, vast windows with heraldic glass, and hammerbeam roof topped by an attractive hexagonal lantern. The gallery is a riot of Jacobean decoration. Henry VIII presides from his portrait above the dais; on his right (looking down the Hall) is his daughter Mary Tudor and beyond her are Masters. On his left is the Duke of Gloucester, aged six, by Reynolds, beyond him distinguished members of the college.

The Screens Passage leads W into NEVILE'S COURT (1612), down steps adjoining the classical rostrum built (possibly to Wren's design) across this side of the hall, to bring it into harmony with the rest of the court, whose Italianate cloisters and Renaissance elegance are an interesting contrast to Great Court. The classical effect of the whole was accentuated by 18C renovations and alterations. At the far end is Trinity's crowning glory, the great *Library, designed by Wren and built in 1676–90 by Robert Grumbold (open Mon–Fri 12–2; Sat in full term 10.30–12.30). In the Baroque style, it is of cream-coloured Ketton stone, and carried on a cloister; along the roof balustrade are statues symbolising Divinity, Law, Physic, and Mathematics (by Cibber). The entrance is in the right corner. The lofty interior (190ft long), with its perfect proportions, great windows, and beautiful furnishings 'touches the very soul of any one who first sees it' (Roger North, 1695). The decorative lime-wood carving is by Grinling Gibbons, and a number of the wonderfully lively busts are by Roubiliac. The window at the far end (by Cipriani, 1774–75) depicts the Muse of the College presenting Newton to George III, who sits enthroned among lightly-draped nymphs, cherubs, and clouds, while Bacon looks on, somewhat askance, notebook in hand. Over all broods Byron; his life-size statue (by Thorvaldsen, 1829) was rejected by Westminster Abbey in disapproval of the poet's morals. Newton's personal library is in the adjacent shelves.

Displayed in covered glass cases down the centre aisle are some of the library's many treasures. Older MSS and books (left, facing up the room) include 8C Pauline epistles, the *Trinity Apocalypse, a leaf from the Gutenberg Bible of 1456 (first printed book), a first folio Shakespeare, and Milton's 'Comus'. Among later MSS and books (right side) are works by Bertrand Russell, Housman's 'Shropshire Lad', Wittgenstein's notebook, and A.A. Milne's 'Winnie-the-Pooh'. Also on show are letters of Robert Louis Stevenson, George Eliot, Trollope, Livingstone, Faraday, and many others. This is just a random selection from an exhibition which repays hours of study.

Beyond the library are the college 'Backs' and a bridge (1765) over the river. To the S (left) are NEW COURT (neo-Gothic by Wilkins, 1823–25) and BISHOPS HOSTEL (1669–71). Arthur Hallam, to whom Tennyson was so devoted, had rooms in New Court; he had wished to go to Oxford, and in an early letter referred to Cambridge disparagingly as 'this college-studded marsh'.

In the 19C Trinity, like Caius later, expanded across Trinity St, into WHEWELLS COURT (Salvin, 1859–68). The Gothic Revival buildings were financed by the energetic and generous Master of the time, Dr Whewell, and are liberally adorned with his insignia. Alongside is the Wolfson Building (1971), and the college also has hostels near the University Library, off Burrell's Walk.

FAMOUS MEMBERS: John Fisher, bishop and martyr (Master of Michaelhouse) 1469–1535; Francis Bacon, philosopher and statesman, 1561–1626; George Herbert, poet and divine, 1593–1633; Andrew Marvell, poet, 1621–78; John Dryden, poet and dramatist, 1631–1700; Lord Melbourne,

Classical Baroque splendour: the interior of the Wren Library, Trinity College

statesman, 1779–1848; Lord Byron, poet, 1788–1824; Lord Macaulay, historian and poet, 1800–59; Alfred, Lord Tennyson, poet, 1809–92; W.M. Thackeray, novelist, 1811–63; J.M. Neale, hymnologist, 1818–66; Charles Stanford, composer, 1852–1924; A.E. Housman, poet and classical scholar, 1859–1936; Bertrand Russell, philosopher and mathematician, 1872–1970; R. Vaughan Williams, composer, 1872–1958; G.M. Trevelyan, historian, 1876–1962; A.A. Milne, writer (creator of Winnie-the-Pooh), 1882–1956; L.J.J. Wittgenstein, philosopher, 1889–1951; Shri Jawaharlal Nehru, first Prime Minister of India, 1889–1964.

Scientists and Nobel Prizewinners (a selection only); Isaac Newton, 1642–1727; George Airy, astronomer, 1801–92; Arthur Cayley, mathematician, 1821–95; Francis Galton (Eugenics), 1822–1911; James Clerk-Maxwell, physicist, organiser of the Cavendish Laboratory, 1831–79; George Darwin, astronomer (son of Charles Darwin), 1845–1913; J.W.S. Rayleigh, physicist, Nobel Prize, 1842–1919; J.J. Thompson (Master), mathematician and nuclear physicist, Nobel prizewinner (as were seven of his assistants), 1856–1940; F.G. Hopkins, biochemist (vitamins), Nobel Prize, 1861–1947; William and Lawrence Bragg, father and son, physicists, Nobel Prize, 1862–1942 and 1890–1971; Lord Rutherford, atomic physicist, 1871–1937; Sir James Jeans, astronomer, 1877–1947; Arthur Eddington, astronomer, 1882–1944; A.V. Hill, physiologist, Nobel Prize, 1886–1977; Sir George Thompson, physicist, Nobel Prize, 1892–1975; Lord Adrian, physiologist, Nobel Prize, 1889–1977.

Members of the Royal Family: Edward VII, George VI, H.R.H. The Prince of Wales.

Also numerous statesmen, bishops, scholars, men of letters and scientists, too many to detail.

North (left) of Trinity College, Trinity St becomes St. John's St. On the right is the *Selwyn Divinity School* (Basil Champneys, 1878–79;

no adm). On the left is *St. John's College (Pl.B5; closed early May–late June), until overtaken by Trinity the largest college in Cambridge, and still second only to its immediate neighbour. It was founded in 1511 with benefactions from Lady Margaret Beaufort; she had died in 1509, shortly after plans for the college were first proposed by John Fisher, who was left to carry out her intentions (for details about both see Christ's College, p 156). It replaced the 13C Hospital of St. John. Rebuilding began at once, only the chapel of the old hospital remaining. Fisher's concern for the new college continued

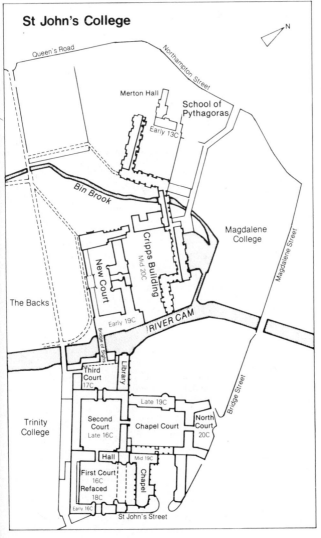

St John's College

until his death on the scaffold in 1535; in his hands both its finances and its scholarship prospered. As an enthusiast for the New Learning and friend of Erasmus he early introduced the study of Greek.

Strongly Royalist in the Civil War, St. John's suffered severely during the Parliamentary occupation of Cambridge; the Master and many of the Fellows were expelled, and the First Court was used as a prison.

During the 19C the college acquired a great reputation for athletic prowess. Its boat club (Lady Margaret Boat Club or LMBC), founded in 1825, is the oldest in Cambridge, and the challenge by one of its members to Oxford in 1829 was the forerunner of the famous Boat Race. The word 'blazer' is said to derive from the scarlet jackets worn by LMBC men.

The magnificent *Gate-tower*, of brick and stone, is best seen from across the street. It carries the emblems of Lady Margaret Beaufort, mythical creatures known as yales supporting the Lancastrian arms, the Beaufort portcullis, and Tudor rose, the background sprinkled' with daisies and forget-me-nots growing from a well-populated rabbit warren. (For further details and explanations see Christ's College.) Above is a statue of St. John (1662); the heavy linenfold-panelled doors are original (1515).

FIRST COURT, though built 1511–20, was much altered in the 18C, when the S side (left) was refaced and sash windows inserted. Over G staircase (no entry) an inscription 'Stag Nov 15 1777' records a stag finally brought to bay by the local hunt half way up the stairs. On the N side (right) is the *Chapel* (usually open Mon–Sat 9–12, and Tues–Fri 2–4. Choral services, during Full Term only, Sun 10.30 am and 6.30 pm; Tues–Sat 6.30 pm). It was entirely rebuilt by Sir George Gilbert Scott in 1866–69; attendance at Chapel was then compulsory, and the college had outgrown the old one. In High Vict-Gothic style, with a polygonal apse, it cannot be said to harmonise with its surroundings. The huge tower, modelled on Pershore Abbey, which is so prominent in the Cambridge skyline, was not part of Scott's design and the expense of its building was for long a heavy financial burden on the college. During this century it has become the custom on Ascension Day (Thursday ten days before Whit Sunday) for a special hymn to be sung from the top (cf Magdalen College, Oxford); the choir has a long tradition of excellence.

In the ante-chapel are relics of the previous building. On the S wall (left) are the three arches of Bp Fisher's chantry (1525), with, set between two of them and protected by glass, a fragment representing the hand of Christ. Opposite is the tomb of Hugh Ashton (1522), one of Lady Margaret's officials. Typical of the time are the corpse below, and the rebus (a kind of visual pun) of ash-tree and barrel, or tun, on the tomb and railings. Other relics of the past, in the chapel itself, are the 13C piscina S (right) of the altar, and the 16C end stalls.

Opposite the main gate a handsomely carved archway surmounted by a statue of Lady Margaret Beaufort leads into the Screens Passage; to the right is the *Hall* (no adm), mostly original though enlarged by Scott in the 1860s, when heating was installed to replace the charcoal brazier then still in use. The hammerbeam roof and much of the linenfold panelling dates from the 1530s; the heraldic glass is mostly Vict. SECOND COURT, built in 1598 partly with benefactions from Mary Cavendish, Countess of Shrewsbury (daughter of the great Derbyshire builder Bess of Hardwick) is the work of Ralph Symonds (see also Trinity, Emmanuel, and Sidney Sussex) and Gilbert Wigge, whose plans, the oldest surviving in Cambridge or Oxford, are in the library. As required in the contract, the style is the same Tudor-Gothic as the First Court before its 18C face-lift. Elizabethan decorations, such as strapwork, alone indicate its later date. A passage on the N side (right) leads to CHAPEL COURT (1885) and NORTH COURT (Sir Edward Maufe, 1939). Over the archway E (right) is a carving of Fisher's coat of arms (Eric Gill).

The gate-tower on the W side of Second Court is embellished with Cavendish and Shrewsbury coats of arms (stag's head and dog respectively) and a late 17C statue of Lady Shrewsbury. Until 1859 its top storey was an observatory. The gateway leads into THIRD COURT. On the N side (right) is the Library (no adm) built in 1624; the interior is unchanged, and it houses a valuable collection of MSS and books. The rest of the court was built after the Civil War, 1669–72. On the W side the famous so-called 'Bridge of Sighs' (closed to visitors) leads to NEW COURT, to which there is also an entrance from the Backs. Leave Third Court by a passage S (left), turn right through the elegant wrought-iron gates (1711) on to Kitchen Bridge (Robert Grumbold, 1709) and go in under the 'Wedding Cake' gateway, which is such a dominant feature of the Cambridge scene. This route gives delightful *views of the Backs, the 'Bridge of Sighs' and New Court (Rickman and Hutchinson, 1824). With its vaulted cloisters, battlements, and pinnacles, in the then newly fashionable neo-Gothick style, it is in complete contrast to the rest of St. John's, a romantic fairy-tale flight of fancy. Its construction on a boggy riverside site was a herculean task; all the waterlogged soil had to be removed and replaced by timber foundations and huge cellars.

Opposite the 'Wedding Cake' a passage leads to the *CRIPPS BUILDING (Powell and Moya, 1964–67), given in one enormous benefaction by the Cripps Foundation. It is an exceptionally attractive composition, almost as much photographed as the 'Bridge of Sighs'. It extends W across the Bin Brook into open ground which until 1959 belonged to Merton College, Oxford. Here stands one of the oldest buildings in Cambridge, the School of Pythagoras (c 1200); the reason for its curious name is unknown. It has recently been converted for modern use, as has Merton Hall (16C) behind it (no adm to either).

FAMOUS MEMBERS: Thomas Wyatt, poet, 1503–42; Roger Ascham, scholar and tutor to Elizabeth I, 1515–68; William Cecil, Lord Burghley, chief minister to Elizabeth I, 1520–98; Robert Herrick, poet, 1591–1674 (also Trinity Hall); Erasmus Darwin, a scientific man of letters and grandfather of Charles Darwin and Francis Galton, 1731–1802; William Wilberforce, who brought about the abolition of the slave trade, 1759–1833; William Wordsworth, poet, 1770–1850; Lord Palmerston, statesman, 1784–1865; John Herschel, astronomer, 1792–1871; Louis Leakey, anthropologist, 1903–72; Nobel prizewinners Sir Edward Appleton, physicist, 1892–1965, and Sir John Cockcroft, nuclear physicist, 1897–1967. Also many archbishops and bishops.

Magdalene College (Pl.A4; pron 'Maudlin'; men only) can be reached through the Porter's Lodge of St. John's Cripps Building or via Bridge St. (a continuation of St. John's St) and Magdalene Bridge (cast iron, 1823) after which the name changes to Magdalene St. The only one of the older colleges across the river, it was charmingly described by Thomas Fuller in 1655 as the 'Trans Cantine Anchoret' (quoted by Edmund Vale, 'Little Guide to Cambridge', p 160). It was founded in 1542 by Thomas Audley, who had recently acquired great wealth through the dissolution of the monasteries. Its history, however, long predates this, since from the mid 15C the Benedictine abbeys of East Anglia (Crowland, Ely, Ramsey, and Walden) had a community here, where their monks could live while studying at the university, each probably maintaining its own 'house' (cf Worcester, formerly Gloucester, College, Oxford, p 84). At some stage this establishment received financial help from the Duke of Buckingham

Modern Cambridge at its best: Cripps Building, St. John's College

(executed for treason in 1484), and acquired the name 'Buckingham College'.

The founder of 1542 gave it little beyond its name, its motto 'Garde ta Foy' ('Keep Faith', or less reverently, 'Watch out for your liver'), and the proviso that its Master should in perpetuity be appointed by the owner of his great property at Audley End, near Saffron Walden (see Environs, p 196). In the early 20C, through a long series of inheritances, this right devolved upon the title-holder of the Braybrooke family, who is also college Visitor.

Magdalene has an interesting link with the United States. In the mid 17C, when it was something of a Puritan enclave, a number of its members settled in New England, where one of them, Henry Dunster, became the first President of Harvard University (see also Emmanuel College, p 173). The post of Master at Harvard had been intended for the Moravian educationist Comenius, though he never took up the appointment. Dunster, however, always regarded himself as Comenius's deputy, and therefore used the title 'President' (a Cambridge term for Vice-Master); hence, possibly, the designation of the President of the United States.

An extremely influential Master (1915–25) was the author A.C. Benson. His books were enormously successful, and he lavished his consequent wealth on the college, being responsible for many of the 20C additions and alterations. He was also responsible for a strong connection with his old school, Eton.

The spelling of Magdalene with a final 'e' which distinguishes it from Magdalen College, Oxford, dates from the early 19C. Before that it was spelt either way indifferently.

An attractive Renaissance gateway (1585) leads into FIRST COURT, which until the 18C comprised the whole college. The N (left) and S (right) sides were the old 15C Buckingham College; over the staircase doorways are modern versions of the coats of arms which indicated to which abbey the 'house' belonged.

The *Chapel* (N side, usually open), though built c 1480, has suffered many changes; 'classicised' in the 18C, it was 're-Gothicised' (largely by Pugin) in the mid 19C. In the ante-chapel, to the right of the entrance, is a small modern bronze of Henry VII, aged seven.

Opposite the entrance gate is the Screens Passage, and (left) the *Hall* (usually open), built in 1519 but inside completely remodelled in the early 18C, when a ceiling was put in, the Royal Arms (Queen Anne's) installed over the dais, and the uncommon double staircase built, leading to the gallery and combination room. It incorporates decorative woodwork from the old hall. There is a fine display of armorial bearings. Behind the dais are those of Audley, Sir Christopher Wray (who built the W side of the court and the gateway) and of the Dukes of Buckingham and Suffolk (also benefactors). Audley's arms appear again in the middle window, E side (16C). Otherwise the heraldic glass is all 20C, and commemorates distinguished members of the college; it was selected and paid for by Benson. Portraits include those of the founder and benefactors (on the dais) and of Samuel Pepys, Charles Kingsley, and Lord Tedder (on the stairs). The hall is still lit only by candles.

In the SECOND COURT is the *Pepys Library* (open Mon–Sat 2.30–3.30, also beginning of Easter Term–end August 11.30–12.30, or as announced on a notice in the gatehouse). The building is a curious mixture of styles, probably accounted for by the changes of fashion occurring during the 60 years it took to build (c 1640–1700). Pepys's Library was installed here, after various moves, in 1742 (as recorded on the facade).

Stringent conditions accompanied Pepys's bequest. The books were to be kept in their specially-made glass-fronted cases, none were to be added, and a periodical inspection was to be made by Trinity College (the other possible legatee). As well as superbly-bound books, the library contains *Pepys's famous diary*, written in his own shorthand (with an account of Charles II's escape after the battle of Worcester as told by the King himself). Also on show are reminders of Pepys's days as Secretary of the Navy Board—Drake's pocket book, Elizabethan charts, and plans of Henry VIII's Navy. In the case between the windows is a manuscript translation of Ovid's 'Metamorphoses' made for Caxton. Pepys acquired the first part. The second, long thought lost, appeared in an auction sale in 1966 and was secured for Magdalene through the generosity of Mr Eugene Power of Ann Arbor, Michigan, USA.

S of the library, facing the river, is Bright's Building (1909, by Sir Aston Webb, who also built Admiralty Arch). N is the *Fellows' Garden* (open 2–4), and W across more gardens is a further block, built and designed by Benson.

Further expansion took place from the 1920s onwards across Magdalene St, both by the adaptation of old houses and by some new building; *Lutyens Building*, 1930, is said to have been paid for from the royalties of 'Land of Hope and Glory', whose words Benson wrote; *Buckingham Court* (David Roberts, 1970) abuts on to St. John's Cripps Building, and is clearly distinguished by its fiery red colour. The conversions (mostly by David Roberts) form an exceptionally attractive miniature townscape; the two 'courts' are named after *Benson* (left) and *Mallory* (right), the climber who perished near the summit of Everest in 1924.

FAMOUS MEMBERS: Henry Dunster, first President of Harvard, died 1659;

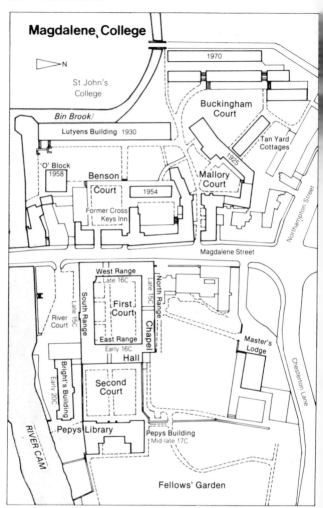

Samuel Pepys, diarist, 1633–1703; Charles Kingsley, novelist, 1819–75; Charles Parnell, Irish Nationalist, 1846–91 (long practically disowned); G.L. Mallory, mountaineer, 1886–1924; Air Chief Marshal Lord Tedder, Deputy Supreme Commander Allied Forces, Second World War, 1890–1967; P.M.S. Blackett, physicist, Nobel prizewinner, 1897–1974.

The neighbourhood N of Magdalene is described on p 179–181. Back in Bridge St, *St. Clement's Church* (usually locked) is on the left between Thompson's Lane and Portugal Passage. Basically EE, it has been much altered by the addition of an incongruous tower in 1821, and by Victorian restorers. Its services are Anglo-Catholic in character. Shortly beyond it, just before Bridge St becomes Sidney St, is the Church of the Holy Sepulchre, usually known as the **'Round**

Church (Pl.B5). Dating from the early 12C, it is one of the few round churches in England. Its Norman appearance, however, is almost entirely due to 19C rebuilding by Salvin, under the direction of the Cambridge Camden Society or 'Ecclesiologists' (see p 14). The conical roof is likewise 19C. It is now the centre of Cambridge's vigorous Evangelical churchmanship. It has a warmly welcoming atmosphere.

The Round Church, 'centre of Cambridge's vigorous Evangelical churchmanship'

Behind it, in Round Church St, is the *Cambridge Union Society*. Founded as a debating club in 1815, it was suppressed two years later for debating politics, but restarted in 1821 on condition that no discussions took place on the politics of the last 20 years. It moved from the Red Lion Inn in Petty Cury to its present building (Alfred Waterhouse at his most strident) in 1866. Debates (nowadays of course on modern issues) are held Mon and Fri at 8.15 pm. Visitors may attend as guests of members, though several days' notice is required.

To the SE of the Round Church is Jesus Lane, on the left of which is the Pitt Club and (in Park St) the *Amateur Dramatic Club* theatre. Further down on the left is *Wesley House*, a Methodist training college, and beyond it ***Jesus College** (Pl.B6), founded in 1496 by John Alcock, Bp of Ely and Comptroller of Works to Henry VII. Its position, somewhat away from the town centre, and its spacious grounds, are a reminder that this was once the site of the Nunnery of St. Radegund (established 1135). By the late 15C, when Bp Alcock suppressed it in order to found his new college in its place, the community had dwindled to two—one of them allegedly imbecile. Alcock retained the conventual buildings, though vigorously adapting and adding to them, and architecturally Jesus is one of the most interesting colleges in Cambridge.

The massive three-storey *Gate-tower*, approached by a long

Jesus College Gate-tower and the 'Chimney' approach

passage known as 'The Chimney' (cf Trinity College, Oxford) was built by Alcock c 1500. Above the central niche is a cock perched on a globe; this is Alcock's rebus and occurs ubiquitously on buildings and in stained glass.

The range W (left) of the gate until 1570 housed the grammar school attached to the college. In FIRST COURT the range opposite the gate is 17C, but deliberately designed to harmonise with the conventual buildings on the E (right) side, where a carved ogee-headed doorway, again surmounted by the cock, leads into *CLOISTER COURT. This was the heart of the old nunnery, to which Alcock added the third storey, the beautiful timber ceiling of the cloisters, and of course his rebus. On the N side is the *Hall* (the first in Cambridge to be placed upstairs), Alcock's rebuilding of the nuns' refectory, with a magnificent chestnut-wood hammerbeam roof, and large oriel window. The heraldic glass on the right was previously in the chapel, that on the left is by William Morris (1875). There are interesting portraits; above the dais the founder (an imaginary likeness), Mary Queen of Scots, and Cranmer. Others of distinguished Jesus men include Flamsteed, Malthus (by Linnell), S.T. Coleridge as an old man, and Steve Fairbairn (d 1938), the great rowing coach who brought Jesus to its pre-eminent position on the river. Outside the hall, steps lead up to the *Old Library* (no adm), which remains much as Alcock left it, complete with his books, and his cock in the window-glass.

Beyond the hall entrance, on the E side of the cloisters, are the beautifully carved EE arches which once led into the Chapter House. Concealed for 350 years by Alcock's alterations, they were rediscovered during restorations in the summer vacation of 1840. Only one undergraduate, Osmond Fisher, and one don were in residence. In spite of Fisher's enthusiasm for the medieval gem orders were given for the arches to be plastered in, and it was not until 1893, when Fisher was himself an Honorary Fellow, that they were again revealed.

The huge and magnificent *CHAPEL on the S side of the court is one of the most exciting in Cambridge. It has a complicated architectural history. Originally the conventual church, also serving St. Radegund's parish, it was a cruciform building of EE design though with Norman work on the N side. Alcock reduced its size by removing the side aisles and converting the W end of the nave into rooms and part of the Master's Lodge. He also installed new windows (in the Perp style) and furnishings.

In the late 18C this interior was 'classicised' but of this phase virtually nothing remains, for in 1845 under the influence of the Gothic Revivalists of the Cambridge Camden Society a complete restoration began whose object was to return the chapel to its 13C pre-Alcock state. What we see now, therefore, is partly genuine Norman and EE, and partly a brilliant realisation of their vision of the ideal medieval church.

Anthony Salvin restored the original choir roof, and built the organ chamber on the site of the old N choir aisle. Later Pugin replaced Alcock's E window with one in EE style, and filled it with glass inspired by the windows of Chartres Cathedral, to which he made a special visit. While there he purchased a sackful of fragments from a window under repair, and incorporated these with his own work, so that parts are in fact 15C Chartres glass. He also designed the floor tiles, organ panels, and some of the stalls, in which he used pieces of Alcock's carved woodwork. This had been sold to Landbeach church (about 5m NE of Cambridge) during the 18C alterations, and the college now made strenuous though only partly successful efforts to recover it. The lectern was given by Lord Brome, and is copied from one in the Brome family chapel.

The second phase of restoration, begun in 1864, provides a feast for admirers of the Pre-Raphaelites, for the delicate and colourful *ceilings were painted by William Morris, and the side-windows designed by Burne-Jones and Ford Madox Brown, except for one in the S transept which is by Morris (bought 1900). The tower, which G.F. Bodley (who took charge after Pugin's death) considered unsafe, was narrowly saved from demolition by the intervention of Sir George Gilbert Scott, whose son was Bodley's assistant.

The striking green and gold altar frontal is by Barbara Dawson (1971); Pugin's frontal is in a glass case in the S transept. Below it, slightly to the right, is the tomb-slab of a 13C benefactor of St. Radegund's. Final reminders of the chapel's 13C origin are the columns (part of the N aisle) outside in the cloister wall. They were exposed when the War Memorial was installed.

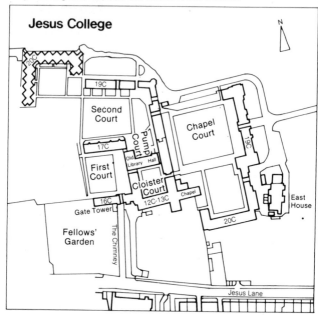

Jesus College

N

19C

Second Court

17C

Pump Court

Old Library   Hall

Chapel Court

19C

First Court

16C

Cloister Court

12C–13C   Chapel

East House

Gate Tower

20C

The Chimney

Fellows' Garden

Jesus Lane

To the N and W of Cloister Court are PUMP COURT and SECOND COURT, both 19C. To the E is the very spacious CHAPEL COURT, also partly 19C, completed on the S side by Morley Horder in 1931 (coat of arms by Eric Gill). The striking building NW of Second Court is by David Roberts, 1963–66.

The grounds of Jesus are open and roomy. Sadly the pleached limes which were such an attractive feature of Chapel Court were cut down in 1979, but the college still possesses a mulberry tree planted for James I, and the great plane trees, from the Vale of Tempe in Greece, planted in 1801 in the Master's and in the Fellows' gardens. Round the latter are massed crocuses, and in spring the gate into Jesus Lane is left ajar so that passers-by can look in.

FAMOUS MEMBERS: Thomas Cranmer, Abp to Henry VIII and Edward VI, compiler of the English prayer book, 'Oxford Martyr', 1489–1556; Laurence Sterne, novelist, 1713–68; Thomas Malthus, economist, 1766–1834; S.T. Coleridge, poet, 1772–1834; Humphrey Davy, chemist, inventor of the miner's safety lamp, 1778–1829; A. Quiller-Couch, man of letters, 1863–1944 (see also Trinity College, Oxford). *Member of the Royal Family*: HRH The Prince Edward.

Opposite Jesus College, in Jesus Lane, is *All Saints* church (1864), designed by G.F. Bodley and decorated by William Morris, Burne-Jones, and Ford Madox Brown. It is now maintained by the *Redundant*

Churches Fund; the keys are obtainable in accordance with the notice outside. Next door is *Westcott House*, a Church of England training college. The wall beyond it is the boundary of **Sidney Sussex College** (Pl.B5) whose main entrance is in Sidney St (left at the top of Jesus Lane). This small college was founded in 1596 under the will of Lady Frances Sidney, wife of the Earl of Sussex. The head of the Sidney family (of Penshurst, Kent) is still the Hereditary Visitor, and the family crest, a porcupine, appears in various places on the buildings. These are on the site of the Greyfriars' convent, dissolved in 1538, whose church had formerly served the university for large gatherings and ceremonies (cf Great St. Mary's, p 134). Nothing remains of the conventual buildings, however, for they had already been demolished to provide material for Trinity College.

The purpose of the new foundation was to train men for ministry in the Reformed Church, and its statutes were closely modelled on those of Emmanuel College. During the religious controversies of the 17C its tendency was strongly Puritan, in spite of which in the Civil War it remained loyal to the King, and suffered the consequent ejection of its Masters and Fellows. Oliver Cromwell did not intervene to spare his old college.

The present appearance of Sidney Sussex is largely due to the restoration and alterations carried out in neo-Gothick manner by Sir Jeffry Wyatville in 1821–32. He built the central Porter's Lodge, covered the old buildings with Roman cement, and added the battlements, crow-step gables, and ornamental chimney-tops which are all such distinctive features. HALL COURT (left, by Ralph Symonds, 1598) stands where the conventual buildings stood. On the NE side is the *Hall* (open when the staff are there, or by arrangement); it was completely remodelled inside in the mid 18C by *Sir James Burrough*, Master of Gonville and Caius College, when a ceiling was put in below the old hammerbeam roof, and the walls panelled. The soft grey of its present decoration is most pleasing. Portraits include one of the three of Oliver Cromwell owned by the college, and may be the one that he instructed should be a true likeness 'warts and all'.

On the N side of the court a passage leads to CLOISTER COURT (J.L. Pearson, 1891). To the right of the Porter's Lodge is CHAPEL COURT. Ahead (S) is Sir Francis Clerke's Building (1628). To the E (left) is the *Chapel*, which replaces two former ones. On the site of the friars' refectory, it runs N and S instead of the usual E and W—perhaps a deliberate Protestant disregard of tradition (cf Emmanuel College). The original simple chapel of 1600 was replaced in the late 18C (by James Essex), and this again was rebuilt and greatly enlarged 1912–23 by T.H. Lyon, in a freely Renaissance style. It has a barrel-vaulted ceiling decorated with the theme of the 'Benedicite'—all God's living creatures. The woodwork is rich in symbolic carvings, and the windows carry the armorial bearings of benefactors. Above the bronze and marble altar hangs a painting of the Holy Family (Giovanni Battista Pittoni, 1687–1767) which was also the altarpiece in Essex's chapel. A statue of St. Francis is a reminder of the medieval friars.

In the ante-chapel windows are mosaics composed of 13–14C glass from the medieval church of the *Greyfriars*; large quantities of fragments were excavated in the garden in 1959, and there are similar mosaics in the old library (no adm). Also in the ante-chapel a tablet records the burial near by of Oliver Cromwell's head, which after many vicissitudes found a resting place in his old college in 1960.

SOUTH COURT (1938) and GARDEN COURT (*T.H. Lyon, 1923*) lie S and E of the chapel. Beyond looms the menacing BLUNDELL COURT (Howell, Killick, Partridge, and Amis, 1969), gloomy in purple brick and dark grey aggregate.

The gardens, once bounded to the E by the King's Ditch, are exceptionally large and beautiful. CROMWELL COURT, at the E end of King St, provides accommodation for both Fellows and undergraduates. Designed by David Roberts (1983), it is faced with buff-coloured brick which harmonises pleasantly with its surroundings. The ground floor is occupied by shops.

FAMOUS MEMBERS: Oliver Cromwell, 1599–1658; C.T.R. Wilson, physicist, Nobel prizewinner, 1869–1959.

On the corner of Sidney St and Market St (S of Sidney Sussex) is *Holy Trinity* church, mostly 14C and 15C. Historically it is linked with the Evangelical movement, a leading protagonist of which, Charles Simeon (died 1836), was vicar for 54 years. Left of the busy road junction, where Sidney St becomes St. Andrew's St, is **Christ's College** (Pl.B8), originally founded as God's House c 1436 by William Byngham, rector of St. John Zachary church in London (burnt down in 1666). The intention was to provide a supply of trained teachers for schools, and studies were secular rather than theological. Established near Clare College, which gave it some assistance, it moved to the present site in the 1440s, when the whole area S of Clare was cleared to make way for King's College.

In 1505 it was refounded, as Christ's College, by Lady Margaret Beaufort, mother of Henry VII, and 'a scholar, a gentlewoman, and a saint', who had already founded professorships of Divinity at both Cambridge and Oxford and was shortly to found St. John's College (see p 145; Lady Margaret Hall, Oxford, is also named after her). Her close friend, confessor, and adviser was the saintly John Fisher, Bishop of Rochester; he was formerly Master of Michaelhouse (see p 140–141), then President of Queens', Vice-Chancellor, and later Chancellor of the University (he was executed in 1538 for refusing to recognise Henry VIII as supreme head of the Church). Both Lady Margaret and Fisher were deeply interested in the New Learning, and classical studies formed part of the new regime.

In Elizabethan times Christ's tended religiously towards Puritanism, but then and later always showed a marked moderation and tolerance of outlook.

The superb *Gate-tower* closely resembles that of St. John's, but the display of Lady Margaret's insignia is even richer and more complicated. The Beaufort arms are supported by yales—fabulous creatures similar to antelopes, but with the great asset of being able to move their horns independently (as made clear by the curious angles at which they are set). Around them are the Beaufort portcullis and coronet, the Tudor rose and royal crown, and at the sides the Welsh dragon and greyhound, supporters of the royal arms. Daisies (marguerites), perhaps recalling Lady Margaret's name, forget-me-nots recalling her motto (souvent me souvient), and plentiful rabbits fill in the background. The linenfold-panelled doors are the originals, but have several inches cut off at the bottom to adjust them to the changed street-level (notice also the staircase steps just inside the gate).

The appearance of FIRST COURT was much altered in the 18C (probably by James Essex) when the brick and clunch used by the 16C builders was cased in Ketton stone, the battlements replaced by balustrades, and the windows sashed. Opposite the entrance is the Master's Lodge, whose oriel window (left) carries the same Beaufort emblems as the gatehouse. This upper floor was Lady Margaret's lodging; the room still has its Tudor fireplace. Next to it was a tiny oratory with an oriel window (rebuilt 1899) opening into the chapel (it can be seen in the chapel S wall; cf New College, Oxford).

The *Chapel* is entered through the black and white door to the left of the large oriel. Like the rest of this range it dates from the old God's House, although it was completely classicised in the 18C. However, some ancient features remain; behind hinged panels on the N and S sides are doorways formerly leading respectively to a side chapel and the Master's Lodge, and in the windows on the N side is some of the oldest glass in Cambridge. The larger figures (c 1475) are possibly St. Gregory and Henry VI, the smaller (c 1505) Henry VII, Lady Margaret, and Edward the Confessor. The magnificent brass lectern is also 15C. Lady Margaret's greyhounds were added later. On the N wall is a handsome monument to two close friends, Sir John Finch and Sir Thomas Baines (Joseph Catterns, 1684). The E window (1912) shows First Court as it appears in Loggan's print of 1688, with above it the Risen Christ, and below Lady Margaret, Bp Fisher, and Edward VI.

The *Hall*, E (right) of the Master's Lodge, was rebuilt in Gothic style by George Gilbert Scott the Younger in the 1870s. Some of the woodwork in the screen was the Tudor hall. The coats of arms over the gallery arches are those of Bp Fisher, with (left) William Byngham and (right) the first Master, John Sycling (Sir Ninian Comper, 1939). There are portraits of Lady Margaret, John Milton (also a bust, copied from an original in the Senior Combination Room), Charles Darwin, Field-Marshal Smuts, and several Nobel prizewinners.

A passage to the right of the hall leads into SECOND COURT. Opposite is the sumptuous classical *Fellows' Building* (1624), in the centre of which a restored 16C doorway opens into the *Fellows' Garden* (open 10–12.30, 2–4). At the far end is a mulberry tree (one of several in the grounds) vaguely associated with Milton. These trees are descendants of some of the 300 planted in 1608 at the request of James I, who wished to encourage silk manufacture. Unfortunately the wrong species was chosen, and all the silkworms died. Near by is an outdoor bathing pool, whose water is still supplied by Hobson's Brook (see p 171 and Emmanuel College). Beside it is a memorial to C.P. Snow.

Additions were made to Second Court in the early–mid 19C, and Third Court was built at various times between 1889 and 1953. N of it, backing on to King St, is NEW COURT (Denis Lasdun, 1970) which inevitably recalls the Mappin Terraces in Regent's Park.

FAMOUS MEMBERS: John Leland, antiquary, 1506–52; John Milton, poet, 1608–74, and his friend Edward King, lamented in 'Lycidas'; Charles Darwin, 'Origin of Species', 1809–82; Jan Smuts, South African statesman, 1870–1950; Lord Mountbatten of Burma, royal sailor and statesman, 1900–1979; C.P. Snow, novelist, 1905–80.

Opposite Christ's College Petty Cury leads back to Market Hill.

2   West and South of Market Hill

From the top side of Market Hill St. Mary's Passage leads to KING'S PARADE, the heart of visitor's Cambridge, dominated by the soaring splendour of King's College Chapel, world-famous alike for the superlative quality of its architecture and of its choral music. **King's College** (Pl.D1; no adm to any building except the chapel) was founded as 'The King's College of our Lady and St. Nicholas in Cambridge' in 1441, by Henry VI (the 'Royal Saint' of Wordsworth's sonnet), and began quite modestly with provision for a Rector and twelve scholars, to be housed in a building N of the chapel, opposite the entrance to Clare. This was the *Old Court*, now part of the University Offices (see p 136). But in 1445 the King devised a much more ambitious scheme, which envisaged a foundation of a Provost and seventy scholars, to be drawn from his newly established school at Eton, with a series of magnificent buildings ranged round a huge court. The whole plan was evidently based on William of Wykeham's New College at Oxford. To clear the chosen site, S of Old Court and Clare, the recently-opened God's House had to be removed (see Christ's College, p 156), the church of St. John Zachary pulled down (see St. Edward's church, p 134), houses and wharves along the river demolished, and roads diverted. Of all the grand plans only the chapel was ever realised, for in 1455 the Wars of the Roses broke out, and in 1461 Henry VI was deposed.

Apart from the completion of the chapel (see below) no more building was done until the 18C, the only living accommodation being the Old Court. In 1724 James Gibbs, then busy with the Senate House, made plans for a new great court, but, history repeating itself, again only one part of the plan materialised, the *Fellows*, or *Gibbs, Building* opposite the entrance gates. Nearly 100 years elapsed before the court was completed, in romantic neo-Gothick style, by William Wilkins, who built the screen and gatehouse facing on to King's Parade, and the S (left) range which includes a splendidly medieval-looking *Hall* (no adm), now rather uneasily accommodating modern bar and self-service arrangements. Outside the gatehouse is a domed Victorian post-box, a much-loved feature of the local scene.

Until the 1870s only Etonians were admitted to King's, and its members were exempt from university examinations. After these somewhat inhibiting privileges were removed the college expanded rapidly and quickly established a tradition of intellectual pre-eminence, particularly on the arts side, which is still maintained. It was one of the first men's colleges to admit women (1972).

Further buildings were added in the late 19C—*Chetwynd Court*, behind Wilkins' S range (1873 by Scott), *River Court* (1893 by G.F. Bodley), and *Webb's Court*, W of Chetwynd (1909 by Sir Aston Webb). Across the river is Garden Hostel (1950), and on Market Hill is Market Hostel (1960). In the late 1960s King's and St. Catharine's next door joined forces to build the complex (by Fello Atkinson) of small courts, dining and concert halls, in and over the narrow space of King's Lane. St. Catharine's College has since added a library, and Junior Common Room social activities buildings. The whole complex is familiarly known as 'Cats and Kings'.

FAMOUS MEMBERS: Christopher Tye, musician, c 1500–73; Francis Walsingham, statesman, c 1530–90; John Harrington, inventor of the water-closet, 1561–1612; Edmund Waller, poet, 1606–87; George Monk (Duke of Albemarle), soldier and statesman, 1608–70; Charles 'Turnip' Townshend, statesman and agriculturalist, 1674–1738; Robert Walpole, statesman, 1676–1745, and his son Horace, wit and man of letters, 1717–97; M.R. James, scholar and writer of ghost stories, 1862–1936; Roger Fry, art critic, 1866–1934; E.M. Forster, novelist, 1879–1970; Maynard Keynes, economist, 1883–1946; A.V. Hill, physiologist, Nobel prizewinner, 1886–1977; Rupert Brooke, poet, 1887–1915; P.M.S. Blackett, physicist, Nobel prizewinner, 1897–1974.

Across a wide expanse of grass is **King's College Chapel**, open as follows: Term: Mon–Sat 9.30–3.45, Sun 2–3 and 4.30–5.45. Vacation: Mon–Sat: October–April 9.30–5, May–September 9.30–5.45; Sun: 10.30–5. Liable to variation. Choral services in term Tues–Sat 5.30, Sun 10.30 and 3.30 (none in vacation).

It is perhaps one of the greatest, as also the latest, medieval buildings of England, and indeed of Europe, Wordsworth's 'immense/And glorious work of fine intelligence'. The richness and variety of its decoration and furnishing reflect the changes in taste, largely due to the Renaissance, which took place during the 100-odd years it took to complete. Perhaps they also reflect the difference in outlook between the founder and his more worldly successors.

Work began in 1446, under Henry VI's master mason Robert Ely, but stopped abruptly in 1461 when the king was defeated at the battle of Towton. One great stone, half cut at the time, remained untouched for over two centuries and was eventually used as the foundation-stone of the Gibbs Building. Some progress was made between 1476 and 1483, but it was not until Henry VII visited Cambridge with his mother Lady Margaret Beaufort (see Christ's and St. John's Colleges, pp 156, 145) in 1506 that vigorous building began again, this time directed by John Wastell. The stonework was finished by 1515, but much remained to be done inside, and it is to Henry VIII that the chapel owes the superb woodwork and windows.

The plan is simple—a great rectangle 289ft long, 40ft wide, and 80ft high, spanned by fan vaults of exquisite delicacy, and lit by windows so enormous that the building seems walled in glass. Over the S porch are the royal arms of Henry VII, supported by Tudor dragon and Beaufort greyhound. These emblems and other insignia of the royal family, Beaufort portcullis, French fleur-de-lis, antelope, Tudor rose, and crown, are the principal motifs of the carving throughout the chapel.

The *screen* which divides the ante-chapel from the choir is an outstanding example of Renaissance woodwork, every inch richly carved. It bears the initial of Henry VIII (the donor) intertwined with that of his queen, Anne Boleyn, whose family crest of a falcon also appears alongside the Tudor rose. Surmounting the screen is the organ; the case dates from 1686–88, but incorporates part of an earlier one. The trumpet-blowing angels were copied from old designs in 1859.

On the E side of the screen in the aisle is an early 16C bronze lectern, engraved on one side with roses and on the other with the four evangelists and their beasts and topped by a small statue of Henry VII. The *stalls* are contemporary with the screen, and by the same craftsmen; above are heraldic panels (1633) showing on the N side (left) royal arms and those of Eton and Oxford, and on the S the arms of King's College and Cambridge. The *altarpiece* is Rubens's 'Adoration of the Magi' (1634) given to King's in 1961. Its installation necessitated the removal of panelling and the steps on which the altar then stood, and at the time aroused much controversy. The modern gold, bronze, and blue altar frontal was designed by Joyce Evans, and embroidered by Elizabeth Geddes. S of the altar is the *War Memorial Chapel*, which contains facsimiles of Rupert Brooke's sonnets 'The Soldier' and 'The Dead'.

All the *windows* (except the W window, a 19C Last Judgement) are by the famous glaziers Bernard Flower and Galyon Hone working with Flemish craftsmen c 1517–47. Each contains four scenes, divided vertically by a light showing prophets and martyrs, horizontally by a stone transom. Beginning on the N side, W end, they tell the story of the Virgin, and the life of Christ up to the Passion, which is depicted in the E window. The theme is continued on the S side with the Resurrection, Pentecost, Acts of the Apostles and finally the Assumption of the Virgin.

Between the chapel and the river is a sweeping lawn, and across

King's College Chapel: 'that branching roof/Self-poised, and scoop'd into ten thousand cells'

the bridge (1871) King's 'Backs', in spring carpeted with crocuses and, later, daffodils. The •view back towards the college and chapel is well worth the short walk.

Immediately S of King's is **St. Catharine's College** (Pl.D1), founded in 1473 by Robert Woodlark, Provost of King's, to serve as a chantry and for the study of philosophy and theology. He provided only for a Master and three Fellows and there were no students until after the Reformation (mid 16C). It was known as Katharine Hall until the 1850s (cf Clare College).

Nothing remains of the original buildings. The three-sided front court, closed on the Trumpington St side only by fine iron railings (1779) was built in various stages between 1675 and 1757; of mellow brick, in restrained Baroque style, it makes a particularly attractive and individual contribution to the local scene. Seats round the sides (many of them memorial) are pleasantly welcoming. The rather unadorned early 18C *Chapel* (right) has a handsome reredos and organ gallery.

Fronting on to Trumpington St on each side of the front court are buildings closely in harmony with it, but in fact dating only from the 20C: *Woodlark* (S, 1951) named after the founder, and *Hobson* (N, 1930) named after Hobson the carrier (see p 171) whose George inn once stood here. Beside it was the Bull inn, bequeathed to St. Catharine's in 1626 by the Master of Caius, Dr Gostlin, much to the chagrin of his own college. Of this only the 1820s facade remains; behind is the new complex built jointly with King's (see p 158). There are more buildings (1870s–1930s) and the Master's garden (no adm), behind the S range of the main court, towards Silver St. On the W side a gate leads out into Queen's Lane. For the college's building in Grange Rd, St. Chad's, see p 177.

FAMOUS MEMBERS: James Shirley, dramatist, 1596–1666; John Addenbrooke, founder of Addenbrooke's Hospital, d 1719.

Almost opposite St. Catharine's W gate is the entrance to **'Queens' College** (Pl.C2; open throughout the year 1.45–4.30, except during examinations, early May–mid June, when it is entirely closed; fee charged end March–mid October; visitors enter and leave by the Queen's Lane gate, and should follow the route described). This college, whose head is President, not Master as elsewhere, has three founders. In 1447 Andrew Dokett, rector of St. Botolph's church, first established it as St. Bernard's College; the following year it came under the patronage of Margaret of Anjou, the young queen of Henry VI (who had just founded King's College next door), and was renamed The Queen's College of St. Margaret and St. Bernard 'to laud and honneure of sexe feminine'. Soon after, the Wars of the Roses broke out; in 1461 Henry VI was deposed and the Yorkist Edward IV became King. His queen, Elizabeth Woodville (a former lady-in-waiting to Margaret), became the college's new patron and 'true foundress by right of succession'. (This is reflected in the position of the apostrophe in *Queens'*, which, however, only became apparent in 1831.) The changes in royal patrons, who also included Richard (III) of Gloucester, account for the many elaborations of the college arms.

Queens' College: the Gate-tower and Old Court

In the early 16C, shortly after the Presidency of Bp John Fisher (see also Christ's and St. John's Colleges. pp 156, 145), Queens' had the distinction of playing host to his friend Erasmus, the great Renaissance scholar who introduced the study of Greek into Cambridge and Oxford. He was a most difficult guest, full of complaints, particularly about the college beer, 'raw, small, and windy ... I am being killed with thirst'. However he found English girls 'divinely pretty, soft, pleasant; gentle and charming as the Muses'.

The magnificent *Gate-tower* has richly carved and coloured vaulting, and on the outer side a statue, possibly of Andrew Dokett. OLD COURT was built in two stages 1448–49; the vertical join in the brickwork can be clearly seen on the S (left) side. On the N (right) is a large sundial (1733) which also tells moon-time, and the old chapel and library (no adm to either).

Over the doorway W, opposite the gate-tower, is the college coat of arms (1575)—those of Margaret of Anjou, showing quarterings of the many countries to which her father laid claim. The door (original) leads into the Screens Passage and (right) the *Hall, recently restored (1980) and a glorious riot of colour and decoration. Although the basic structure is 15C, the interior has been radically altered twice, first by James Essex in the 1730s, to which date belong the panelling, screen, and 'reredos' behind the high table, and secondly by G.F. Bodley in the 1850s and 1860s. He removed the 18C plaster ceiling, restored the timber roof, exposed the old fireplace, and built a central louvre (which the hall, having a fireplace, would never in fact have needed). This was removed in 1951. Roof and walls were decorated by William Morris, who also, with Ford Madox Brown, designed the exceptionally attractive tiles over the fireplace; they represent the months of the year, the saints of the college, and the two queens. Through the Screens Passage is *CLOISTER COURT (1460–95), with its warm red brick and intimate atmosphere one of the most pleasing in Cambridge. On the N side (right) is the 16C half-timbered *President's Gallery*, built at a time when long galleries were a fashionable feature of gentlemen's houses.

On the S side (left) is *Pump Court* (James Essex, 1756); its rather gaunt appearance is in marked contrast to the cosiness of the cloisters. Behind it (E corner) can be seen the tower where according to oral tradition Erasmus had his rooms (no adm). The passage on the W side leads on to the wooden bridge (often, though wrongly, called the *Mathematical Bridge*); it is copied from the original Chinese-style design of 1749. Straight ahead is the striking new CRIPPS COURT (Powell and Moya 1972; cf St. John's College, Cambridge, and Wolfson College, Oxford), while to the left is *Fisher Court* (1936), of which there is a better view from Silver St. There is a short riverside walk (right) to the Grove.

Back over the bridge in Cloister Court a passage NE (left) under the President's Gallery leads into WALNUT TREE COURT, of which the E side (right) was built in 1617–19 (restored after a fire, and enlarged 1778). Beyond it is FRIARS COURT (1886, the W side by Sir Basil Spence, 1959). Between is the *Chapel, built 1889–91 to replace the old chapel, which the college had outgrown. It was designed by G.F. Bodley in Gothic style similar to his restoration of the Hall, and like the Hall it presents a brilliant spectacle of colour. Three windows on the S side, and the brasses in the ante-chapel, come from the old chapel, and three painted panels incorporated in the reredos were previously in the President's Lodge. They were originally part of a large altarpiece painted in Brussels in the late 15C.

Queens' Lane is reached by returning to Old Court through the passage immediately opposite the chapel door.

FAMOUS MEMBERS: Erasmus, scholar (resident c 1511–14), 1466–1536;

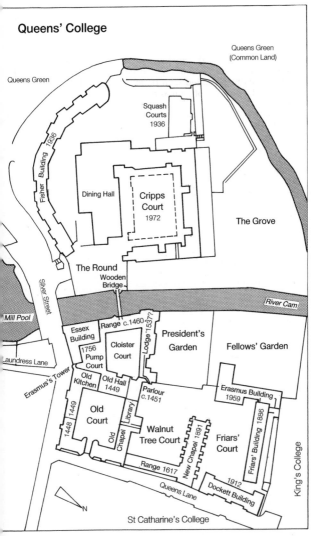

Queens' College

Queens Green
(Common Land)

Queens Green

Fisher Building 1996

Squash Courts 1936

Dining Hall

Cripps Court 1972

The Grove

The Round

Wooden Bridge

Silver Street

Mill Pool

River Cam

Essex Building

Range c.1460

Lodge 1537?

President's Garden

Fellows' Garden

Laundress Lane

1756 Pump Court

Cloister Court

Erasmus's Tower

Old Kitchen

Old Hall 1449

Parlour c.1451

Erasmus Building 1959

1448

1449

Old Court

Old Chapel

Library

Walnut Tree Court

New Chapel 1891

Friars' Court

Friars' Building 1886

King's College

Range 1617

1912

Dockett Building

Queens Lane

N

St Catharine's College

John Fisher, bishop and martyr, 1469–1535; Thomas Smith, statesman and scholar, died 1577; Thomas Fuller, antiquarian, author of 'Worthies of England', 1608–61; Isaac Milner, mathematician and divine, 1750–1820; Osborne Reynolds, mathematician and engineer, 1842–1912; Charles Villiers Stanford, composer and organist, 1852–1924; T.H. White, author ('The Once and Future King'), 1906–64.

At the SE end of Queens' Lane (to the right out of Queen's) is Silver St; across the street are various university offices and lecture rooms, once part of the Cambridge University Press, whose Pitt Building

(1821) is at the top of the street. Its architecture is so ecclesiastica
that it has been called the 'Freshmen's Church', from the old joke o
directing newcomers to it on Sunday. It was built with money le
over from subscriptions collected for a memorial to William Pitt.

A short way N (left) along Trumpington St, across the road, i
Corpus Christi College (Pl.D1; familiarly 'Corpus'), which wa.
founded in 1352 by the united religious guilds of Corpus Christi and
the Blessed Virgin. It was strongly religious in character; all member.
were in holy orders, and chantry duties were incumbent on them
These were carried out in the neighbouring church of St. Benedic
or Bene't (see below) which served as the college chapel until 1579
and the foundation was long known as Bene't's College.

In the riots of 1381 the college was a particular object of attack
this was perhaps due to resentment of its prosperity and the wealth
of the guilds which supported it, and also to the extreme unpopularity
of its patron the Duke of Lancaster. The buildings were sacked and
college records burnt on Market Hill.

The entrance gate leads into New Court, in the NE (far left) corner of which i
a passage into *OLD COURT, completed in 1377 and until the 19C the college'
sole building. Though buttressed for strength in the 15C and 17C, it remain
outwardly much as it was in the 14C, and is the best example in Cambridge o
a medieval college court. A passage on its N side leads to some 20C additions
NEW COURT was built by William Wilkins (1823–27), in the neo-Gothic style
he had also adopted at King's. His plans involved the complete destruction o
the old chapel given to Corpus in 1597 by Nicholas Bacon, and subscribed to
(it is said) by Sir Francis Drake. The new *Chapel*, extended 1870, has stall-backs
from the old one (no adm, but it can be seen through a locked glass door
installed after serious thefts). In the *Hall* (N, or left) which has a richly decorated
timber roof, is a fine collection of portraits among which perhaps the mos
interesting is a painting on wood, dated 1585, of a young man thought to be
Christopher Marlowe. It was found among builders' rubbish during repair work
in 1955.

On the S side (right) is the *Old Library* (for opening times enquire at Porter's
Lodge). It houses the priceless collection of MSS and books bequeathed by
Matthew Parker (Master 1554, and later Abp of Canterbury), and containing
much material rescued from monastic libraries dispersed after the Dissolution
Among its treasures are a MS of the Anglo-Saxon Chronicle, Geoffrey of
Monmouth's 'Historia Britanniae', the 12C rhymed chronicle 'Brut', and a 12C
'Life of Charlemagne'. Parker left strict instructions for its care, which included
an annual surveillance by Caius and Trinity Hall. In the 1960s Corpus established
a postgraduate hostel, Leckhampton House, off Grange Rd (see p 177).

FAMOUS MEMBERS: Matthew Parker, Abp of Canterbury, 1504–75
Nicholas Bacon, statesman, father of Sir Francis Bacon (Trinity), 1509–79
Christopher Marlowe, dramatist, 1564–93; John Fletcher, dramatist, 1579–1625
Sir George Thomson, physicist, Nobel prizewinner, 1892–1975.

On the N side of Corpus Christi is *St. Bene't's* church (entrance in
Bene't St); the tower is early 11C and the tower arch at the W end a
particularly good example of Saxon work. The rest of the church is
mainly 13C and 14C, much restored. The elegant little font is 18C.
In c 1500 Dr Cosyn, Master of Corpus, added two chapels, one above
the other, on the S side, and connected them with the college by a
gallery. They now serve as a vestry and a college room. Fabian
Steadman, who perfected the art of change-ringing, and after whom
various 'changes' are named, was parish clerk in the 17C (tablet).
Until the 1940s the incumbent was nearly always a Fellow of Corpus.

S of Corpus Christi is the church of *St. Botolph* (14–15C, heavily restored late
19C). He was a patron saint of travellers and churches of this dedication were
usually near city gates, in this case Trumpington Gate. The four bells are exactly

as they came from the foundry in 1460, and there is a particularly handsome font-case and cover (1637).

Beyond St. Botolph's, Pembroke St, becoming Downing St, runs E (left), a rather cheerless thoroughfare on each side of which is a large complex of Science Faculty buildings of many dates from the 1860s to the 1970s. THE NEW MUSEUMS (N side, left) came first, built on the site of the old Botanical Garden. Embedded in this gloomy and confusing medley is the *Zoology Museum* (open Mon–Fri 2.15–4.45 except public holidays) and the small white semi-circular *Mond Laboratory*, decorated with a crocodile in tribute to Lord Rutherford (nicknamed 'The Crocodile'). Near it a passage leads into Free School Lane, where the *Whipple Museum of the History of Science* (open Mon–Fri 2–4 except public holidays and sometimes during vacation; May–October: open 1st Sun in month 2–4) is housed in the original hall of the Perse School (17C). On the Downing site (S side, right), through the Vict-Gothic portal, are (left) the *Sedgwick Museum of Geology* (open Mon–Fri 9–1, 2–5, except public holidays; Sat 9–1 in term only) and (right) the *Museum of Archaeology and Ethnology* (open Mon–Fri 2–4, Sat 10–12.30).

On the corner of Pembroke St is **Pembroke College** (Pl.D3), founded in 1347 by Marie de Valence, widowed Countess of Pembroke, and close friend of Lady Elizabeth de Clare, founder of Clare College. It was known as Pembroke Hall until the 1850s.

Although it is one of the oldest colleges in the university, only its 14C gateway on to Trumpington St still presents its medieval appearance. The N and NW sides of OLD COURT are basically the original, but the crumbling clunch walls were refaced partly in brick (1633) and more extensively in stone c 1712, the first to receive this treatment, afterwards employed so widely elsewhere in Cambridge. Pembroke was also the first to have its own chapel, licensed in 1398. In 1663–65 a new *Chapel* was built (S side, right, in Old Court). The donor was Matthew Wren, Bp of Ely (died 1667), who had studied at Pembroke and later became Master of Peterhouse (qv). His High Church sympathies earned him eighteen years in the Tower; soon after his release at the Restoration in 1660 he commissioned his nephew, Christopher Wren, to design a chapel for his old college. It was Wren's first building to be completed (he was also then working on the Sheldonian Theatre in Oxford), his first church, and the first classical building in Cambridge. The sanctuary, entered between massive Corinthian columns of Italian marble, was added by G.G. Scott the Younger in 1880. On its S side (right) is the 14C piscina from the old chapel, and the chair of Nicholas Ridley, Bp of London and one of the 'Oxford Martyrs' (see p 12), a former Master. Matthew Wren's cushions of turkey-work (a particular kind of stitchery) are still in use in the stalls.

The old chapel (NW corner, left, in Old Court) was converted into a *Library* (now used for various gatherings; open by written appointment). It was given a *plasterwork ceiling of exceptional gaiety and charm: scrolls and swags, open books and putti and birds flying across a pale blue sky (by Henry Doogood, 1690).

Opposite the entrance gate is the *Hall* (usually open in the morning). This, and the buildings S of the chapel (c 1890) are by Alfred Waterhouse, who had recently done Tree Court at Caius. As there, he made no attempt to harmonise his designs with their surroundings. The hall was lengthened and a ceiling installed in 1925, and the whole much simplified in the late 1940s. The admirable Master's Chair (David Pye, 1965) is the first piece of official Cambridge furniture in the mid-20C style. As well as many interesting portraits there are busts of William Pitt and the famous 19C mathematician Sir George Gabriel Stokes, who founded a number of Pembroke scholarships.

Behind the hall is IVY COURT; the N (left) side is of 1614. The S side (1659) is named after Sir Robert Hitcham of Framlingham, with whose bequest it was built, and carries his coat of arms. On the upper floor are the *rooms occupied by the poet Thomas Gray* from 1755 till his death in 1771 (open by written appointment; see Peterhouse for the story of his migration to Pembroke). During restoration work wall-paintings were discovered behind the panelling; there are two life-sized drawings of decorations on Wren's chapel (perhaps the working drawings of the architect or his master mason), and a picture of a red-haired, bearded man, whose presence is an intriguing mystery.

To the E of Ivy Court are more buildings by G.G. Scott the Younger (1878) and Caröe (1907), and a few 20C additions. The gardens are extensive and beautiful; on a mound near the pond in the Fellows' Garden (private) is a mulberry tree descended from that associated with the poet Edmund Spenser.

FAMOUS MEMBERS: Nicholas Ridley, bishop and martyr, 1500–55; Edmund Spenser, poet, c 1552–99; Richard Crashaw, poet, 1613–49; Thomas Gray, poet 1716–71; William Pitt the Younger, statesman, 1759–1806; George Gabriel Stokes, mathematician and physicist, 1819–1903; and many archbishops and bishops.

Shortly beyond Pembroke, across Trumpington St, is the 14C church of *St. Mary the Less* (Pl.D3), or Little St. Mary's, a beautiful example of Dec style architecture; until 1632 it served as the college chapel for Peterhouse, which takes its name from the former church on this site—St. Peter without Trumpington Gate. On the N and S side are the remains of chantry chapels (presumably for Masters of Peterhouse); the present vestry, below which is a tiny rib-vaulted crypt, was also at one time used as a chantry, and an oratory built over it connected with the college by a covered gallery (cf St. Bene't's and Corpus Christi). At the W end on the N wall is a memorial to Godfrey Washington, vicar 1705–29, who from his coat of arms was evidently of the same family as the first President of the United States.

At the bottom of Little St. Mary's Lane is the new Ward Library and Theatre of Peterhouse. The building was formerly occupied by the Museum of Classical Archaeology, now in Sidgwick Av.

Peterhouse (Pl.D3; never Peterhouse 'College') is the oldest college in Cambridge, founded by Hugh de Balsham, Bp of Ely, in 1284, on much the same lines as Merton College, Oxford, founded 20 years earlier. From the first its studies were to be secular rather than theological, perhaps reflecting the Benedictine founder's wish to counteract the influence of the Friars, so dominant in Cambridge at the time. Initially de Balsham lodged his students in the Hospital of St. John which preceded St. John's College, but this was not a success, and after three years they moved to houses on the present site.

During the religious and political upheavals of the mid 16C the fortunes of Peterhouse were guided by Dr Andrew Perne (Master 1553–89), who so skilfully adjusted his opinions to the many changes of wind that the weather-vane he put up was regarded as something of an emblem, and his initials 'A.P.' which formed part of its design were said to signify 'A Protestant', 'A Papist', or 'A Puritan' (it is now on the church of St. Peter in Castle St). He was an early advocate of improved sanitation for the town (see p 132, and Hobson's Conduit, p 171). In the Civil War Peterhouse paid dearly for its High Church and Royalist sympathies, and its chapel was a particular target for the iconoclasts.

The buildings are mostly much older than they appear, the 15C and 16C walls having been faced with stone on the inner side in the 18C. The original medieval walls can still be seen outside, from Little St. Mary's Lane. In FIRST COURT, immediately left of the 18C entrance gate, is the Old Library (adm by written arrangement only), in which until recently was housed the splendid collection of MSS and books, 'the worthiest in all England', bequeathed by Dr Perne. Some of the old fittings survive. Opposite (right side) is the *Burrough's Building* (1738–42) designed by the talented amateur architect Sir James Burrough, Master of Caius. On its top floor the poet Gray had rooms in 1742–56; he had a morbid dread of fire, and the iron bar for his fire-escape can still be seen from the street, near Little St. Mary's church. Heartier members of the college made him the butt of practical jokes, and it was their raising of a false fire-alarm that eventually precipitated his departure to Pembroke. The story that he descended into a tub of water is, alas, fictional.

The court is dominated by the *Chapel*, built 1628–34 while Matthew Wren, who later gave Pembroke its chapel, was Master. It is a most interesting mixture of Gothic and Renaissance styles. Originally of brick, it was, like the rest of the buildings, later refaced in stone. The attractive flanking colonnades were rebuilt by Robert Grumbold c 1709. Many of its decorations and most of its windows were destroyed in 1643 by William Dowsing, who 'pulled down two mightie great Angells with wings and divers other Angells, and the four Evangelists, and Peter with his Keies over the Chappell Dore, and about 100 cherubims'. The E window (1639), based on Rubens's 'Le Coup de Lance' and possibly by Bernard van Linge, happily survives. The remaining windows have 19C Munich glass, which greatly darkens the interior. Over the altar is a Gothic 'Pietà' by Postan, installed in 1941 in memory of the social historian Eileen Power.

On the S side (left) of Old Court is the *Hall* (entered from the Screens Passage). It dates from 1290, but was virtually rebuilt by George Gilbert Scott the Younger in 1870, and decorated by William Morris, who also designed the daisy-pattern tiles of the fireplace (itself early 16C, with a 17C fireback carrying the arms of James I). The windows are by Morris, Burne-Jones, and Ford Madox Brown, and commemorate benefactors and distinguished members of the college. Eighteen small portraits on wood (16C) also record benefactors, Fellows, and Masters. On the right side of the high table a doorway, probably 16C, once led to a spiral stairway connecting with the Master's apartments.

To the W of Old Court are Gisborne Court (neo-Gothick, 1825) and Fen Court (1939); S, through the Screens Passage, a path leads into the *Deer Park* or *Grove*, once the grounds of the ancient Friary of the Penance of Jesus. There have been no deer since the 1930s. At the far end, in the Scholars' Garden, is an eight-storey brick tower-block (Sir Leslie Martin, 1953), given by and named after an old scholar of Peterhouse, William Stone, who died in 1958 aged 101. A path leads out into Trumpington St.

FAMOUS MEMBERS: Sir John Paston of the 'Paston Letters', 1442–79 (also Trinity Hall); Thomas Campion, poet and musician, 1567–1620; Richard Crashaw, poet, 1613–49; Thomas Gray, poet, 1716–71; Henry Cavendish, scientist, after whom the Cavendish Laboratory (where his library is housed) is named, 1733–1810; Charles Babbage, scientist, 1792–1871; William Kelvin, mathematician and physicist, 1824–1907.

The handsome building backing on to Peterhouse gardens is the **•Fitzwilliam Museum** (Pl.D3; open Tues–Sat downstairs only 10–2, upstairs only 2–5; Sun all rooms 2.15–4.55), one of the oldest public

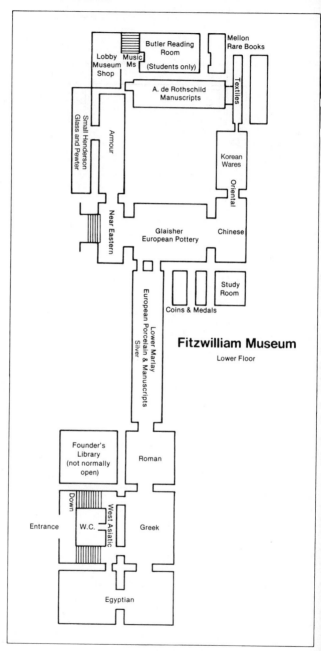

Mellon Rare Books

Butler Reading Room

(Students only)

Lobby Museum Shop

Music Ms

A. de Rothschild Manuscripts

Textiles

Armour

Small Henderson Glass and Pewter

Korean Wares

Oriental

Near Eastern

Glaisher European Pottery

Chinese

Study Room

Coins & Medals

Lower Marlay European Porcelain & Manuscripts Silver

Fitzwilliam Museum

Lower Floor

Founder's Library (not normally open)

Roman

Down

West Asiatic

Entrance

W.C.

Greek

Egyptian

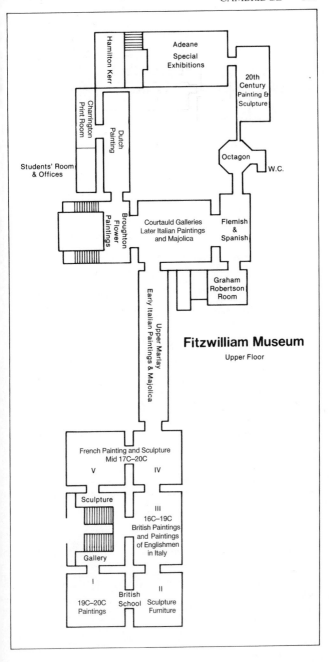

Hamilton Kerr

Adeane Special Exhibitions

20th Century Painting & Sculpture

Charrington Print Room

Dutch Painting

Octagon

W.C.

Students' Room & Offices

Broughton Flower Paintings

Courtauld Galleries Later Italian Paintings and Majolica

Flemish & Spanish

Graham Robertson Room

Upper Marlay Early Italian Paintings & Majolica

Fitzwilliam Museum

Upper Floor

French Painting and Sculpture Mid 17C–20C

V

IV

Sculpture

III 16C–19C British Paintings and Paintings of Englishmen in Italy

Gallery

I 19C–20C Paintings

British School

II Sculpture Furniture

museums in Britain, and certainly among the finest. It was founded by the bequest of Viscount Fitzwilliam in 1816; the massive neo-classical building was designed by George Basevi, and started in 1837. Later work was done by C.R. Cockerell (cf the Ashmolean Museum, Oxford) and the interior completed by E.M. Barry in 1875. There have been many additions since, as the museum's collections have grown.

As only half the museum is open at a time, except on Sunday afternoon, a visit needs to be planned with some care, and the pleasant coffee and snack bar over the museum shop (S end, left) can be useful here. The floor plans show how the exhibits are grouped; the following guide to 'highlights' is necessarily both selective and somewhat subjective.

Lower Floor. At the bottom of the stairs is the WEST ASIATIC ROOM, with Syrian and Phoenician ivories and reliefs (9C–5C BC) including the huge Ashurnasirpal II, King of Assyria. In the EGYPTIAN ROOMS (right) are exhibits from the pre-Dynastic to the pre-Coptic periods; specially striking are the *Shrine of Nekbet* and the *sarcophagus lid of Ramasses III*, King of Egypt 1198–1166 BC. The GREEK ROOM contains pottery, statuary, grave-reliefs (a charming one of two boys with hoops), and seals. In the window is the *Dexamenos gem*. Among the exhibits in the ROMAN ROOM are: the Pashley sarcophagus, and a child's sarcophagus (early 2C AD); the mosaic fountain niche from Baiae (c AD 50), and an Etruscan funerary couch carved in bone. The LOWER MARLAY GALLERY has European porcelain and silver, and in cases down the centre a superb *collection of books and MSS which includes a first edition of Milton's 'Paradise Lost', a second folio of Shakespeare, Keats's 'Ode to a Nightingale', letters of Shelley, Tennyson, A.E. Housman, Walter de la Mare, and Rupert Brooke. Music MSS include works of Vivaldi, Bach, Handel, Mozart, and Purcell. At the far end of the gallery is the great marble *figure of 'Glory' by Baratta. The GLAISHER ROOM is devoted to European pottery; almost opposite the entrance is the first perfect copy by Wedgwood of the 'Portland Vase', which he gave to Erasmus Darwin.

The ORIENTAL ROOMS (right) display Chinese lacquer, carvings, and ceramics, and beyond are Korean ware, Japanese weapons, lacquer, and Chinese snuff boxes. Through the TEXTILE GALLERY is the ANTHONY DE ROTHSCHILD ROOM, with more marvellous MSS both European and Islamic, ivories, crystals and jewellery, and the most ancient works in the museum, Paleolithic drawings from the Dordogne (far end, left). The ARMOURY (off which is the SMALL HENDERSON ROOM, displaying English and Irish table glass, stained glass and pewter) leads into the NEAR EASTERN ROOM where the most interesting exhibits are a Persian painted 'Hawk', and the glass lamp cover of Emir Shaikhu from his mosque in Cairo. From here are steps to the entrance hall.

Upper Floor. This floor is devoted to pictures. At the top of the stairs (right) are three galleries of the British school, late 16C–mid 20C, displayed with contemporary furniture, ceramics, drawings, and busts. The collection includes works by *Hogarth, Reynolds, Constable, Sickert* and *Augustus John*. In desk cases are notable drawings by *William Blake*. In the central bay of ROOM III (at the top of the stairs), are portraits of Englishmen in Italy. ROOMS IV AND V (left) contain French paintings of mid 17–20C; in ROOM IV are works by *Oudry, Vouet* (Entombment), *Poussin* (*Eliezer and Rebecca), *Corot, Delacroix* (*Odalisque), *Rousseau*, and *Decamps*, and in ROOM V

by *Boudin, Fantin-Latour, Degas* (*Au Café), *Renoir* (*Coup de Vent),
Monet, Cézanne, Gauguin, Pissarro, Sisley, Matisse and *Picasso*
*Man's Head). The UPPER MARLAY GALLERY displays early Italian
paintings, notably part of *Simone Martini's* polyptych showing Sts.
Geminianus, Michael and Augustine, (left side), *Domenico
Veneziano's* Annunciation and *Lorenzo di Credi's* Martyrdom of St.
Sebastian. This room leads back into the COURTAULD GALLERY,
where there are later Italian pictures with work by *Tintoretto, Bassano,
Palma Vecchio*, (Venus and Cupid), *Titian* (Venus; Tarquin and
Lucretia), *Veronese* (Mercury, Herse and Aglauros), and drawings
by *Leonardo da Vinci, Michelangelo, Titian, Tintoretto*, and *Tiepolo*.
  In the FOUNDER'S ROOM, left past the *Broughton flower paintings*
at the top of the stairs, are beautiful Dutch landscapes by *Cuyp,
Ruisdael, Hobbema, Aert van der Neer* and *Van Goyen*, and a portrait
by *Frans Hals*. At the other end of the Courtauld Gallery (right) are
pictures of the *Flemish and Spanish schools*, including a *Murillo*, oil
sketches by *Rubens*, and three *Van Dycks* (notably a Madonna and
Child). The OCTAGON ROOM has changing displays of watercolours
and drawings, and the final room is devoted to 20C works; especially
striking are *Graham Sutherland's* *Deposition and *Ben Nicholson's*
*White Relief. There are bronzes and drawings by *Henry Moore*.
Special exhibitions are mounted in the ADEANE GALLERY beyond
(normally entered from the other end, up stairs from S lobby).

Opposite the Fitzwilliam Museum are the buildings of the old *Addenbrooke's
Hospital*, founded with a bequest from John Addenbrooke (d 1719), a Fellow
of St. Catharine's, and opened in 1766. It closed in the early 1980s; New
Addenbrooke's Hospital is in Hills Rd, on the outskirts of Cambridge. Further
on (right) are the Engineering Laboratories and the *Leys School*, founded (for
Methodist boys) in 1875. In Lensfield Rd (left) is the *Scott Polar Research
Institute and Museum* (open Mon–Sat 2.30–4; may be closed on Bank Holidays).

At the junction of Trumpington St and Lensfield Rd stands *Hobson's
Conduit* (Pl.D6), moved here in 1856 from its original site on Market
Hill, where it had been dispensing fresh water since 1614. Beyond
it, beside Trumpington Rd, flows the pleasant little watercourse
which is all that can now be seen of the Cambridge New River, or
Hobson's Brook, constructed in 1610, shortly after the making of
London's New River. It carries water from springs about 3m. S to this
point; from here, in the past, an open stream flowed down
Trumpington St (its memory survives in the very wide roadside
channels) to wash out the King's Ditch, and pipes took supplies of
drinking water to the conduit on Market Hill. Another leet was made
in 1630 which flowed E to St. Andrew's St, from which water was
piped to Emmanuel College and thence to Christ's (whose pools still
make use of it). A moving spirit in the scheme was Thomas Hobson
(d 1631), a prominent Cambridge citizen, landlord of the George inn,
the 'University carrier' on whose death Milton wrote two semi-
humorous poems, and the originator of the expression 'Hobson's
choice', from his insistence that clients hiring his horses should take
the one that had been longest in the stable, and not select their own
mount.

About a quarter of a mile further on are the *University Botanic Gardens* (open
Mon–Sat 8–7.30 or dusk if earlier; Sun in summer 2.30–6.30 except from
Trumpington Rd gate; other gates in Hills Rd and Bateman St). The gardens
began in the 17C on the site now occupied by the New Museums and were
moved in 1846.

Also opposite the Museum, Fitzwilliam St runs E to Tennis Court Rd Just to the right is an entrance to **Downing College** (Pl.D4) but the main gate is in Regent St (turn left to Downing St, then right into Regent St). It was founded in 1800 under the will of Sir George Downing (1683–1749) grandson of Emmanuel Downing, who was one of the founders of Massachusetts, and son of George Downing one of the first graduates of Harvard. He himself was not an admirable character. The provisions of his will were so complicated, and gave rise to so much litigation, that 50 years elapsed between his death and the establishment of his college. By that time the money available had greatly dwindled.

Neo Classicism: Downing College

The outstanding feature of Downing is its parkland setting, unique in Cambridge. The main buildings form three sides of a huge grassy court with a long vista to the nearby Roman Catholic church. The original design, on a grand scale, was by William Wilkins in neo-Grecian style. Of his plans, only the E and W ranges were ever built (finished 1875 by E.M. Barry). In the centre of the N side (Sir Herbert Baker, 1931) is the *Chapel*, designed by A.T. Scott and completed in 1953. Its cool simplicity and pale woodwork are restful and pleasing. In the apse windows is a semi-abstract depiction of the 'Four Horsemen of the Apocalypse' (L.C. Evetts, 1963) and let into the floor on the S side of the altar is a small square of Greek marble from a Byzantine church in Sparta, the site of which was excavated by W.L. Cattle, Senior Tutor of the college. The beautiful altar frontal is by Barbara Dawson. In the ante-chapel is an attractive sculpture—'Mother and Child'.

The *Hall* (left at the far end of the great court), recently enlarged, has a portrait of the first Sir George Downing, on loan from Harvard, of the second Sir George (the founder), and various other members of the family.

FAMOUS MEMBERS: J.M. Neale, hymnologist, 1818–66 (Chaplain); C.M. Doughty, explorer and poet, author of 'Arabia Deserta' 1843–1925; E.R. Lankester, zoologist, 1847–1929; F.R. Leavis, literary critic, 1895–1978; also a number of distinguished lawyers, including Edward Christian, 1758–1823, C.S. Kenny, 1847–1930, and F.M. Maitland, 1850–1906.

Opposite Downing College is one of the many open commons in Cambridge, *Parker's Piece* (Pl.D2/4). It belonged originally to Trinity College, and takes its name from an early tenant, Edward Parker, the college cook; in 1613 it was exchanged with the town for some land which is now Trinity 'Backs'. During the 19C it was much used as a games field. Just S is *Fenner's*, the university cricket ground, overlooking which, in Mill Rd, is *Hughes Hall*, founded in 1885 as a women's teacher-training college, but now admitting both men and women graduates to study a variety of other subjects as well. It became an Approved Foundation of the university in 1985. About 1¼m. up Hills Rd is *Homerton College*, an Approved Society (since 1977), whose students all read for the Education Tripos (B.Ed). Its origins go back to an 18C academy for training Congregationalist teachers, but it has for many years been non-denominational.

A few minutes' walk N (to the left coming out of Downing) is **Emmanuel College** (Pl.D2; familiarly 'Emma'), founded in 1584 by Sir Walter Mildmay, a former member of Christ's College, and a staunch Puritan, to train men for a preaching ministry in the church. Questioned by Elizabeth I, to whom he was Chancellor of the Exchequer, about his 'Puritan foundation', Mildmay replied 'No Madam, far be it from me to countenance anything contrary to your laws; but I have set an acorn, which, when it becomes an oak, God alone knows what will be the fruit thereof'. Perhaps significantly his acorn was planted on the site of a friary of Dominicans, the Order of Preachers (dissolved in 1538), of which the chapel, correctly oriented, became the college dining hall, while another building, which ran N and S, became the college chapel. This may have been a deliberate demonstration of Puritan disregard for ritual and religious tradition (cf Sidney Sussex College).

During the 1630s when, under Abp Laud's regime, Puritans were in great disfavour, many Emmanuel men sought religious liberty in America; of the first hundred graduates who settled in New England a third were from this college. New Town, Massachusetts, was renamed Cambridge in honour of one of them—the preacher Thomas Shepherd—while another, John Harvard (BA, 1632), was the major benefactor of the first university in America, which bears his name. The link between Harvard and Emmanuel is preserved in the Lionel de Jersey Harvard Studentship, awarded each year to a graduate of Harvard to study at Emmanuel, and a graduate of Emmanuel to study at Harvard.

Emmanuel's Puritanism found favour during the Civil War and the Commonwealth, when it supplied no less than eleven heads of colleges to replace those Masters ejected for their High Church and Royalist sympathies. But with the Restoration, and the Mastership of William Sancroft (later Dean of St. Paul's, and then Abp of Canterbury), it gradually lost its original aura of religious nonconformity.

The job of converting and adding to the friary buildings was given to Ralph Symonds, and was his first major undertaking in Cambridge (cf St. John's, Trinity, and Sidney Sussex), though little is now visible of his work. On the N side (left) of FRONT COURT is the *Hall* (originally the friary chapel, see above). Reconstructed by Symonds in 1584, in the mid 18C it was refaced in stone by James Essex and given its handsome plasterwork ceiling (the old timber-trussed roof survives above). The panelling and wrought-iron gates also date from c 1760, but the furniture mostly from 1694, the high table having 'barley-sugar-twist' legs typical of the period. Over it is a portrait of the founder. In the lobby to the Upper Hall and kitchens (no adm) are remains of a window and door-arch of the priory church. Essex also built the W (entrance) side of the court, with the facade to St.

Andrew's St.

Opposite the gateway is the *Chapel*, with its most attractive flanking cloister, initiated by William Sancroft and completed in 1677. It was designed by Sir Christopher Wren (cf Pembroke College), who was also then working on St. Paul's Cathedral in London. Most of the woodwork is original (carved by Cornelius Austin); the altar rails were formerly three-sided, and when the side-rails were moved in the 1880s to accommodate a third step the panels of the central gates

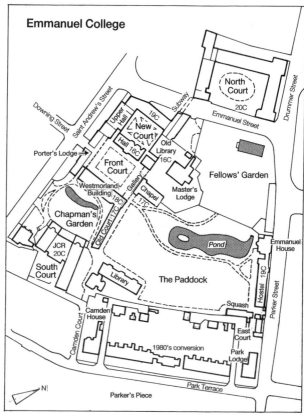

Emmanuel College

North Court
20C

Downing Street

Saint Andrew's Street

Upper Hall

New Court

Subway

Emmanuel Street

Drummer Street

19C

Hall   16C

Old Library   16C

Porter's Lodge →

Front Court

Westmorland Building   18C

Gallery

Chapel 17C

Master's Lodge

Fellows' Garden

Chapman's Garden

Old Court 17C

JCR 20C

South Court

Library

The Paddock

Pond

Emmanuel House

Hostel 19C

Parker Street

Camden Court

Camden House

1980's conversion

Squash

East Court

Park Lodge

N↓

Park Terrace

Parker's Piece

were reset in a credence in the SE corner. The altar-piece is 'The Return of the Prodigal Son' (Amigoni), presented in 1734. On the altar is a war-memorial cross (1951) matching the 1764 candlesticks, and a strikingly beautiful modern *frontal (by Beryl Dean) with the CHI RHO monogram surrounded by flames and palms in silver raised-work.

On the S side (right) of the court is the *Westmorland Building*, which in the early 18C replaced Symonds's original range. It was named after the Earl of Westmorland, descendant of the founder, who largely paid for it, and whose coat of arms is over the doorway. Running S at right-angles to it is the pleasant

Old Court (formerly the Brick Building) of 1633. Beyond this is the modern *South Court* (1966) and the Library (1910 and 1930) with a new wing added in 1972–74.

A passage to the left of the chapel leads to NEW COURT (actually the oldest part of the college) on the right of which is the *Old Library* (no adm). This was the original college chapel; it became the library when the Wren chapel was built. It is now used for concerts and social gatherings. Behind a hinged panel can still be seen the ancient clunch and rubble of the medieval wall, and between ante-room and main room the chapel screen of 1584. The neo-Tudor N side of the court is early 19C; from this side a subway leads under Emmanuel St into NORTH COURT (1914). The charming Elizabethan herb garden was laid out in 1961.

To the E are spacious gardens; the pools here and in Chapman's Garden (W of the Old Court) are fed with water from Hobson's Brook (see p 171). Near the great pond in the Paddock, E of the Chapel, is a bronze statue, 'Warrior with Shield', by Henry Moore.

The buildings of Park Terrace S of the Paddock were acquired in 1982 for adaptation as part of the College accommodation.

FAMOUS MEMBERS: John Harvard, principal benefactor of Harvard University, 1607–38; William Sancroft, Dean of St. Paul's during much of its building, Abp of Canterbury, one of the 'Seven Bishops' who defied James II, 1617–93; William Temple, diplomat and essayist, to whom the 'Letters of Dorothy Osborne' were written, 1628–99; William Law, divine, author of 'The Serious Call to a Devout and Holy Life', 1686–1761; Thomas Young, physicist, egyptologist, polymath, 1773–1829. Nobel prizewinners: Gowland Hopkins, biochemist, discoverer of vitamins, 1861–1947; R.G.W. Norrish, chemist, 1897– 1978. Swift's Gulliver, of 'Gulliver's Travels' (published 1726) went to 'Emanuel College in Cambridge at Fourteen Years old, where I resided three years, and applied myself close to my Studies'.

Shortly N beyond Emmanuel College, Petty Cury leads back to Market Hill. On the left is the church (shared with the Greek Orthodox Church) of *St. Andrew the Great* (19C), grim, gloomy, and usually locked. It contains monuments to Captain Cook, 'circumnavigator of the globe' (d 1779) and his family, transferred from the earlier church on this site.

3   Across the River

Cambridge began to spread west of the river only in the late 19C, and of the buildings described in this route the majority are 20C, and in the main belong to the great period of university expansion after the Second World War. Visitors only interested in historic Cambridge, and with limited time, need not in fact cross the river at all (except to see Magdalene College, for which see pp 147–150). Nevertheless, not to look at what has happened in the last hundred years, and especially in the last forty, would be to go away from Cambridge with a very unbalanced picture, and to miss some stimulating visual experiences.

From Silver St to Castle Hill (about 1m.)

It is worth pausing on the bridge in Silver St to look up-river at the old mill-pool, the weir, the 'island', and—usually—boats. On the E side (left) is *Laundress Green*, where much of the university's washing used to be hung out to dry, and the *University Graduate Centre* (no adm; designed by Howell, Killick, Partridge, and Amis, 1964).

Across the water is **Darwin College** (Pl.C4; no adm), of which the best view is from the bridge, or the terrace of the Anchor Inn. It is a graduate college, established in 1965 by Caius, St. John's, and Trinity; its buildings incorporate Newnham Grange, the former home of Sir George Darwin and his family, and the Hermitage, both so vividly described in 'Period Piece' by Gwen Raverat (Darwin). The Hermitage was also the first home of New Hall (see p 180). Straight ahead is Sidgwick Avenue, on the left of which is *Ridley Hall*, an evangelical Church of England training college, and immediately beyond it **Newnham College** (Pl.C3), founded for women (and still for women only) in 1875, largely under the aegis of Henry Sidgwick, a leading figure in the women's education movement in Cambridge (for details of which see History, pp 14–16). His ideas were more liberal and flexible than those of Girton's founder, Emily Davies, and their differences of opinion led to the almost simultaneous establishment of two separate women's colleges. Newnham's life began in 1871 with five students in a house in Regent St (Sidgwick's 'little garden of flowers') presided over by Miss A.J. Clough, who became the first principal. She was succeeded by Mrs Sidgwick, and the college became the Sidgwicks' home. His liberal outlook and genial personality seem to have left their mark on Newnham, whose buildings are on a deliberately domestic scale, and, uniquely, are arranged in a series of self-contained houses (linked by passages), so that students belong to the smaller community of a house as well as the larger community of the college.

The *original entrance* was in Newnham Walk (turn right at the end of Ridley Hall Rd), which ran right through the college site until Sidgwick Avenue was made (largely at Henry Sidgwick's expense). It still provides the best approach. The early buildings (1875–1910) were all by Basil Champneys, Dutch red brick with white dressings and shaped gables (cf his work at Lady Margaret Hall, Oxford). The *Hall* of the house known as Clough (seen by arrangement) has a ceiling by Sir George Frampton, designer of the Peter Pan statue in Kensington Gardens, and the Edith Cavell statue in St. Martin's Place, London. In the gardens, on whose grass you may walk, is the *old laboratory* used by science students before they were admitted to university facilities. It is now used as a studio by the university's Artist-in-Residence. Additional buildings belong to 1938 (W side) and the 1960s (E side).

Harvard University's first woman professor (of Astronomy, 1956) was an old Newnhamite—Mrs C.H. Gaposchkin (Payne).

Opposite Newnham is the **University Arts Faculties** site (the 'Sidgwick site'), a complex of individually-styled buildings (Sir Hugh Casson and Neville Conder, 1952 onwards) providing libraries, lecture rooms, two halls and a buttery, loosely grouped round a podium which, with its benches and tables and newly-planted trees, has something of the village-green community atmosphere. The roof-lines offer some visual excitement. The Classical Faculty Building houses, on its upper floor, the Museum of Classical Archaeology (open Mon–Fri 9–1 and 2.15–5, Sat 9–1 during university term; free). On the N side is the controversial *History Faculty Building* (James Stirling, 1965; cf the Florey Building of Queen's College, Oxford, p 62), two six-storey blocks of fiery red brick set at right angles, with a receding pyramid of glass between. The effect is not improved by venetian blinds hanging at crazy angles behind most of the 'windows' and the patchy first aid which has had to be applied to the exterior (1986). In the NE corner of the site is Caius College *Harvey Court* (Sir Leslie Martin, 1960), an inward-facing three-sided court with rooms in stepped-back terraced tiers, an arrangement affording the occupants little privacy.

On the corner of Sidgwick Avenue and Grange Rd, beyond the Sidgwick site, is **Selwyn College** (Pl.C3), founded in 1882 to provide a university education for young men of the Church of England unable to afford the fees of the older colleges (cf Keble College, Oxford). It is named in honour of George Augustus Selwyn, first Bp of New Zealand, an influential and greatly admired man (d 1878). Its denominational character, and somewhat unusual charter, which made no provision for Fellows, long delayed Selwyn's full acceptance as a college. It was recognised as an Approved Foundation in 1923, and as a college in 1958. Although never confined to theological studies, a very high proportion of Selwyn men did, until recent times, go on to take Holy Orders.

The red-brick Tudor-style buildings, set round a spacious court, were mostly designed by Sir Arthur Blomfield. Opposite the entrance is the *Chapel*; the side windows (Kempe) depict saints and church leaders, the E window Christ in Majesty. Behind the altar, against a white wall, is a sculpture of Christ ascending (Karin Jonzen, 1958). Set into the altar is the pectoral cross of Bp Patteson of Melanesia, friend and colleague of Bp Selwyn. His combined bible and prayer book are in the vestry, and his staff in the chapel above. The trowel used at the laying of the foundation stone is on the N wall below the sanctuary steps. On some of the stalls are carved the heads of contemporary statesmen (1895). On the S side of the court is the *Hall* (1905), approached up a double flight of steps over which appears the rebus, three apples and a tun, of the then Master, Richard Appleton. Across Grange Rd, just past Cranmer Rd, is the attractive *Cripps Court*, in brick, concrete, and knapped flint (1969, by Cartwright, Woollatt, and Partners).

Opposite Selwyn a private road leads to *Leckhampton House* (no adm) a graduate hostel for Corpus Christi College. In the grounds is a sculpture, 'Seated Figure' by Henry Moore. Also opposite Selwyn is a graduate hostel of King's.

Turning S (left out of Selwyn) along Grange Rd, and then right at Barton Rd, one comes to (right) **Wolfson College** (Pl.C5) founded in 1965 as University College and renamed in 1973 in recognition of a large benefaction from the Wolfson Trust. It is principally a graduate college, fostering connections with Continental and other overseas universities, and with business and administrative circles. The buildings (Ferrey and Mennim) incorporate Bredon House, formerly occupied by a professor of botany and consequently having beautiful gardens. The grounds are open to visitors (keep to the paths).

To the N (right) of Selwyn, on the corner of Grange Rd and West Rd, is *St. Chad's*, a hostel of St. Catharine's College. It consists of a large Edwardian brick house with modern additions, providing living accommodation and, at the S end, the Octagon, used for concerts, lectures, etc. (James Cubitt, Fello, Atkinson and Partners 1977–81). A little further on, in Herschel Rd (left) is *Clare Hall* (Pl.A7), a graduate establishment founded in 1966 by Clare College, but now independent. The buildings (by a Scandinavian architect, Ralph Erskine) provide both single and family accommodation.

Immediately beyond Herschel Rd is **Robinson College** (Pl.A7), the first in Cambridge to be founded for both men and women. The college was entirely financed by a Cambridgeshire businessman, Mr David Robinson. The first graduates were admitted in 1977, and undergraduates in 1979. It was formally opened by the Queen in 1981.

The red-brick L-shaped buildings, with very large grounds beyond, were designed by Gillespie, Kydd and Coia (and at a later stage by Yorke, Rosenberg, and Mardall). The massive gatehouse, approached by a ramp, is reminiscent of a castle; the *Chapel*, with John Piper glass, is to the right, the Hall straight ahead. Communal rooms face outward to the roads, private ones inwards to the quiet of the court.

On both sides of Grange Rd beyond Robinson are college sports grounds, and on the left *St. John's College Hostel* and Girton's *Wolfson Court* (in Clarkson Rd; by David Roberts, 1969).

Opposite Robinson, Burrell's Walk leads back to Queen's Rd past (left) *Trinity College Hostel* (no adm). On the right is the **University Library** (Pl.A7; open Mon–Fri 9–7.05, Sat 9–1. Accompanied visitors admitted; unaccompanied visitors shown round Mon–Fri 3 pm, the tour lasting about $\frac{1}{2}$ hr). Built in 1931–34 by Sir Giles Gilbert Scott, it is one of the country's most important libraries, with over four million books, MSS which include the 6C Codex Bezae, one of the five great uncial MSS of the Gospels, and a magnificent collection of Caxtons including his 'Historyes of Troye' (1475–76), the first book printed in English, and the only perfect copy of his 'Golden Legend' (1483). There is often a special exhibition in the long first floor corridor.

Immediately next to the library, facing on to Queen's Road, are *Clare College Memorial Buildings*, which commemorate members of the college killed in the First and Second World Wars. The original buildings, dating from the 1920s and 1930s, were designed by Sir Giles Gilbert Scott, in neo-Georgian style. They are now divided into two courts, *Memorial Court* (E) and *Ashby Court* (W) by a new building of 1985 designed by Sir Philip Dowson, which contains a library and other amenities. On the S side in *Thirkill Court*, built in 1950 in a style similar to Scott's. The sculptures are Henry Moore's 'Falling Warrior' and Barbara Hepworth's 'Two Forms (Divided Circle)'. Clare Bridge, and shortly N, Garrett Hostel Lane, lead back to the city centre.

About a third of a mile N of Clare Memorial Buildings Queen's Rd joins Northampton St (right) and Madingley Rd (left). Opposite the junction is *Westminster College*, a Presbyterian training college (1899), and in Lady Margaret Rd (to the right off Madingley Rd) *Lucy Cavendish College*. This began informally in the early 1950s, to provide a social focus for senior women graduates working in the university but not attached to a college. In 1985 it became an Approved Foundation of the university. A few (mostly mature) undergraduates are now also admitted.

About one third of a mile along Madingley Road is **Churchill College** (off Pl.A3; entrance in Storey's Way), founded in 1960 to promote scientific and technological studies, though not exclusively devoted to them. As a national memorial to Sir Winston Churchill it attracted benefactors and gifts from all over the world. Now one of Cambridge's largest colleges, Churchill was also one of the first three men's colleges to admit women (1972).

The low brick, wood and concrete buildings (Richard Sheppard Robson) follow the traditional plan of connecting courts, and form an intricate complex. From the massive entrance through aluminium gates, presented by the British Aluminium Company, the wide corridor runs for part of the length of the main central block of the College. The *Dining Hall* is to the right up a wide flight of stairs on which there is an impressive bust of Sir Winston Churchill (Oscar Nemon). The Hall is the largest in Cambridge. Its roof consists of three concrete tunnel-vaults, resting on exposed beams; the walls are wood-slatted, and it is lit by high and low level lights concealed in copper beams. In the *Bracken Reading Room*, built in memory of Brendan Bracken, is a magnificent Lurçat tapestry presented by General de Gaulle. The Bevin Library, given by the Transport and General Workers' Union in memory of Ernest Bevin, a great trade unionist and wartime statesman, contains a collection of Hepworth prints and Sir Winston's books on Napoleon. The *Churchill Archive Centre*, built to house his priceless collection of papers and also containing papers of many of his political, intellectual, and scientific contemporaries, is approached through bronze doors designed by Geoffrey Clarke. It was funded by US ambassadors to London, and other prominent American donors. The sculptures on the lawns and courts are by Henry Moore, Barbara Hepworth, Sean Crampton, Bernard Meadows, Peter Lyon and Denis Mitchell.

At the western end of the grounds is the *Chapel*. Although a Chapel was included in the original plan, the College decided that it should not be built as part of the main College buildings as it was considered inappropriate in a community devoted to secular studies. The Chapel was, therefore, privately subscribed for and is maintained by a separate Trust. It is a Byzantine-style building with central altar; the windows, designed by John Piper and made by Patrick Reyntiens, are a memorial to the first Master, Sir John Cockcroft, and the bell was given by the Board of Admiralty, of which Sir Winston was several times First Lord.

Near the Chapel are flats providing accommodation for married couples (Richard Sheppard) and some way beyond (NE) graduate flats and maisonettes (David Roberts).

The sports grounds are part of the main College site and extend to the boundary with the University Observatory.

Northampton St runs E (right) from the junction with Queen's Rd. On the right is the back entrance to St. John's Merton Hall and Cripps Building (see p 147), on the left is *Kettle's Yard Art Gallery*, which contains a fine collection of 20C art including work by Henri Gaudier-Brzeska, David Jones, Henry Moore, Ben Nicholson, Alfred Wallis and Christopher Wood. The gallery's collection of artifacts and found objects helps to create a domestic atmosphere. The original building was converted from four 17C and 18C cottages, and a modern extension with an adjoining temporary exhibitions gallery, designed by Sir Leslie Martin, was added in 1971. There is a continuous programme of temporary exhibitions of modern art and crafts. (Open daily 2–4 except BH and Christmas–New Year; also 12.30–5.30 (7 on Thurs) Tues–Sat during exhibitions.) On the corner of Castle St, is the *Cambridge and County Folk Museum*, housed in the 16C former White Horse Inn (open Tues–Sat 10.30–5; Sun 2.30–4.30; closed most Bank Holidays).

From Castle Hill to Girton (about 2m.)

On the right of Castle St is the great artificial grassy mound of Castle Hill, thrown up in 1068 to form the base of the keep of the castle built by William I. The earthworks extending eastwards are remains of the second castle built by Edward I in 1285, remodelled by the Parliamentarians in 1643. The mound, approached from the southern edge of the car park of Shire Hall (Cambridgeshire County Council headquarters), affords an excellent view of the city. Below it is St. Giles Church, 19C, but incorporating fragments of its 12–13C predecessor, beyond which (in Chesterton Lane) is Clare College *Castle Hill Hostel*, consisting of two older houses and a new building by David Roberts (1957–58). On the left is the tiny church of St. Peter (Redundant Churches Fund), early 13C but rebuilt with the old materials c 1780. The Norman font is decorated with mermen.

Further on (about 6–7 minutes' walk), down Mount Pleasant, is *St. Edmund's House*, which began in 1895 as a residential centre for Roman Catholic priests studying in Cambridge. It is now an Approved Foundation (1975) of the university and as well as some priests admits lay men and women graduates and a few mature undergraduates, who need not be Roman Catholics. It remains an essentially Christian community.

About 5 minutes' walk beyond is *New Hall (Pl.A1; call at the Porter's Lodge), founded in 1954 as Cambridge's third college for women, and still admitting only women as graduates and undergraduates, though the Fellowship is mixed. It began life at The Hermitage in Silver St (see Darwin College, p 176) and moved to its present site in 1962. The eye-catching buildings (by Chamberlain, Powell, and Bonn) are faintly reminiscent of the Taj Mahal, of pure white brick and concrete, and arranged round sunken courts with pools and fountains. In the centre rises the segmented dome of the hall roof, surrounded by four half-domed towers which contain the four staircases that approach the *Hall*, a cruciform room hung with modern pictures and lit with grey-glass-shaded lamps. The Library (no adm) is on two levels, arcaded bookshelves above, reading cubicles below. The undergraduates' rooms, arranged in pairs, are also on two levels, the upper one reached by ladder-like steps—a novel, if hardly practical, idea (of course no adm).

Next door is **Fitzwilliam College** (Pl.A1) whose history begins in 1869 with the Non-Collegiate Students Board, set up to administer the affairs of men who wanted to study at the university but who could not, or did not wish to, belong to a college (cf St. Catherine's College, Oxford). The first premises were in Trumpington St, opposite the Fitzwilliam Museum, from which it takes its name, and as Fitzwilliam Hall, later House, it became a centre for non-collegiate students, who always included a high proportion of graduates studying for higher degrees. It moved to its present site in 1963, and became a full college in 1966.

The buildings are by Denis Lasdun, long low uniform ranges of dark-grey brick, in marked contrast to the white curves of their neighbours. Over the *Hall*, which has a flat roof, is a distinctive fluted canopy on slender concrete columns.

Fitzwilliam has three Nobel prizewinners among its past members, including Sir Charles Sherrington, physiologist, 1857–1952 (also Caius).

On the outskirts of the city (about 1½m.) is **Girton College**, the first residential college in Britain to offer a university education for women. It was founded in 1869 by the educational pioneer Emily Davies, with the support and encouragement of such leaders of the Women's Movement as Barbara Leigh Smith (afterwards Mme Bodichon) and a number of liberal-minded Cambridge men (see p 14–16) for details on the history of women in the universities). Miss Davies's insistence on women fulfilling exactly the same examination requirements as men, and the rigid discipline she imposed, led in time to some conflict with both her colleagues and her students; she resigned in 1904.

The College began at Hitchin, a place discreetly removed from Cambridge, yet accessible to visiting lecturers from the university. It was greatly disapproved of by the more conservative, and even referred to by an indignant clergyman as 'that infidel place'. In 1873 it moved to its present spacious site on the outskirts of Cambridge near the small village of Girton, from which it took its name. Men are now admitted.

The original red brick Vict-Tudor buildings were designed by Alfred Waterhouse (see also Caius and Pembroke Colleges), and the same style was followed in subsequent additions (some by his son Paul, and grandson Michael, with Sir Giles Gilbert Scott). An innovation was the arrangement of rooms on corridors, instead of staircases as in the older colleges. In the large Hall are portraits of, among others, Emily Davies, looking deceptively mild, Mme Bodichon, and Lady Stanley of Alderley, an early benefactor. The chapel has embroidered kneelers and an altarfrontal designed by Jennifer Gray (1965) and another frontal by Leila Kerr (1978). The college also owns a fine set of embroidered wall-panels (1902) by Lady Carew (seen by prior arrangement). The beautiful grounds were originally laid out c 1900 by the then Mistress, Miss Elizabeth Welsh.

In 1969 Girton's centenary was marked by the opening of the new residential block, Wolfson Court, in Clarkson Rd (see p 178).

ENVIRONS OF CAMBRIDGE

The Immediate Vicinity

On foot

The various commons on the edge of the city centre offer some pleasant short walks. On the E side are *Jesus Green*, and *Midsummer Common* where a path beside the river, opposite the college boathouses, runs from Victoria Bridge to Elizabeth Way (about ¾m.). On the SW side there are numerous paths across *Lammas Land*, *Sheep's Green*, and *Coe Fen*, beginning in Mill Lane (left, just before Silver St Bridge).

With transport

The *American Military Cemetery* is about 4m. NW of the city, along Madingley Rd past Churchill College. It commemorates American servicemen based in Britain who were killed on operations. It has beautifully landscaped gardens and a chapel in which is a mural map of the war in Europe.

Stourbridge Chapel is about 1½m. SE along Newmarket Rd, on the left immediately over the railway bridge, at the edge of Stourbridge Common, which was once the scene of the great annual fair (see p 132). It is now a dreary industrial wasteland, though the tiny 12C church stands in an oasis of green. It was the chapel of the leper hospital maintained by the monks of Barnwell Priory. It was evidently re-roofed in the 14C, but not very skilfully, as many of the vertical timbers have no supporting corbels below. For long it was used simply as a store, and at fair-time as a beer-house. Through the enthusiasm of Westcott House students, one of whom 'discovered' it while walking on the common, the chapel was in the mid 19C restored to religious use, and completely renovated by Sir George Gilbert Scott, who inserted the Norman-style W window. It is now cared for by the Cambridge Preservation Society, and well worth a visit in spite of its bleak surroundings (key at house near by).

The *Gog Magog Hills*, about 4m. SE (leave Cambridge by Hills Rd), rising to 222ft, are the highest ground for miles. They are crossed by the old Roman 'Via Devana', and on top is Wandlebury Camp, an Iron Age fort. The area is maintained by the Cambridge Preservation Society; there are nature-trails and picnic places.

Trumpington is about 2½m. SW, the old village lying to the right of the busy main Trumpington Rd. In the church is the second oldest brass in England—Sir Roger de Trumpington, 1289. Past the church, on the Grantchester road, a footpath to the left (about quarter of a mile) leads to *Byron's Pool*, where 'his ghostly lordship' swam in his undergraduate days. The close proximity of the M11 motorway is not conducive to poetic imaginings.

Grantchester, immortalised by Rupert Brooke, can be reached from Trumpington (1m.), from Grantchester Rd, left off Barton Rd past Wolfson College, or—most pleasantly—by a footpath near the river, which starts at the end of Grantchester St (beyond the junction of Newnham Rd and Fen Causeway). In the church are memorials to the poet, whose name is also recalled by an inn and various tea-gardens etc. in the village. The Old Vicarage (private), at which he lodged for a time, is below the church near the river, where

'The chestnuts shade, in reverend dream,
The still unacademic stream.'

Further Afield

Cambridge, with good public transport and, in the holiday season, a number of organised tours (details from the Information Office) is an excellent centre from which to explore East Anglia and the East Midlands. However, it is clearly beyond the scope of this book to cover such a wide field (consult *Blue Guide England*), and the places described in the following pages are, therefore, all within about twenty miles of the city, and suitable for a half-day (or leisurely full-day) expedition.

Mileages in brackets after a place-name indicate the distance from Cambridge.

North of Cambridge

THE FENS

Cambridge is on the southernmost edge of the Fen District; almost totally flat, criss-crossed by dykes and drainage channels, with huge skyscapes, and a curious translucency of atmosphere, it is an area unique in England. It is not beautiful, but it has a strange and compelling attraction.

Much of the land is below sea-level, and was for centuries either under water, or waterlogged. Some drainage was carried out by the Romans, and a few remains of their work still exist in the fragments of Carr Dyke, but after their departure the land was re-flooded. Determined attempts at reclamation, vigorously opposed by the local 'fen-slodgers' who earned their living by fishing and wild fowling, began in the 17C. Much of the work was carried out by the Dutch engineer Cornelius Vermuyden (d 1677; see also Fen Drayton, p202) under the aegis of the Earl of Bedford, after whom the Bedford rivers and Bedford level are named. The reclaimed land is extremely fertile.

It is noticeable that the scattered towns and villages are always built on rising ground, to lift them above flood level, and to provide a solid foundation. Ely in particular, on a slight hill, is visible from a great distance in this flat country.

THE ROUTE TO ELY

Leave Cambridge by Chesterton Rd and A10.

Chesterton, now a suburb, has a 14C church with a Doom (Last Judgement) painting over the chancel arch. Two of the 15C carved bench-ends portray young men in the fashionable costume of the day (c 1430). For over 300 years the living was in the gift of the abbey of Vercelli in Italy, for whose representative Chesterton Tower (mid 14C, restored 1949) was probably built. At *Waterbeech* (4½m.) is a short length of Carr Dyke (see above).

Just outside the village of *Stretham* (12m.) is the *Old Pumping*

Engine (turn right in the village on A1123, then right again down a signed side road). It is the sole surviving example of a steam-powered fen-drainage engine, built in 1831 to lift water from the surrounding channels into the river Ouse, and last used in 1941. Its vast boilers, valves, pistons and flywheel give an impression of enormous power. Display panels and leaflets clearly explain its workings. There are long views from the top floor of the engine house, where some old eel traps are on show, reminders of a past trade (open daily, small fee).

Wicken Fen (17m. NT) lies just S of A1123 3½m. E of Stretham. 500 acres of primaeval wet land, last surviving remnant of the Great Fen, it is one of the most important nature reserves in Europe. It provides habitats for a wide variety of flowers, birds, insects and butterflies. Even the uninitiated can enjoy its quiet and mystery (open daily; fee).

Ely (16m.) on the River Great Ouse, is a small cathedral city and market town, described by Bede in the early 8C as resembling 'an island surrounded by water and marshes ... it derives its name from the vast quantity of eels that are caught in the marshes'. It was the stronghold in which Hereward the Wake, 'The last of the English', made his final stand against the Normans (1070–71) after the Conquest. It is dominated, as is the surrounding countryside, by the great **Cathedral**. With its massive W tower, rare and intricate Octagon, and immense length (517ft), it is one of the most impressive and interesting medieval buildings in England, and represents an architectural history of four centuries.

HISTORY: The first building at Ely was a Benedictine abbey for both monks and nuns, established by St. Etheldreda (or Audrey), Queen of Northumbria (d 679), who retired from the world, here to the home of her girlhood, and became abbess in 673. Soon after her death miracles were being reported from the shrine set up to her, and Ely became a goal of Saxon pilgrimage. In 870 the Danes sacked the abbey; but in the 10C it was refounded by King Edgar (959–75) as a Benedictine monastery. William the Conqueror appointed as abbot a Norman, Simeon, who began the present structure in 1083; the transepts and E end were completed by 1106, and three years later the church became the cathedral of a new diocese. The Norman nave seems to have been finished c 1189, and the Galilee (W porch) was added by Bp Eustace (1198–1215). Bp Hugh of Northwold (1229–54) lengthened the choir by six exquisite bays in the EE style, which provided a worthy setting for St. Etheldreda's shrine. In 1322 the collapse of the central tower wrecked the Norman choir and gave the sacrist Alan de Walsingham and his team of craftsmen the chance to build the lovely and original Dec octagon and the three W bays of the present choir; at the same time work began on the building of the Lady Chapel, which was not completed until after 1350. The chantry chapels at the E end of the church belong to the Perp period (1486–1533). The incomplete, asymmetrical appearance of the W front is due to the fall of the NW tower in a storm in 1701.

Exterior: A walk round the outside of the Cathedral gives a constantly changing vista of shapes and surfaces, from the forthright Norman style of most of the building, to the fanciful pinnacles of the octagon and the graceful lines of the Lady Chapel. The most prominent part is the *W Front*, including the castellated W tower, the *Galilee porch*, and the *SW transept*. Except for the octagonal top storey and corner turrets, which are Dec, the whole of the striking tower (215ft) belongs to the Transitional Norman period (1174–89), though the lack of the

Ely Cathedral: the great lantern

NW transept robs the facade of its full dignity. The unique Central Octagon is one of the marvels of medieval building; the timber lantern was restored in the 19C by Sir George Gilbert Scott.

Interior: The EE *Galilee Porch* consists of two simply vaulted bays, with blind arcades; the doorway leading from the porch into the nave is richly moulded. From the W entrance there is an impressive vista of the full length of the church; the original Norman screen dividing nave from presbytery and E end was pulled down during mid-18C restorations. The architecture increases in richness as the eye travels on to the stained glass of the E end lancets. *The W Tower* (visitors may climb the tower; no fixed times, but roughly on the hour during the holiday season; fee), with its arcaded galleries, has a 19C painted roof. The pattern in the floor is a labyrinth or maze, the distance from its entrance to its centre the same as the height of the tower, 215ft. On the left is a modern sculpture 'Christus' by Hans Feibusch. The *SW Transept*, in the Norman Transitional style, has richly arcaded walls, triforium and clerestory. It is adjoined by the semicircular *St. Catherine's Chapel* (rebuilt 1848).

The narrow *Nave*, nearly 250ft long and consisting of 12 bays, is an imposing example of late Norman work. The triforium arcade is nearly equal in height to the main arcade, both in nave and transepts. Massive though the piers are, they are light in comparison with the earlier work of the transepts. The old unadorned roof has been replaced by a 19C painted ceiling, but the S aisle vaults in the four E bays retain their original 12C colouring. The windows in the N aisle are Perp insertions, and those in the S aisle have been restored to their original Norman form.

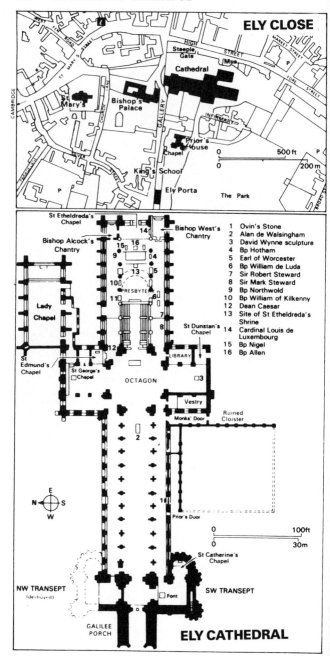

ELY CLOSE

1   Ovin's Stone
2   Alan de Walsingham
3   David Wynne sculpture
4   Bp Hotham
5   Earl of Worcester
6   Bp William de Luda
7   Sir Robert Steward
8   Sir Mark Steward
9   Bp Northwold
10 Bp William of Kilkenny
12 Dean Caesar
13 Site of St Etheldreda's
    Shrine
14 Cardinal Louis de
    Luxembourg
15 Bp Nigel
16 Bp Allen

ELY CATHEDRAL

In the S aisle is the *Prior's Doorway* (c 1140), normally kept closed in winter; on the outside it is richly carved on the tympanum with Christ in Majesty, and on the pilasters with fanciful figures of men and beasts. The capitals of the door posts are carved with an interlaced pattern known as Solomon's Knot, symbolic of infinity. Near the door is the base of a Saxon Cross, called 'Ovin's Stone', erected to Ovinus, a leading East Anglian thane and a vassal of Queen Etheldreda. The inscription on the pedestal reads: *Lucem tuam Ovino da Deus et requiem amen* ('O God, grant Ovinus thy light and rest, amen'). He eventually renounced the world and joined St. Chad's brotherhood at Lastingham in Yorkshire. The S Doorway, also richly decorated outside, at the E end of the S aisle, was the monks' entrance from the cloisters. Near the W end of the nave lies Alan de Walsingham, builder of the octagon, under a marble slab from which the brass has disappeared.

The lower parts of the *Great Transepts*, which have aisles on both sides, display the oldest work in the cathedral (1083–1107). In the E aisle of the N arm is *St. Edmund's Chapel*, with a 14C screen and a 12C wall painting of St. Edmund's martyrdom at the hands of the Danes. The adjoining *St. George's Chapel* was restored as a war memorial by Sir George Dawber (1922). The NW corner of the transept was restored by Sir Christopher Wren; the outer side of the N door is of classical design. In the triforium above is a *museum of stained glass* (open weekdays 11–3.30, Sun 2–4, fee). The bronze group, 'Christ and Mary Magdalene', in the S arm is by David Wynne (1963). The hammerbeams of the transept ceilings are adorned with brightly painted carved angels (15C).

The great **Central Octagon, with its lantern that seems to be poised in space, has been called 'perhaps the most beautiful and original design to be found in the whole range of Gothic architecture'. The lantern is of wood, set with its angles opposite the faces of the stone octagon below. It weighs 400 tons and all England was searched to find oaks large enough for the corner posts, which are 63ft long. The weight is distributed by a wooden framework, on the principle of the hammerbeam, out of sight behind the vaulting. The master carpenter of the octagon—the inspiration of Alan de Walsingham (see above)—was almost certainly William Hurle or Hurley, who was the most famous carpenter of his age, and worked at Westminster and Windsor on the royal palaces. High up on the arches of the octagon are stone carved heads, including those of King Edward III and Queen Philippa, Alan de Walsingham, Prior Crauden and Bishop Hotham.

The *Choir* is separated from the octagon by a 19C screen. There is a clear division between Hugh of Northwold's EE bays and the three Dec ones built by de Walsingham adjoining the octagon. The vaulting has some superb carved bosses. Of the choir stalls, the upper ones are 14C with some lively carved misericords, but the other furnishings are 19C. On the high altar a cross (1964) by Louis Osman stands between candlesticks of 1661. In the N and S Choir aisles are a number of monuments, mostly to past bishops (see plan). An inscribed slate slab in front of the high altar marks the site of *St. Etheldreda's shrine*. Her chapel is at the E end of the N aisle, beyond *Bp Alcock's Chantry*; Alcock (d 1500) founded Jesus College, Cambridge (see p 151), and the chantry is decorated with his rebus of a cock standing on a globe. In the corresponding position to the S is *Bp West's Chantry* (West, d 1534), a graceful combination of classical and medieval styles.

To the NE of the N transept is the elegant and spacious *Lady Chapel, started c 1321 and completed c 1353, which served as a parish church from 1566 to 1938. It is elaborately decorated, but most of the statuettes are badly damaged, mainly due to the clunch (soft limestone) of which they are made, though they also suffered at the hands of the Duke of Somerset, Lord Protector during the reign of Edward VI, in the 1540s. The complex lierne vault, which spans 46ft, is the widest medieval vault in England.

The *Cloisters* are now represented mainly by the E walk, which forms the S entrance to the nave. A tombstone to William Pickering and Richard Edger (both died in 1845 in an accident during the building of the local railway) is inscribed with a delightfully naive poem called 'The Spiritual Railway'. To the E of the S transept are parts of the Infirmary (fine examples of Norman work).

The remains of the Conventual Buildings, S of the cloisters, include the *Prior's House* and the exquisite *Prior Crauden's Chapel* (1324, with a 13C undercroft), built for the prior by Alan de Walsingham. These now form part of the King's School, refounded in 1541, after the monastery was dissolved, as 'The King's New College at Ely' and the successor to the monastic school at which King Edward the Confessor (d 1066) was a pupil. The Deanery was constructed from the old guest-hall and retains some of its 13–14C work and remains of the 12C monks' kitchen. On the S side of the precinct is an attractive park, from which *Ely Porta* (the great gateway of the monastery, built c 1394) leads into a street called The Gallery and back to the W front of the cathedral. The Bishop's Palace facing the cathedral is mainly late 17C, but retains wings built by Bp Alcock and a long gallery built by Bp Goodrich (d 1554). It was used as the bishop's residence until 1939. After wartime years as a convalescent home, and later as a school for handicapped children, it has now (1986) been taken over by the Sue Ryder foundation.

On Palace Green, in front of the cathedral W end is a cannon captured from the Russians at Sebastopol, and presented to Ely by Queen Victoria in 1860.

W of Palace Green is St. Mary's Church (EE and Dec) and the half-timbered Cromwell House, now the vicarage, where Cromwell lived while MP for Cambridge 1636–47. Along the High St (N) beyond Steeple Gate (16C timber and plaster) are a number of buildings originally connected with the cathedral: The *Sacrist's Gate* and *Goldsmith's Tower* both built by Alan de Walsingham 1325, and the *Almonry*, once used as a monk's dormitory. The Sacrist's Gate now houses *Ely Museum* (open 2.15–5 Sat, Sun, and Thur, June–September; small fee). The displays illustrate local themes: ancient trades such as brewing and eel fishing, archaeological finds, the histories of the Cambridgeshire and Suffolk regiments. There is also a Victorian and Edwardian exhibition, including a complete Victorian parlour. The street eventually leads to the river, where there are boats for hire and pleasant walks. The Cambridge University trial eights practise here during the Lent term.

The small market town of **March** (about 30m.) is about 20m. NW of Ely, across a fenland landscape of drains, dykes, and isolated farms (leave Ely by Cambridge road A10, then turn right on to A142 to Chatteris, and A141 to March). The 14C–15C parish church, uniquely dedicated to St. Wendreda, sister of St. Etheldreda of Ely, has one of the most splendid double hammerbeam angel *roofs in England—118 angels with outspread wings.

East of Cambridge

East of Cambridge the landscape becomes slightly undulating, and varied with clumps of woodland. There are many pleasant villages, characteristically set on rising ground.

THE ROUTE TO NEWMARKET

Leave Cambridge by Newmarket Rd and A1303.

Anglesea Abbey (6m. NT) lies just W of the village of Lode (take B1102 at junction of A1303 and A45 about 4m. E of Cambridge). Outwardly a modest Jacobean manor, within it is sumptuously decorated and a treasure house of pictures, furniture, objets d'art and collector's items. It is set in 100 acres of gardens which combine sweeping grandeur of design with intimacy of detail.

From its foundation in the mid 12C until the Dissolution of the Monasteries in 1539 Anglesea Abbey (properly Priory) was a house of Augustinian Canons. Of the conventual buildings only the Chapter House and Common Room remain as part of the early 17C house we see today. The property had many owners, including two who had special links with Cambridge University—Thomas Hobson (see p 171) and Sir George Downing, founder of Downing College (p 172). The present splendour of the house and grounds are, however, entirely due to its last private owner, Huttleston Broughton, 1st Lord Fairhaven, who bought it in 1926. His father, an Englishman, had made a fortune in the USA in mining and railways, and his mother was a New York heiress, so that he was an extremely wealthy man. By his will the property passed to the National Trust on his death in 1966.

Lord Fairhaven completely remodelled the interior of the house, and over the years enlarged the old Common Room block and added picture galleries and a library wing. The rooms are richly decorated, some with carved panelling or ornamental plasterwork, and filled with treasures collected over 40 years. They include furniture, tapestries, sculpture, bronzes, clocks, jewelled crosses, armour, ceramics, and paintings, among which are two by Claude Lorraine (*The Father of Psyche sacrificing at the Temple of Apollo* and *The Landing of Aeneas*) deemed of such importance that when first brought to England in 1799 they received a naval escort. In the library are over 9000 books, many specially bound. A number of visits would be required properly to appreciate the collection.

The gardens, where visitors are free to walk and picnic anywhere, were laid out by Lord Fairhaven from 1926 onward. Near the house are various flower gardens, enclosed by clipped beech hedges; beyond are vistas of grass, trees and water, enhanced by statuary and classical ornaments. In the NE corner of the grounds is Lode Mill, restored and again grinding corn. (House and Grounds open 2–6 Wed–Sun and BH Mon late April–mid October; fee.)

Bottisham (right off B1102), *Swaffham Bulbeck* and *Swaffham Prior* (both on B1102), are attractive villages near Lode. At Swaffham Prior two churches stand side by side on a hill, St. Mary's below, St. Cyriac's above. In medieval times they served separate parishes; in 1667 these were united and St Cyriac's was demolished except for the tower. A hundred years later the tower of St. Mary's was struck by lightning, and the parishioners insisted on moving to St. Cyriac's, rebuilt in Georgian-Gothick style. This eventually deteriorated so much that in the 1880s St. Mary's had to be restored for use. The work was completed only in 1982. The windows are most curious: those in the N aisle, showing battle scenes, are a First World War memorial, those in the S aisle were moved from St. Cyriac's and depict, *inter alia*, Wicken Fen and the Statue of Liberty. St. Cyriac's, renovated in the 1970s by the Redundant Churches Fund, serves as a hall.

About 1m. beyond Swaffham Prior the road crosses the line of the Devil's Ditch (see below). Newmarket can be reached by turning right on to B1103 at Burwell.

Newmarket (13m.) stands on the edge of a chalky upland whose light, well-drained soil provides conditions ideal for horse racing, of which it has been the centre for over 300 years. James I was its earliest royal patron, and it was especially favoured by Charles II, who, with his court, was a frequent visitor. Much of the town was

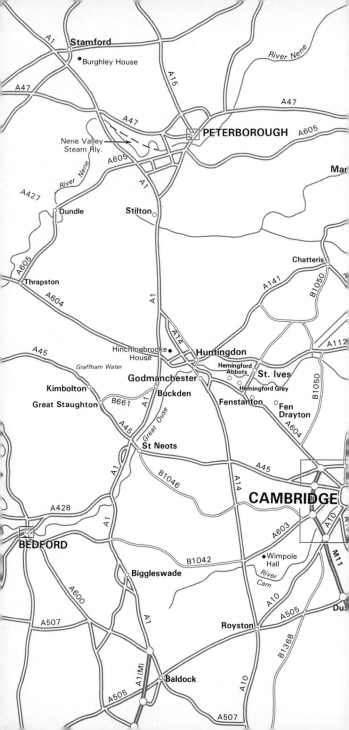

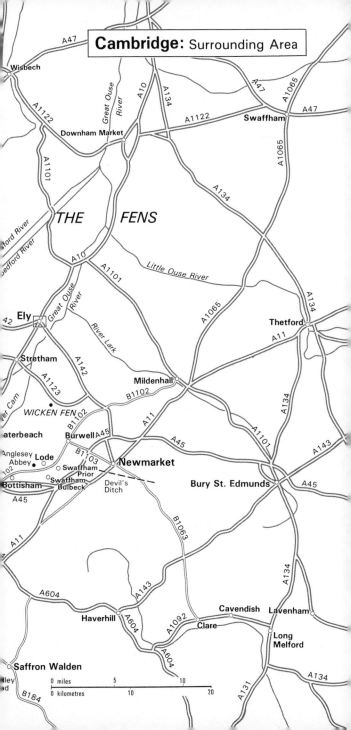

destroyed by a fire in 1683; the precipitate departure of the royal party frustrated the plans which were being hatched to assassinate the King and his brother James as they returned to London (the Rye House Plot). The racecourses, where many of the classic flat races take place, notably the Cambridgeshire and the Two Thousand Guineas (both October) and the Caesarewitch (spring), and the National Stud, lie between the bypass A45 and the Cambridge road A1303. There are many other studs and training stables in the vicinity, and horses may be seen on the gallops (mostly NE of the town, on each side of A1304) in the early mornings up to about 9.30 am.

On the right of the High St are the Georgian-style Jockey Club (by Sir Albert Richardson 1933) and next door the *National Horseracing Museum* which is housed in the elegant Old Subscription Rooms. All aspects of horseracing and its history are lucidly explained and illustrated, from royal patronage to the sign-language of the tick-tack man, blood-stock breeding to famous racecourse entertainers. Exhibits include old prints and paintings, blown-up press photographs, racing trophies and memorabilia, a weighing-in room and a horse-drawn ambulance, and such curiosities as the telegram sent by Queen Alexandra to the royal jockey Herbert Jones after he and his horse were brought down in the Derby of 1913 by the militant suffragette Emily Davidson, described as 'that lunatic brutal woman'. (she was killed, the horse and jockey recovered). The displays are varied from time to time, and are constantly being added to. They are supplemented by a video film. (Open 10–5 Tues–Sat, 2–5 Sun early March–mid December, also BH Mons, and Mon in June, July and August, fee.)

Further up the High Street is the handsome Georgian Rutland Arms Hotel, and behind it, in Palace St Nell Gwynn's house (so called; c 1640), Palace Mansion, built on the site of James I's palace, and (left) the gateway into a racing stable. Here, in the heart of the town, you may glimpse horses, saddlery, straw, and buckets, and catch an authentic whiff of the horseracing world. At the end of the Avenue (right, just short of the Jockey Club) are *Tattersall's Sales Paddocks*. Regular horse sales were started by Richard Tattersall in 1776 at Hyde Park Corner in London. In 1865 they were moved to Knightsbridge (where sales were held until 1939), and the firm established itself at Newmarket in 1870. One reminder of the London days is the Fox Rotunda in the Park Paddocks Lower Parade Ring; the base was originally a fountain at Hyde Park Corner; this supports a bust of the Prince Regent (George IV), who was a friend of Mr Tattersall. Another is the Arch (Vict) at the top of the driveway, which was formerly the entrance to the Knightsbridge sale yard. On top of the Sales Ring (Sir Albert Richardson; completed 1966) is a beautiful copper weathervane of Pegasus, over 200 years old. The classical 'lead' plant holders round the outside of the ring are modern imitations.

Just SE of Newmarket, intersected by A45 and A1303, runs the *Devil's Ditch*, one of the three great defensive earthworks of Cambridgeshire, built some time between the withdrawal of Rome (c 420) and the Anglo-Saxon wars of the 7C and 8C (the others are Fleam Dyke and Bran's Ditch). It extends from Reach, NW of Burwell, SE to Stetchworth. A foot-path along the top provides wide views in all directions, and in spring a rich variety of wild flowers flourish in its chalky soil.

Mildenhall (25m.; 12m, NE of Newmarket on A11) is a busy market town; the large parish church of St. Mary (mostly EE and Perp) has a magnificent hammerbeam angel roof. Many of the angels are peppered with small shot, presumably a Puritan attempt to deface them. In 1942 ploughing turned up a great hoard of Roman silver able-ware in nearby fields. It is now in the British Museum (the Mildenhall Silver). NE is a US Air Base, which accounts for the American voices and uniforms in the streets on this small East Anglian town.

S and E of Newmarket are many attractive small towns and villages typical of East Anglia, with noble Perp churches and houses either Georgian brick, or characteristically of timber and colourwashed plaster (often decorated with pargeting) and steeply-pitched roofs, often thatched. At *Bury St. Edmunds* is a ruined abbey, a small cathedral, and two interesting museums: Moyes Hall, local history, and the Gershom Parkinson Collection of Clocks and Watches. *Lavenham, Long Melford, Clare,* and *Cavendish* have particularly splendid churches. For details see *Blue Guide England.*

South of Cambridge

The countryside is pleasantly undulating, even quite hilly over the borders into Essex and Hertfordshire. There are extensive plantings of oilseed rape; in late spring its metallic yellow makes patches of brilliance in the landscape and its sickly-sweet smell invades the air.

THE ROUTE TO SAFFRON WALDEN

Leave Cambridge by Trumpington Rd and A1301.

At *Duxford* (12m.; turn right on to A505 about 10m. S of Cambridge) there has been a military airfield since the First World War. During the Second World War it served as a Battle of Britain fighter base. It is now the centre of the *Imperial War Museum's air display*. Historic aircraft from both wars are on view, and some modern civilian aeroplanes, including Concorde 01. A video tells the history of the airfield. Pleasure flights are available at weekends, and there are occasional air displays. (Open 10.30–5.30 daily mid March–early November except Good Friday and May Day BH, fee.)

Saffron Walden (15m.) is one of the most attractive, and typical, of East Anglian small towns. In the late Middle Ages its prosperity was based on the cloth trade, and on the cultivation of the autumn-flowering saffron crocus, which was used for dyeing, also medicinally, and from which the town derives its name. The flower is carved in the spandrel of an arch in the S aisle of the church, facing the S door (c 1495).

The church, nearly 200ft long, is one of the largest in Essex; it was almost entirely rebuilt between 1450 and 1525, and is therefore late Perp in style. The exterior, with its battlements and pinnacles, is strongly reminiscent of King's College Chapel (p 159); the same master masons, Simon Clerk and John Wastell, are known to have worked on both. The tall spire (193ft) was added in 1831 by Rickman and Hutchinson, designers of St. John's College, Cambridge, New Court (p 147). The interior is lofty and light, the roof-vaults richly decorated with tracery, bosses, and heraldic badges, among which the Tudor Rose and portcullis are prominent (again cf King's College Chapel).

Just E of the church are the remains of a 12C castle, and the *Museum*. This contains exhibitions of ethnography, ceramics, glass, woodwork, costumes, and natural history. In the archaeology section is the famous 9C Saffron Walden necklace, unearthed in the nearby Saxon cemetery. The interesting Local History display illustrates many local houses which can still be seen, and the materials and methods used in their construction (open 11–5 (4 pm October– March Mon–Sat, Sun and BH 2.30–5).

In High St. (W of the church) and its northerly extension Bridge End, are a number of 14C and 15C timbered houses, their plaster lavishly adorned with pargeted birds, swags of foliage, and figures. Outstanding are the Eight Bell Inn and, on the corner of Myddleton Place, the Youth Hostel. On the corner of Church St (S of the church) and Market Hill the old Sun Inn has a splendid display of pargeting which includes the Saffron crocus, and a battle between a local man Thomas Huckathrift and the Wisbech giant.

In the spacious Market Square, where an open market is still regularly held, are the 19C Corn Exchange (now converted into arts centre and library, and housing the Information Office) and the Town Hall. A heavily Tudor-style building of 1874 has a parapet richly decorated with plasterwork. On the wide Common, E of Market Square, are traces of a medieval (or older) earth-cut maze, one of some half-dozen surviving in Britain. It was re-cut for the sum of 15 shillings in 1699; its brick lining dates from 1911.

At the end of Abbey Lane (W of the High St) are the lines of Pell (or Battle) Ditches, which indicate a 13C extension of the town. Over 200 Roman graves have been found here. A footpath leads W across the park to the great mansion of Audley End.

Audley End (from Cambridge: by car leave A1301 at Stump Cross and take B1383; by train to Audley End Station, from which a 1½m. walk) is one of the largest and most important Jacobean houses in England. It must also be one of the most architecturally confusing, having endured radical alteration at almost every change of family circumstances and contemporary fashion.

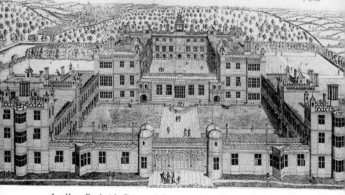

Audley End: 'A General Prospect' by Henry Winstanley, c 1676

HISTORY: Nothing remains of the abbey of Walden which originally stood here, and which was granted to Sir Thomas Audley, Speaker of Parliament, in 1538 for his part in the Dissolution of the Monasteries (see also Magdalene College, Cambridge, p 148). His grandson, Sir Thomas Howard, Earl of Suffolk and Lord Treasurer to James I, replaced the medieval buildings with a house so vast and palatial that King James is said to have remarked wryly that 'it was too big for a king, but might do very well for his treasurer'. Suffolk also built the stables (across the lakes), now much altered, and almhouses in Audley End village, now St. Mark's College, a home for retired clergy. In 1618 Suffolk, convicted of embezzlement, retired in disgrace, and died in 1626, leaving his successors burdened with enormous debts and a totally unmanageable house. In 1701 the 6th Earl called in Vanbrugh to reorganise and reduce it to practical proportions. The outer court (W side) was demolished; also, in 1725, the council chamber and chapel (E side). The last Howard owner, the 10th Earl, in 1733 enclosed the Jacobean loggia (S side) and radically altered the first floor rooms.

The property was bought in 1781 by the Countess of Portsmouth, a remote relative of the Howards, who made further alterations. It was her heir, Sir John Griffin Griffin (later Lord Howard de Walden and 1st Baron Braybrooke) who made the impact on Audley End most clearly apparent to and understood by the visitor today, for he engaged Robert Adam to redesign the reception rooms (S wing) and Lancelot ('Capability') Brown to landscape the park. The third and final reshaping of the house was carried out by the 3rd Lord Braybrooke, who inherited in 1825, and his wife Lady Jane Cornwallis. An enthusiastic antiquarian, he attempted, in tune with current fashion, to restore to the rooms their Jacobean character. Hence for the visitor the confusion: not only through 450 years has the size, shape, and function of practically every room been altered, re-altered and altered again, but much of what might be assumed to be early 17C in fact only dates from the mid 19C.

During the Second World War Audley End was requisitioned and became the HQ of the Polish section of Special Operations (Polish memorial SW of the house, 1983). Both Lord Braybrooke's sons were killed in action and the house passed to the DOE in 1948. Many of its contents still belong to the Braybooke family.

Tour: Over 20 rooms are open, and renovation is in constant progress on others. Practically every one evidences the drastic changes which succeeding owners imposed on the work of their predecesors.

GROUND FLOOR: The Vestibule, or Bucket Hall, so called from the leather fire buckets of 1833 hung from the beams, is the screens passage of the original house. It opens into the *Great Hall*, where the roof, plasterwork, oak screen and panelling are Jacobean, but greatly restored and embellished in the 19C. The stone screen, beyond which rise the twin gilded staircases (c 1725), is a relic of 'the bad taste of Sir John Vanbrugh' according to the 3rd Earl. Among historic suits of armour and weapons on display are the swords and helmets of two Braybrooke sons killed in the Crimean War (1853–56). Portraits of the first owner, Sir Thomas Audley, and his wife hang to the left of the chimneypiece, and between them their daughter Margaret, whose marriage brought the house to the Howard family. The *Great Apartments* which follow are the work of Robert Adam (1760s and '70s) who converted a number of small inconvenient rooms into a grand succession of elegant apartments which provided a fit setting for entertaining in the formal and sumptuous manner of the period. The rooms open into one another in a series of vistas which give an illusion of size and space, and are embellished with columns, niches and plasterwork (by Joseph Rose) of neo-classical design. Many of the contents are faithful modern reproductions but the furniture in the Great Drawing Room is Adam's original work, although the silk coverings, like those of the walls, are modern copies. The colourful *Little Drawing Room* is decorated by Biagio Rebecca, who did much work at Audley End during this phase of alteration. Adam's Library was converted into three smaller rooms in the 19C, but a modern trompe l'oeil painting indicates its original splendid appearance, and one of his bookcases remains, filled with books bound to his special design. The grisaille friezes (two of the original six) are by Cipriani, and the chimney board (one of five originals) by Biagio Rebecca. At the foot of the S stair is a very large painting of the house as it was c 1676. The *Long Gallery*, now housing part of the 4th Lord Braybrooke's collection of stuffed birds, links the two wings of the house; at the far end the

N stair leads to the first floor.

FIRST FLOOR: *North Wing*. In the Jacobean house this wing contained the State Apartment and many of the beautiful plasterwork ceilings and friezes survive. Further friezes were added during the 1708 (Vanbrugh) alterations, in the much bolder style then fashionable, and more again in 1736, these of greatly inferior workmanship. The three groups are clearly distinguishable. Most of the furniture was previously in the S wing bedrooms (see below), but the magnificent State Bed, made for an anticipated royal visit in the 1780s, remains in its original position, and retains its hangings of blue silk decorated with flowers appliquéd on with matching thread. These may have been re-used from a court dress of Lady Portsmouth's. These rooms were used by Lord and Lady Braybrooke in the 19C, and Lady Braybrooke's sitting room, redecorated and with most of its original contents replaced, presents almost exactly its mid 19C appearance. Across the N stair is the *Chapel* (basically of 1725, when the Jacobean chapel was demolished), which was remodelled 1768–71 by the successful joiner John Hobcraft in 'Gothick' style. The window above the altar is by Biagio Rebecca.

The *Picture Gallery*, with ceiling by Joseph Rose in Jacobean 'fret' style (1762) is hung with Cornwallis family portraits and contains more cases of mounted birds. It leads to the S wing.

South Wing. Previously bedrooms, this was redesigned by the 3rd Lord Braybrooke (1825 onward) to form a set of reception rooms which could house the pictures, libraries, and family treasures of the three different family properties owned by him and his wife. Adam's Grand Apartments on the floor below, completed little more than 50 years previously, were relegated to use as bedrooms. In accordance with the 3rd Lord Braybrooke's antiquarian tastes, the remaining Jacobean ceilings were preserved, and new ones created to match; the style throughout is Jacobean, though many of the furnishings are antique French. The *South Lobby* contains five portraits by Lely, the *Dining Room* full-length portraits of George II and of Lord Cornwallis, commander of the British forces during the American War of Independence, and later governor general in India and lord lieutenant of Ireland (by Sir William Beechey). In the *South Library* are portraits of Sir John Griffin Griffin and his two wives (both portrayed as sybils) by Sir Benjamin Wrest. The 16C walnut chair once belonged to Alexander Pope, the poet and satirist (d 1744). Lord Braybrooke's *Sitting Room* contains some of the best of the families' picture collections and many pieces of late 18C furniture designed for the adjoining saloon. This beautiful room substantially retains its 18C character; it was last painted in 1786. The ceiling, whose panels depict sea monsters, merfolk, and ships, is Jacobean. The portraits illustrate the lineal descent of Sir John Griffin Griffin from Thomas Audley; the earlier ones (necessarily imaginary) and those of Henry VIII and Queen Elizabeth I are by Rebecca.

The Park, originally much larger, was laid out 1762–97 by Lancelot 'Capability' Brown. The Palladian bridge is by Adam, who also designed the Temple of Victory on Ring Hill (W beyond the road B1383). The Temple of Concord (E towards Saffron Walden) is by R.W.F. Brettingham, 1832. (Open 1–5.30 April–September. Closed Mon except BH. Grounds daily 12–6.30.)

South West of Cambridge

Leave Cambridge by The Fen Causeway, Barton Rd and A603. Shortly after Barton village is a striking group of white dish radiotelescopes (not open to the public). They belong to Cambridge University Cavendish Laboratory.

Wimpole Hall (8m.; NT) is the largest house in Cambridgeshire; in spite of its immense size it is essentially domestic in character. It has experienced many changes of owner, and both house and grounds have been remodelled many times; some of the most famous 18C architects and landscape designers are associated with its development.

HISTORY: The estate was inherited in 1640 by Sir Thomas Chicheley, whose forebears were wealthy City merchants. He built (and may have designed) 'an extraordinary curious neate house' which is the core of the one we see today. He sold the property in 1686. Between 1693 and 1710 its owner was the 2nd Earl of Radnor, who added a detached service wing and orangery on the E and W sides; elaborate formal gardens in the French and Dutch styles then fashionable were created N of the house (possibly by George London and Henry Wise), and avenues planted E and W. According to Defoe it contained 'all the most exquisite contrivances which the best Heads could invent'. The cost of all these alterations forced Lord Radnor to sell. After various vicissitudes Wimpole passed in 1713 to Edward Harley, 2nd Earl of Oxford, one of a brilliant intellectual circle of poets, writers, and artists. His collection of books and manuscripts constituted the largest private library ever assembled in England (his manuscripts are all now in the British Library, though his books are scattered). Harley engaged James Gibbs (see Index for reference to his work in both Oxford and Cambridge) to enlarge the house, and Charles Bridgeman (of Stowe gardens fame) to enlarge the gardens. To this period belong the W wing, the Chapel (E wing) and the Library block (N side). Of Bridgeman's garden lay-out of avenues and ha-has, canals and 'cabinets' of woodland linked by serpentine paths (S side) nothing remains but the line of the great South Avenue, now being replanted, and the octagon pond (beyond A603). The original trees, together with hundreds of others in the park, succumbed to the recent epidemic of Dutch Elm disease.

In 1740, again owing to the owner's extravagance, Wimpole once more changed hands. It was bought by Philip Yorke, 1st Earl of Hardwicke, a leading lawyer and politician, and Lord Chancellor 1736–56. It remained in the family until 1894. He engaged the architect Henry Flitcroft, who re-faced Chicheley's central block (giving it its present appearance), created a long gallery in the W wing, and rebuilt the parish church. The interior was completely redecorated, with much carving by Sefferkin Alken, and plasterwork by Guiseppe Artari. In tune with contemporary taste the process of replacing the formal gardens with a 'natural' landscape also began, first under Robert Greening (who created the Walled Garden, N) and continued by 'Capability' Brown, who among other things built the Gothic Tower on Johnson's Hill (N) and replaced Bridgeman's N avenue with clumps of trees which still survive. Further alterations were made to the house for the 3rd Lord Hardwicke by the original and romantic architect Sir John Soane, who designed the beautiful Yellow Drawing Room, the Bookroom, and the Bath House. Humphrey Repton, the most fashionable garden 'improver' of the time, planned alterations for the grounds, though not many were carried out. His 'Red Book' for Wimpole is exhibited in the Red Room.

Final extensive alterations were made in the 1840s for the 4th Lord Hardwicke, to designs by H.F. Kendall. Most of his grandiose additions have since been demolished; those remaining are the central chimney stack, the stables, the Arrington gateway (on the Huntingdon road, A14), the Dining Room (now the Tea Room) and much interior decoration (principally plasterwork ceilings). Socially this was Wimpole's hey-day; Queen Victoria and Prince Albert stayed there, and the Prince of Wales (Edward VII) visited frequently while an undergraduate at Cambridge. The extravagant life-style of the 5th Lord Hardwicke (nicknamed Champagne Charlie) forced him to

Wimpole Hall: Sir John Soane's Bath House

sell in 1894, after which the fortunes of Wimpole declined. When Captain and Mrs Bambridge (the daughter of Rudyard Kipling) bought it in 1938, it was empty and in sad disrepair. They dedicated themselves to its restoration and refurbishing; after his death in 1943 she continued alone, bequeathing it to the National Trust at her death (1976).

Tour: The Entrance Hall, part of the original 1640s house, was remodelled and divided by a screen of columns by Kendall in the 1840s. The four large animal pictures are some of the 40-odd painted for the 2nd Lord Oxford by Wootton, eleven of which are at Wimpole on loan. The doorway to the right leads into the *Family Pew*, where prayer books surviving from Lord Oxford's great library (see above) are displayed. The doorway to the left leads in to the *Ante Room* (doorcases and panelling by Sefferin Alken, cornice and ceiling by Kendall). The pictures here are mostly 18C and 19C 'conversation pieces'. On the W wall is a marquetry table painted in trompe l'oeil with cards, coins, and manuscripts. *The South Drawing Room* (Gibbs; carvings by Alken, plasterwork Kendall) contains much S German painted furniture. The portrait of Lady Newcomen and her daughter is probably by Angelica Kauffman. Notice the comical 'Apotheosis of the Royal Family' (George Brittain 1829).

The Gallery is a long, elegant room created by Flitcroft 1742 (plasterwork of wall panels by Guiseppe Artari, ceiling by Kendall). The curtains are 'reefed' as in the 18C. The frames of the pier-glasses and the marble toppped side tables survive from the 1st Lord Hardwicke's time. Most of the pictures relate to the history of Wimpole. Wootton's *'Stag Hunt'* is set in the overmantle; on each side are portraits of Sir Thomas Chicheley and his wife (after Lely).

The Book Room, partly by Gibbs, was enlarged c 1806 by Soane, who also installed the projecting bookcases with their linking ellitptical arches. The impressive library was designed by Gibbs to house Lord Oxford's vast book collection. It has since been considerably altered. Notice the oak pulpit on castors (c 1745) providing access to the upper shelves. *The Red Room*, redecorated by Kendall, but with a few survivals from Flitcroft and Soane, contains a display of drawings and plans relating to the development of the house and grounds. Near the back staircase hangs *'The Dun Arabian'*, again by wootton.

The Yellow Drawing Room, highly original and dramatic in design, is entirely the work of Soane (1790s). Most of the settees and armchairs are original to this room.

The Saloon, by Flitcroft, has carvings by Alken and a ceiling by Kendall. The bay windows afford a good view of the park and Gothic Tower. The portrait of the Duchess of Manchester and her son is by Reynolds.

In the Staircase Hall are three landscapes by Wootton; the Grand Staircase has decorations principally by Gibbs.

UPSTAIRS: In the *Lord Chancellor's Room* is a magnificent state bed; the central canopy is c 1780, the rest, including recently restored hangings, dates from 1852. *Mrs Bambridge's* rooms are hung with a large collection of 19C narrative pictures, drawings of carriages, fashion plates, flower paintings, and Gillray cartoons, reflecting the characteristic personal tastes and enthusiasms of both Captain Bambridge and his wife. Down the back stairs is Soane's highly original and elegant *Bath House* (c 1792), and beyond is the baroque *Chapel*, designed by Gibbs and decorated in trompe l'oeil by Sir James Thornhill. The communion rails are by Thomas Warren (see also Clare College gates).

Alongside the house is the *Parish Church*. Apart from the 14C Chicheley Chapel, with its remarkable collection of monuments which includes work by some of the most famous 18C monumental sculptors such as 'Athenian' Stuart, Bacon, Banks, and Westmacott, the church was entirely rebuilt in 1749 by Flitcroft. The three gallery windows contain 18C glass; they are part of a set the rest of which was removed in 1887 to Erdigg, near Wrexham, another Yorke family house.

E of the gardens is *Park Farm*, recently developed as a centre for rare breeds of farm animals. The beautiful buildings are by Soane, and the barn houses a museum.

Open: House, garden and park 2–6 daily except Fri, end March–early November; fee. Farm 11–5.30 same days and dates; separate fee.

North-West of Cambridge

The northern part of this area is very flat. The frequent occurrence of the word 'fen' in place-names itself indicates the character of the countryside. Through it meanders the slow-moving River Ouse. Southward and westward low undulating hills add a little variety to the landscape.

THE ROUTE TO HUNTINGDON

Leave Cambridge by Magdalene St, Castle St, and Huntingdon Rd (A604), which follows the line of the Roman Via Devana. New Hall, Fitzwilliam College, and Churchill College are on the left and Girton College (1½m.) on the right.

Fen Drayton (8m.), lying just N (right) off the main road, is a pleasant village associated with Sir Cornelius Vermuyden, the Dutch engineer responsible for much of the drainage and reclamation of the Fens (see also p 183). The house in which he is thought to have lived, opposite the church, was burnt down in the early 1970s, only the stone doormantle and pillars surviving. These have been retained on the house now occupying the site, and bear the inscription '1713 Niet Zonder Arbyt' (Nothing Without Work). The Dutch motto has been 'adopted', and is set into the floor in Shire Hall in Cambridge.

Fenstanton (9m.) is also a pleasant village. Sir Lancelot ('Capability') Brown, the great landscape-garden designer, lived here and was Lord of the Manor 1767–83. There are monuments to him, and his wife, in the church. The inscription on his begins:

Ye Sons of Elegance, who truly taste
The Simple charms that genuine Art supplies,
Come from the sylvan Scenes his Genius grac'd,
And offer here your tributory Sigh's ...

The late 17C lockup survives, brick built with a clock turret.

St. Ives (13m., turn right on B1040 just beyond Fenstanton) lies on the N bank of the Ouse; its old quay and wharves bear witness to a once-busy river trade. The river still gives the town great character and charm, and provides facilities for pleasure-boating and fishing. St. Ives, named after a legendary 6C (?) bishop Ivo, grew up in the Middle Ages in consequence of the great Easter Fair (one of the four most important in England) granted to the local village by Henry I in 1110. Hence, perhaps, the origin of the nursery-rhyme 'As I was going to St. Ives,/ I met a man with seven wives ..', etc. Open-air markets are still held on Bank Holidays. Oliver Cromwell, whose statue is in the market place, lived here for five years. Among the most interesting buildings is the early 15C bridge carrying a small chapel, one of very few remaining in England. The history of the town is well told and illustrated in the *Norris Museum* (in Broadway, beside the river; open 10–1 and 1–5 Tues–Fri, also Mon 2–5 and Sat 10–12). Beside the river, between St. Ives and Godmanchester, are the attractive villages of *Hemingford Grey* and *Hemingford Abbots*, most enjoyably reached by boat.

Godmanchester (16m.) also derives its main character and charm from its setting on the river Ouse and its many branches, which loop along the little town's western edge, forming islands and backwaters. Beyond the river is the Meadow of Portholme, over 200 acres of open grassland, providing pleasant walks, originally a common pasture, later used, at different times, as a racecourse and a cricket ground. Cobbett described it in 1822 as 'so pretty a spot, so level, so smooth, so green, and of such an extent I never saw, and never expected to see ...'. Godmanchester, as its name suggests, grew up in Roman times, at the river-crossing of three important roads, and Roman gateways, foundations, a bath house, and artefacts have been un-earthed. It is a small place, best explored on foot (car park in Post St; approaching from Cambridge on A604 turn right at the river). In the mainly Perp church are stalls, and misericords richly carved with animals both real and mythical, believed to have come from Ramsey Abbey. S of the church, beside the river, is the Tudor brick Queen Elizabeth Grammar School (1559) and Flemish-gabled Town Hall (1844) both now used for community purposes. A very pretty wooden Chippendale Chinese bridge (1827) leads on to the islands, from whose waterside pathways there is a good view of many attractive houses and gardens, also large flotillas of swans and ducks. The Causeway and streets behind it (turn left from the bridge as you face the river) contain a number of interesting 17C and 18C houses; in West St is Farm Hall (1746), a very handsome classical style brick mansion facing on to lime avenues and the river. At the N end of the town in Post St (near the car park) is *Island Hall*, built c 1740 for John Jackson, Receiver General for Huntingdon. It is of mellow brick in classic Georgian style, with identical facades front and back. After some disastrous alterations, and a fire, it has now been restored to its original state. The interior decoration and furnishings are particularly elegant and beautiful, and there are many pictures and photographs showing the house as it was at various times since the early 1800s. It is owned and lived in by descendants of the family who bought it from the Jacksons in 1802 (open 2.30–5.30 Sun, Tues, Thurs, early June–mid September, also May and August BHs. Guided tours, often by the family; fee).

Huntingdon (16m.) on the N side of the river Ouse, is linked to Godmanchester by a bridge 'lately built' in 1327. Differences in the cutwaters on the N and S sides indicate that it was jointly constructed by the two communities, each following its own ideas. Modern bridges now serve modern needs. In the past Huntingdon was the administrative capital of the county of Huntingdonshire (merged with Cambridgeshire 1974), and in coaching days an important staging post, adjacent to the Great North Road. In recent years it has been greatly developed, but the old town centre retains much of its 18C charm, as a walk through the Market Square and the High Street will show (car parks immediately alongside). Buildings of particular interest are, in Market Sq: the Town Hall (1746), All Saints Church (Perp) and Walden House (late 17C) just behind the church. In the High St, SE (towards the river) is Cowper House (early 18C) where the poet William Cowper lived with his friends the Unwins 1765–67, St. Mary's church, with an ornate Perp tower, and the Old Bridge Hotel (18C). In the NW half of the High St is the George Hotel, refronted after a fire in the mid 19C, but behind retaining its original courtyard and surrounding gallery, used from time to time as a setting for Shakespearian productions. Beyond are Ferrar House (early 18C), Whitwall House (1727) and Montague House (1800).

Huntingdon's chief claim to historical fame is its connection with Oliver Cromwell, whose uncle Sir Oliver then owned Hinchingbrooke (see below). He was born in *Cromwell House* (virtually rebuilt in the 19C), which is in Ermine St, just N of High St. In All Saints church is the register of the old church of St. John (now demolished), which records his birth. He was educated, as was Samuel Pepys, the diarist, at the old Grammar School. What survives of this building, on the side of Market Sq, is now the *Cromwell Museum*; it contains a splendid collection of Cromwell memorabilia, letters, documents, books, and portraits (open 11–1 Tues–Sun, 2–5 Tues–Fri, and 2–4 Sat and Sun, April–October; 11–1 and 2–4 Sat, 2–4 Sun, 2–5 Tues–Fri, November–March; fee).

W of the town, off Brampton Rd (A604) beyond the bypass flyover (A14), is **Hinchingbrooke House**, now a school, but formerly the seat of the Cromwell family, and later of the Earl of Sandwich. Hinchingbrooke is on the site of a 12C nunnery, acquired in 1538 by Richard Cromwell, nephew of Thomas Cromwell, Henry VIII's chief minister at the time of the Dissolution of the Monasteries. Its reconstruction into a house followed the lines of the existing buildings, and many of the old materials were re-used, so that Hinchingbrooke's ecclesiastical origins are still discernible today, in spite of numerous subsequent alterations. It was Richard Cromwell's son Henry, and his grandson Oliver (uncle of the more famous Lord Protector) whose enthusiasm for building and uninhibited extravagance turned it into a grandiose mansion capable of fitly receiving frequent royal visitors, Queen Elizabeth I in 1564, and James I, in 1603 as he progressed from Edinburgh to London to ascend his new throne, and many times thereafter. To this period belong the impressive *gateway* (brought from another Cromwell acquisition, Ramsey Abbey), the *Kitchen Range*, and most of the exterior of the house, notably the SW Tower, and the Great Bow Window; this was moved from its original position (on the E side) to the S front in 1830. Inside little remains of the Cromwells' time apart from the fireplace in the Senior Common Room, and the ceiling and remnants of wall painting in the School Office. The vast expenditure entailed eventually ruined Sir Oliver (as he became) and in 1627 Hinchingbrooke was sold to the Montagu family, in whose possession it remained until 1962 (see Kimbolton for another branch of the family).

The next extensive alterations were made by Edward Montagu shortly after the Restoration in 1660; he had fought for Cromwell in the Civil War, but was later instrumental in arranging the return of Charles II after Cromwell's death, for which service he was created Earl of Sandwich and Viscount Hinchingbrooke. The rebuilding is vividly chronicled in his diary by Samuel Pepys, who was a distant cousin and frequent visitor; he had some hand in planning the gardens. The alterations were almost entirely to the interior of the house; in consequence of the fire in 1830 (see below) and subsequent changes and modernisations little remains from this late 17C era except the library door frame and panels at the foot of the stairs. Edward Montagu was killed at the battle of Sole Bay against the Dutch in 1672. A stained glass window in the library records the scene (William Peckitt 1759). In 1718 the property was inherited at the age of eleven by John Montagu, 4th Earl of Sandwich (after whom the sandwich is named); he died in 1792, and it was during his long ownership that Hinchingbrooke reached its apogee of social fame. 'Few houses were more pleasant and instructive than his lordship's. It was filled with rank, beauty, and talent and everyone was at his ease'. The only alteration at this stage was the insertion of Gothick windows with heraldic glass in the SE corner (Library and Senior Common Room). In 1830 the NE corner of the house, containing the finest rooms created by Sir Oliver Cromwell, was burnt down; though painstakingly restored in Elizabethen style by the architect Edward Blore, much of its former glory and interest was inevitably lost. In the late 1800s a new dining room was added on the W side, and in 1909 the central courtyard (originally the nunnery cloister garth) was roofed in.

Although used and furnished as a school Hinchingbrooke is still architecturally a most interesting (if confusing) house, since something of every period in its long history can be seen. Visitors are guided in small groups. (Open 2–5 Sun, also on BH Mons, April–end August; fee.)

West of Huntingdon runs the historic Great North Road (A1), along whose route lie a number of attractive small towns, in the coaching days of the 18C and 19C important stages in the journey between

London and Edinburgh, and in the mid 20C a series of traffic jams for the frustrated motorist. Now bypassed by the modern dual carriageway which replaces the ancient highway, they have regained their former peace and dignity.

Distances given are from Huntingdon, which is on the route from Cambridge to any of these places.

South and West

Buckden (4m.) has a fine EE and Perp church, and immediately alongside remnants of a palace of the medieval Bishops of Lincoln. In the Great Tower, recently restored, Henry VIII's discarded queen, Katherine of Aragon spent a year of her lonely banishment before her final move to Kimbolton Castle.

Kimbolton (11m.; take B661 from Buckden along the side of Grafham Water reservoir, and at Great Staughton turn right on A45). Originally a fortified manor of the 12C, Kimbolton Castle was rebuilt by Sir Richard Wingfield early in the 16C. Queen Katherine of Aragon was confined here from 1534 until her death in January 1536, but the rooms she used bear no resemblance to their appearance in her time. In 1615 the property was bought by the Montagu family, Earls and Dukes of Manchester (see Hinchingbrooke for another branch of the family), and remained in their ownership until 1950. The house was entirely remodelled in the early 1700s for the 4th Earl by Sir John Vanbrugh, who 'thought 'twas absolutely best, to give it Something of the Castle Air, tho' at the same time to make it regular ... I'm sure this will make a very Noble and Masculine Shew'. It contains magnificent murals by the famous Venetian decorator Pelligrini. The gatehouse is by Robert Adam. Since 1950 Kimbolton has been a school (open 2–6 Sun in August, Sun and Mon Easter, Spring, and late Summer BHs; fee).

North

Stilton (10m.) is chiefly renowned for the cheese which bears its name. This cheese was never actually made here, but further west, in Leicestershire, and was brought to Stilton to be loaded on to coaches going up and down the Great North Road, which until 1964 ran through the village.

Stamford (26m.) was described by Celia Fiennes in 1697 as being 'as fine a built town all of stone as may be seen' and this description still holds good. In the late 13C and early 14C it had many religious houses, and a university which at one point threatened the supremacy of Oxford (see Brasenose College, Oxford, p 74); later it grew prosperous on the wool trade. These factors account for the large number of medieval churches, five intact and the remains of two more. There were once seventeen. It also boasts two ancient almshouses, *Browne's Hospital* (1480s) in Broad St, and *Lord Burghley's Hospital* (1597) near St. Martin's. In the 18C Stamford became locally a great social centre; from this period date the Town Hall, Assembly Rooms, theatre, and numerous handsome houses, which blend happily with their older neighbours to make an exceptionally pleasing townscape.

On the S side is *Burghley House*, the magnificent mansion built 1580–87 by William Cecil, Lord Burghley, Queen Elizabeth I's great chancellor (his grand monument is in St. Martin's church). The well-known Burghley Horse Trials ('Three Day Event') are held in the park in early September. House and grounds are open April–October.

Peterborough (26m., 5m. E of A1) although a city of ancient origin, now presents an almost wholly modern appearance. At its centre is a great Norman cathedral remarkably unchanged since its building in the early 12C. The painted ceiling of the nave dates from c 1220. Queen Katherine of Aragon is buried in the N choir aisle; her tomb was destroyed by the Puritans in 1612. Opposite is the burial place of Mary Queen of Scots (executed 1586). Her body was later moved to Westminster Abbey by her son James I. Tablets commemorate these two sad queens.

SE of Peterborough is the preserved *Nene Valley Steam Railway*, which operates between Orton Mere station (off A606) and Wansford station (off A1) at weekends and holiday periods, March–October. An extension into the centre of the city is under construction (1986).

INDEX

Figures in *italic* denote illustrations, those in **bold** type denote principal references, where there are two or more. Asterisks indicate pages on which a person's name appears among the 'famous members' of a college (see Preface). Persons of the same surname share an entry, even when unrelated.

Typeset by MCL Computerset Ltd, Ely, Cambs, England

Printed and bound in Great Britain by
Butler & Tanner Ltd, Frome and London